"*The Gospel according to God* is a beautifully written exposition of the gospel of Jesus Christ as it is revealed through the prophet Isaiah. Like Philip in the chariot of the Ethiopian court official, MacArthur takes up his pen and, beginning from Isaiah, preaches Jesus to us! The work is scholarly yet devotional—a resource for teaching the gospel to the church and a tool for the evangelization of both Jew and Gentile."

> **Paul David Washer,** Director, HeartCry Missionary Society; author,
> Recovering the Gospel series; *Knowing the Living God*; *Discovering the
> Glorious Gospel*; and *Discerning the Plight of Man*

"John MacArthur's skillful exposition of Isaiah 53 brings us face-to-face with the gospel of Christ crucified. In the death of our divine substitute, we behold the height of God's love and the depth of our iniquity. The clarity of this prophecy is all the more astonishing when we realize that God revealed it to Israel seven centuries before Jesus came. Though Christians hold to different understandings of God's covenant and the end of the age, we find ourselves drawn together as we bow at the foot of the cross in adoration and humble joy."

> **Joel R. Beeke,** President, Puritan Reformed Theological Seminary

"MacArthur gets better and better. *The Gospel according to God* is sure to become the definitive treatment of Isaiah 53 for years to come. An outstanding achievement by one of our leading pastor-theologians."

> **Derek W. H. Thomas,** Senior Minister, First Presbyterian Church,
> Columbia, South Carolina; Teaching Fellow, Ligonier Ministries;
> Chancellor's Professor, Reformed Theological Seminary

"This master expositor and skilled theologian has spent his entire ministry defining and defending the gospel of Jesus Christ. In these pages you will discover the biblical basis for the good news of salvation found in the person and work of the Son of God, Jesus Christ. Your heart will be thrilled as you behold the glory of God in the image of him who is the only Savior of sinners, the Lord of heaven and earth. Here is yet another doctrinally profound yet easily accessible book by this best-selling author. Whatever MacArthur writes, read it for the good of your soul. This book is no exception."

> **Steven J. Lawson,** President, OnePassion Ministries, Dallas, Texas

"*The Gospel according to God* is John MacArthur's powerful, clear, scriptural exposition of Isaiah 52:13–53:12. It is a particular delight to 'listen' in these pages to MacArthur preach the gospel from the Old Testament. Linger here awhile and learn of Christ from the passage God used to transform the life of the Ethiopian eunuch (Acts 8:27–38)."

> **Ligon Duncan,** Chancellor, CEO, and John E. Richards Professor of
> Systematic and Historical Theology, Reformed Theological Seminary

"Isaiah 52:13–53:12 shows the height, depth, and width of the wisdom of God and even the infallibility of his Word. And all that richness is made clear in this book by one of the most gifted and Bible-saturated teachers of our times. MacArthur has done it again; this is the result of searching, believing, and exposing the Scriptures for almost half a century. As you read this profound study, our Redeemer looks more gracious, merciful, desirable, and worthy. This is a must-read!"

Miguel Núñez, Senior Pastor, International Baptist Church of Santo Domingo; President and Founder, Wisdom and Integrity Ministries; Council Member, The Gospel Coalition

"As an eight-year-old boy in a Scottish state school I was 'forced' to learn Isaiah 53 by heart. The teacher said it was about Jesus. She was right. But I wish she had been able to read *The Gospel according to God*. Then she could have shown me how Isaiah's prophecy would be fulfilled in detail. And she could have helped me to understand the meaning of the terrible loneliness, violence, shame, and rejection the Savior endured for me. That's what *The Gospel according to God* does. And it does it with all the Bible-saturated boldness we have come to expect from its author, John MacArthur."

Sinclair B. Ferguson, Chancellor's Professor of Systematic Theology, Reformed Theological Seminary

"We have all gained immensely from the pen and preaching of John MacArthur for almost half a century due to his unflinching fidelity to the Scriptures. In *The Gospel according to God* he is again in his element as he deals with a matter at the very heart of the Christian gospel—Christ's atoning sacrifice. Isaiah 53 is a rare but amazingly rich vein of gospel truth, and Dr. MacArthur mines it with his usual precision and evangelical warmth. If you want to gain a fresh view of Calvary's love to enlarge your mind and heart, this is the book to buy and read!"

Conrad Mbewe, Pastor, Kabwata Baptist Church; Chancellor, African Christian University in Lusaka, Zambia

THE GOSPEL
ACCORDING
TO GOD

THE GOSPEL
ACCORDING
TO GOD

Rediscovering the Most Remarkable
Chapter in the Old Testament

John MacArthur

WHEATON, ILLINOIS

The Gospel according to God: Rediscovering the Most Remarkable Chapter in the Old Testament

Copyright © 2018 by John MacArthur

Published by Crossway
          1300 Crescent Street
          Wheaton, Illinois 60187

Cover design: Josh Dennis

Cover image: Agnus Dei, c.1635–40 (oil on canvas), Zurbaran, Francisco / Bridgeman Images

First printing 2018

Printed in the United States of America

Unless otherwise indicated, Scripture quotations are from the ESV® Bible (The Holy Bible, English Standard Version®), copyright © 2001 by Crossway, a publishing ministry of Good News Publishers. Used by permission. All rights reserved.

Scripture quotations marked KJV are from the *King James Version* of the Bible.

Scripture quotations marked NASB are from *The New American Standard Bible®*. Copyright © The Lockman Foundation 1960, 1962, 1963, 1968, 1971, 1972, 1973, 1975, 1977, 1995. Used by permission.

Scripture references marked NKJV are from *The New King James Version*. Copyright © 1982, Thomas Nelson, Inc. Used by permission.

All emphases in Scripture quotations have been added by the author.

Hardcover ISBN: 978-1-4335-4957-1
ePub ISBN: 978-1-4335-4960-1
PDF ISBN: 978-1-4335-4958-8
Mobipocket ISBN: 978-1-4335-4959-5

Library of Congress Cataloging-in-Publication Data

Names: MacArthur, John, 1939- author.
Title: The Gospel according to God : rediscovering the most remarkable chapter in the Old Testament / John MacArthur.
Description: Wheaton : Crossway, 2018. | Includes bibliographical references and index.
Identifiers: LCCN 2017022968 (print) | LCCN 2017051970 (ebook) | ISBN 9781433549588 (pdf) | ISBN 9781433549595 (mobi) | ISBN 9781433549601 (epub) | ISBN 9781433549571 (hc)
Subjects: LCSH: Bible. Isaiah, LII, 13-LIII—Commentaries.
Classification: LCC BS1520 (ebook) | LCC BS1520 .M27 2018 (print) | DDC 224/.106—dc23
LC record available at https://lccn.loc.gov/2017022968

Crossway is a publishing ministry of Good News Publishers.

LB		28	27	26	25	24	23	22	21	20
15	14	13	12	11	10	9	8	7	6	5	4	3	2

To Stan Broder,
my friend and beloved fellow bondservant—
an Israelite indeed, in whom there is no deceit.
Stan founded the international ministries of Grace to You nearly
four decades ago, extending the outreach of my preaching ministry
to India, South Africa, Australia, New Zealand, Singapore, England,
and ultimately every English-speaking region of the world.
No worker in our ministries has served longer,
seen more fruit, or been more faithful, and no one
on our team is more universally beloved.
"The hearts of the saints have been refreshed
through you, brother" (Philemon 7).

Contents

Introduction

The Whole Story of Salvation in Prophecy

Mr. Moody was once asked whether his creed was in print. In his own prompt way, he replied, "Yes, sir; you will find it in the fifty-third of Isaiah." A condensed Bible is in this chapter. You have the whole gospel here.

Charles Spurgeon[1]

Isaiah means "The Lord is salvation." It's a fitting name for the prophet, because he foretold the gospel message in thorough, vivid, accurate detail.

So far, every prediction Isaiah wrote down has come to pass. The only prophecies that have not yet been fulfilled are those that pertain to the future reign of Messiah, when "the Lord GOD will cause righteousness and praise to sprout up before all the nations" (Isa. 61:11). People "shall beat their swords into plowshares, and their spears into pruning hooks; nation shall not lift up sword against nation, neither shall they learn war anymore" (2:4). And finally, all of redeemed humanity will enter into an eternity of perfect bliss in which heaven and earth will be united, when God "create[s] new heavens and a new earth, and the former things shall not be remembered or come into mind" (65:17).

In that regard, Isaiah provides a ringing endorsement for the value of knowing Scripture well enough to see prophecy fulfilled.

---

1. Charles H. Spurgeon, *The Metropolitan Tabernacle Pulpit*, 63 vols. (London: Passmore & Alabaster, 1893), 39:22.

Taking all the Old Testament's messianic prophecies collectively, the side-by-side themes of suffering and glory were understandably mysterious prior to the crucifixion of Christ. Even after the resurrection, when Christ appeared to two of his disciples on the road to Emmaus, they were puzzled and clearly discouraged about what had happened. "We had hoped that he was the one to redeem Israel," they said (Luke 24:21).

Jesus's answer was a mild rebuke: "O foolish ones, and slow of heart to believe *all* that the prophets have spoken! Was it not necessary that the Christ should suffer these things and enter into his glory?" (vv. 25–26). And then he began to talk them through the Old Testament's many messianic prophecies: "Beginning with Moses and all the Prophets, he interpreted to them in all the Scriptures the things concerning himself" (v. 27).

Scripture does not record the substance of that discourse, but we can be absolutely sure that the risen Messiah took them to Isaiah 53. He very well might have spent a significant amount of time there, showing them that everything he suffered was clearly foretold. His death on the cross was neither an accident nor an interruption in the plan of God, but he was "delivered up according to the definite plan and foreknowledge of God" (Acts 2:23), in order once for all "to put away sin by the sacrifice of himself" (Heb. 9:26).

Throughout the New Testament, Isaiah is the most quoted of all the Old Testament prophets. Jesus and the New Testament writers quote him at least sixty-five times, and he is mentioned by name twenty-two times in the New Testament. (By contrast, the prophet's name appears only sixteen times in the Old Testament's Historical Books.) We have very little information about the man himself. We will survey his life and the times in which he ministered in part 2 of this book.

Isaiah's prophecies are rich and riveting, full of imagery and doctrinal themes that constitute the cardinal truths of the Christian gospel—human depravity, divine grace, justification, substitutionary atonement, and more. Jerome, the fourth-century theologian and historian who translated most of the Bible into Latin, famously said Isaiah "should be called an evangelist rather than a prophet, because he describes all the mysteries of Christ and the church so clearly that one would think he is composing a history of what has already happened rather than prophesying what is to come."[2]

In fact, Isaiah foretold coming events with such remarkable accuracy that rigid rationalists and skeptics in the academic community stubbornly *insist* the book that bears his name must have been written by at least three authors living centuries apart, and that they were actually writing history rather than prophecy. One such critic arrogantly asserted that "virtually no one maintains that the entire book (or even most of it) was written by one person."[3]

That statement seethes with the foolish conceit of modernism. *All* faithful believers who accept the Bible as the Word of God (together with countless Jewish scholars) hold to the single authorship of Isaiah. In fact, for at least 2,400 years after the prophet's lifetime, *no one* of any significance ever suggested that more than one person wrote Isaiah. Jesus himself, together with all the New Testament Gospel writers, clearly maintained that Isaiah was a single individual. Matthew's Gospel quotes from many diverse parts of Isaiah and always attributes the words to the prophet.[4]

Modern criticism is rooted in the rationalism of Dutch philosopher Baruch Spinoza (1632–1677). Spinoza famously questioned the Mosaic authorship and early date of the Pentateuch. Over the next century various European scholars experimented with Spinoza's agnostic, conjectural approach to the biblical text (known today as *the historical-critical method*, or *higher criticism*). Finally that approach was adopted and developed further by German theologian Friedrich Schleiermacher (1768–1834). By the middle of the nineteenth century, higher criticism had decimated the religious academic communities of Europe. They in turn helped spawn the theological

---

2. From Jerome's prologue to Isaiah in the Vulgate, *Biblia Sacra: Iuxta Vulgatam Versionem*, ed. Robert Weber, 2 vols. (Stuttgart: Deutsche Bibelgesellschaft, 1975), 2:1096.

3. David L. Petersen, *The Prophetic Literature: An Introduction* (Louisville: Westminster John Knox, 2002), 48.

4. Matt. 13:14–15 is a quotation from Isa. 6:9–10, and Matt. 15:8–9 quotes Isa. 29:13. In both places Jesus specifically credits the prophet Isaiah with the words. Matthew himself quotes repeatedly from Isaiah (Matt. 3:3 cites Isa. 40:3–5; Matt. 4:15–16 is from Isa. 9:1–2; Matt. 8:17 quotes Isa. 53:4–5; and Matt. 12:18–21 comes from Isa. 42:1–4). In each case Matthew says this "was spoken by the prophet Isaiah." John's Gospel includes a short passage (12:38–41) where the apostle quotes from Isa. 53:1 and Isa. 6:9–10. Without exception, every liberal critic would claim those two sections of Isaiah must have been written by different authors, but John attributes them both to "the prophet Isaiah."

liberalism that wrecked so many mainstream denominations in the twentieth century.

Isaiah is a favorite target of higher critics precisely because they cannot maintain their anti-supernatural skepticism if they acknowledge the uncanny accuracy of the prophet's predictions. And nowhere is the supernatural origin of the biblical text more obvious than Isaiah 53, with its powerful prophetic portrayal of Messiah's suffering and death.

A serious blow to critical skepticism came when the Dead Sea Scrolls were discovered in 1947. One of the first and best-preserved documents discovered was a complete scroll of Isaiah. (Known as the Great Isaiah Scroll, it is now on permanent display at the Shrine of the Book, a special wing of the Israel Museum.) The scroll is more than a thousand years older than any other extant manuscript. It dates from more than a century before Christ—sometime between 150 and 125 BC. A second Isaiah scroll was also found. It is not quite as ancient (but still from a time no more recent than the late first century BC). It is well preserved but not quite complete. Subsequent research has identified fragments from at least twenty other Isaiah scrolls. The existence of so many Isaiah fragments confirms what the New Testament suggests: Isaiah's prophecy was highly prized and well known in the first century.

Evangelical scholar Gleason Archer meticulously examined the Isaiah scrolls from the Dead Sea collection. He wrote:

> Even though the two copies of Isaiah discovered in Qumran Cave 1 near the Dead Sea in 1947 were a thousand years earlier than the oldest dated manuscript previously known (A.D. 980), they proved to be word for word identical with our standard Hebrew Bible in more than 95 percent of the text. . . . The five percent of variation consisted chiefly of obvious slips of the pen and variations in spelling.[5]

Notice, first of all, that nearly two hundred years before the time of the apostles, the book of Isaiah was already well established and thoroughly documented *in exactly the same form and content we have today.* It was universally regarded as one piece, the work of an individual author, not an anthology compiled over time.

---

5. Gleason Archer, *A Survey of Old Testament Introduction*, rev. ed. (Chicago: Moody, 2007), 29.

Furthermore, the modern critics' argument hinges largely on the claim that no one could possibly foresee future events with the level of accuracy reflected in the book of Isaiah. For example, Isaiah 13:17–22 is a prophecy declaring that the Medes would destroy the city of Babylon: "Babylon, the glory of kingdoms, the splendor and pomp of the Chaldeans, will be like Sodom and Gomorrah when God overthrew them. It will never be inhabited or lived in for all generations" (vv. 19–20). When Isaiah made that prophecy, Assyria was the dominant empire, and the Medes were weak and divided. Within a hundred years after Isaiah's death, Babylon grew to become the world's largest city. To any observer of world politics at the time, Isaiah's prophecy might have seemed to paint an impossible scenario.

But more than three hundred years after Isaiah recorded it, the prophecy was indeed fulfilled. The fall of Babylon began in Daniel's time. "The Chaldean king was killed. And Darius the Mede received the kingdom" (Dan. 5:30–31). Babylon was ultimately destroyed by the Medes just as Isaiah predicted, and to this day the site (some 50 miles south of Baghdad) remains uninhabited. Although attempts to rebuild have been made (most recently from 1983 through 2003 by Saddam Hussein), Babylon today is largely a mound of debris with some unfinished brick structures. There hasn't been a sustainable city there for centuries, just as Isaiah predicted.

Scattered prophecies throughout the book of Isaiah accurately describe several other events that came to pass after Isaiah's lifetime. The exactitude of those oracles is frankly the only reason critics have for claiming that parts of Isaiah must have been written after Isaiah's time by multiple authors separated by centuries of time.

But Isaiah 53 debunks their hypothesis because of the detailed way it perfectly presages the most epic event (the crucifixion of Jesus) that happened nearly two hundred years *after* the earliest extant scroll of Isaiah. That, of course, is the passage we will focus on in this book. It would take a cold heart of willful unbelief to study Isaiah 53 with any degree of care and conclude that it has nothing whatsoever to do with the events described in the New Testament Gospel accounts. One commentator rightly says Isaiah 53 "speaks so eloquently of the work of Christ that even the inclusion of his name could add but little more to the extent of its disclosure of him."[6]

Chapter 53 may be more familiar to Christian readers than other parts of Isaiah, but the entire book has significant implications for the Christian faith. Many doctrines essential to Christianity are illuminated by passages in Isaiah.

The book of Isaiah is sometimes called the "fifth Gospel." It's really more than that. It contains in microcosm the whole range of redemptive truth. It is like a miniature compendium of the Bible. In fact, there are some interesting parallels between how the book of Isaiah is laid out and the arrangement of the Bible as a whole.

There were of course no chapter breaks or verse numbers in the original Hebrew manuscripts. (Those were added in the middle of the sixteenth century, when Bibles were first being mass-produced on printing presses in order to make Scripture accessible to common people.) Nevertheless, the chapter and verse divisions do generally follow the logical composition of the text, and they can sometimes reveal the amazing symmetry of the Bible's structure in an extraordinary way.

Isaiah is divided into two sections, the first containing thirty-nine chapters and the second twenty-seven chapters. The Bible also is divided into two sections: the thirty-nine books of the Old Testament and the twenty-seven books of the New.

That second major division of Isaiah begins and ends exactly where the New Testament begins and ends. It opens with the ministry of John the Baptist (Isa. 40:3–5), as does the New Testament (Matt. 3:3; Mark 1:3; Luke 3:4–6; John 1:23). It concludes with the new heavens and the new earth (Isa. 65:17; 66:22), which is also how the New Testament ends (Revelation 21–22). So Isaiah's incredible prophecy accurately anticipates and foreshadows the flow of the New Testament, even though it was written centuries before the birth of Messiah.

Isaiah's second part includes four prophetic songs about the Messiah, who is called the servant of the Lord. The first one is found in 42:1–9. It reveals that he will be chosen by God and empowered by the

---

6. Geoffrey W. Grogan, "Isaiah," in *The Expositor's Bible Commentary*, Frank E. Gaebelein, ed., 12 vols. (Grand Rapids, MI: Zondervan, 1986), 6:305.

Holy Spirit. The servant will bring justice, righteousness, and salvation to the world, delivering blind prisoners from the dungeon of sin.

The second Servant Song is found in 49:1–13. Here we see the servant's authority over the Gentile nations, whom he commands to listen and give attention to him. He will be a man, not an angelic being, since God calls him while he is still in his mother's womb. He will bring salvation to both Israel and the Gentiles, and he will be glorified.

The third song (50:4–11) introduces the servant's suffering, through which he will ultimately be vindicated. The details given about him in this song are more complete and more astonishing than those in the earlier songs.

The fourth and final Servant Song is the text we are most concerned with in this volume: Isaiah 52:13–53:12. This passage reveals precise details of the servant's mission that could not have been known to anyone but God. Here it becomes clear that the servant is more than merely someone chosen by God and empowered by the Holy Spirit, learning obedience through humiliation and suffering. He is the Messiah, the one who will bring justice and salvation to the world—and he will die as a sacrifice for sin.

His full glory would not be revealed until after he suffered. That fact alone was astonishing, unexpected, and baffling to most Jewish readers. They found it impossible to imagine that the Lord's Anointed One would be a suffering slave before he would appear as a conquering king.

Even more scandalous was the idea that the servant of the Lord would suffer not for any evil he had done, but for the sins of others. He would be a substitute, dying as a surrogate for others who (unlike him) deserved the fate he would suffer. "They made his grave with the wicked and with a rich man in his death, although he had done no violence, and there was no deceit in his mouth. Yet it was the will of the LORD to crush him . . . when his soul makes an offering for guilt" (Isa. 53:9–10). He bore the guilt of his people. "He was crushed for our iniquities" (v. 5).

Today Isaiah's words remain just as unbelievable to unrepentant ears, and his message just as vital for their salvation. These pages represent my best effort to explain Isaiah 52:13–53:12 in a readable volume of manageable size. As we walk through the text together, I hope to shine a clear light on the historical and prophetic context of this passage, point out some of its amazing features that you may never have seen, and (by comparing Scripture with Scripture) attempt to infer the gist of what Jesus might have said about this text on the day of his resurrection as he sought to explain to his disciples on the road to Emmaus that the Messiah had to suffer these things before he could enter into his glory.

Part I

THE SUFFERING SERVANT

I

The Most Remarkable Chapter
in the Old Testament

This is one of the chapters that lie at the very heart of the Scriptures. It is the very Holy of holies of Divine Writ. Let us, therefore, put off our shoes from our feet, for the place whereon we stand is specially holy ground. This fifty-third of Isaiah is a Bible in miniature. It is the condensed essence of the gospel.

Charles Spurgeon[1]

" We must know the "
essence of the gospel

No text in the entire Old Testament is more momentous than Isaiah 52:13–53:12. It is a prophecy that begins and ends with the voice of Yahweh himself. He calls our attention to a singular individual: "Behold, my servant . . . " (52:13) and "the righteous one, my servant" (53:11).

The servant is the Anointed One of Israel—the Messiah. We know that for several reasons. To begin with, those opening words are a clear echo of Isaiah 42:1: "Behold my servant, whom I uphold, my chosen, in whom my soul delights; I have put my Spirit upon him; *he will bring forth justice to the nations.*" In the introduction we noted that Isaiah wrote four psalm-like passages prominently featuring a person the prophet calls the servant of Yahweh: Isaiah 42:1–9; 49:1–13; 50:4–11;

---

1. Charles Spurgeon, *The Metropolitan Tabernacle Pulpit*, 63 vols. (London: Passmore & Alabaster, 1903), 49:189.

and 52:13–53:12. All of them (often referred to as Isaiah's Servant Songs) speak of the servant's gentle manner and his worldwide mission. All four are clearly messianic prophecies.

Those passages from Isaiah ring the same note as Zechariah 3:8, another famous messianic prophecy: "*Behold,* I will bring *my servant* the Branch." Of this same individual, Isaiah had previously written, "The government shall be upon his shoulder [and] of the increase of his government and of peace there will be no end, on the throne of David and over his kingdom, to establish it and to uphold it with justice and with righteousness from this time forth and forevermore" (9:6–7).

So the introductory words of Isaiah 52:13 make clear that what follows is a prophecy concerning the Messiah, the promised Redeemer from Israel: "Behold, my servant shall act wisely; he shall be high and lifted up, and shall be exalted."

The entire passage then focuses on the servant of the Lord—described in plain terms as a specific individual. The passage is not about any nation, tribe, people group, or general category of oppressed persons. This is about the suffering of one person, the Lord's servant, and he remains the singular focus of the passage through the end of Isaiah 53.

As we also observed in this book's introduction, the chapter and verse divisions in our modern Bibles aren't found in the original manuscripts. Though generally useful and convenient, the chapter breaks and verse numbers were not divinely inspired. In the case of our text, the break between chapters has been inserted in a rather unfortunate place. The prophecy clearly shifts from one topic to the next after Isaiah 52:12. Both the context and the content make clear that the final three verses in Isaiah 52 actually introduce (and belong to) the passage that spans all of chapter 53. So for convenience's sake, please understand that throughout this book when I speak in general terms of Isaiah 53 without citing specific verses, I have in mind the entire pericope, including those final three verses in chapter 52.

The Text

Here is the complete passage, formatted to reflect the fact that Isaiah is writing in poetic verse:

Behold, my servant shall act wisely;
    he shall be high and lifted up,
    and shall be exalted.
As many were astonished at you—
    his appearance was so marred, beyond human semblance,
    and his form beyond that of the children of mankind—
so shall he sprinkle many nations.
    Kings shall shut their mouths because of him,
for that which has not been told them they see,
    and that which they have not heard they understand.

Who has believed what he has heard from us?
    And to whom has the arm of the LORD been revealed?
For he grew up before him like a young plant,
    and like a root out of dry ground;
he had no form or majesty that we should look at him,
    and no beauty that we should desire him.
He was despised and rejected by men,
    a man of sorrows and acquainted with grief;
and as one from whom men hide their faces
    he was despised, and we esteemed him not.

Surely he has borne our griefs
    and carried our sorrows;
yet we esteemed him stricken,
    smitten by God, and afflicted.
But he was pierced for our transgressions;
    he was crushed for our iniquities;
upon him was the chastisement that brought us peace,
    and with his wounds we are healed.
All we like sheep have gone astray;
    we have turned—every one—to his own way;
and the LORD has laid on him
    the iniquity of us all.

He was oppressed, and he was afflicted,
    yet he opened not his mouth;
like a lamb that is led to the slaughter,
    and like a sheep that before its shearers is silent,

so he opened not his mouth.
By oppression and judgment he was taken away;
    and as for his generation, who considered
that he was cut off out of the land of the living,
    stricken for the transgression of my people?
And they made his grave with the wicked
    and with a rich man in his death,
although he had done no violence,
    and there was no deceit in his mouth.

Yet it was the will of the LORD to crush him; *Lord's will Not*
    he has put him to grief;   *MANS*
when his soul makes an offering for guilt,
    he shall see his offspring; he shall prolong his days;
the will of the LORD shall prosper in his hand.
Out of the anguish of his soul he shall see and be satisfied;
by his knowledge shall the righteous one, my servant,
    make many to be accounted righteous,
    and he shall bear their iniquities.
Therefore I will divide him a portion with the many,
    and he shall divide the spoil with the strong,
because he poured out his soul to death
    and was numbered with the transgressors;
yet he bore the sin of many,
    and makes intercession for the transgressors.

That brief but pivotal portion of Isaiah is a crystal-clear prophecy about the ministry, death, resurrection, and coronation of the Messiah, written more than seven centuries before he came. It is the gospel according to God. Of all the Old Testament's messianic prophecies, this one stands out for its sublime richness and unparalleled clarity. In particular, Isaiah paints a precise prophetic portrait of Messiah's sufferings. He also explains in vivid detail the true meaning of Messiah's death as an atoning sacrifice for the sins of his people.

Many key historical details from the events surrounding the death of Messiah are expressly stated in this passage. For example, Isaiah speaks of the savage brutality of the wounds that were inflicted on him (52:14), his utter silence before his accusers (53:7), his death (vv. 8–9), the place of his burial (v. 9), and the ultimate triumph of his finished work (v. 11). The prophet even alludes to his resurrection from the dead: "He shall prolong his days [and] the will of the LORD shall prosper in his hand" (v. 10).

The passage is also loaded with doctrinal themes: substitutionary sacrifice (vv. 4–6, 10), the forgiveness of sins through the shedding of Messiah's lifeblood (v. 5), the sinlessness of this "despised and rejected" servant who dies for his people (v. 9), the sovereign initiative of God in providing atonement for sinners (vv. 10–11), the justification of many (v. 11), and the intercessory work of the one who offers himself as a sacrifice (v. 12).

Who Is This Suffering Servant?

Ancient Jewish commentators recognized and acknowledged the messianic significance of Isaiah 53. An early belief among some rabbis was that Messiah would be pale and sickly—regarded as a leper—because of how the suffering servant is described in Isaiah 53:3: "despised and rejected . . . as one from whom men hide their faces." The Talmud is a massive compendium of rabbinical teaching covering several centuries of tradition, commentary, legal opinions, philosophy, ethics, and other matters of Jewish custom. It dates from the fifth century after Christ but includes a record of oral traditions from as early as two or three centuries before Christ. One section of the Talmud features a discussion about Messiah and what he was to be called. "What is his name?" the writer asks. Someone answers "Shiloh," based on Genesis 49:10 ("The sceptre shall not depart . . . until Shiloh come," KJV). However, the writer says, "[our] Rabbis maintain that his name is 'the leprous one of the school of Rabbi Judah the Prince,' as it is said 'Surely he hath borne our griefs, and carried our sorrows; yet we did esteem him stricken, smitten of God, and afflicted.'"[2] Clearly those rabbis recognized the messianic significance of Isaiah 53, even though they misunderstood key details of it.

Here, for example, is how Isaiah 53 was used in a formal Jewish

---

2. Talmud Bavli, tractate Sanhedrin 98b. This translation is cited in Yehoiakin ben Ya'ocov, *Concepts of Messiah: A Study of the Messianic Concepts of Islam, Judaism, Messianic Judaism, and Christianity* (Bloomington, IN: Westbow, 2012), 34.

prayer taken from a ninth-century (AD) liturgy for the Day of Atonement:

> Messiah our righteousness (or "our Righteous Messiah") has departed from us: Horror hath seized upon us, and we have none to justify us. He hath borne the yoke of our iniquities and our transgressions, and is wounded because of our transgression. He beareth our sins on His shoulder, that He may find pardon for our iniquities. We shall be healed by His wound at the time the Eternal will create Him (Messiah) as a new creature. O bring Him up from the circle of the earth, raise Him up from Seir to assemble us the second time on Mount Lebanon, by the hand of Yinnon.[3]

A learned and highly esteemed sixteenth-century rabbi surveyed Jewish literature on Isaiah 53 and noted that from a strictly Jewish perspective, the passage is "difficult to fix or arrange in a literal manner." He nevertheless acknowledged that "our rabbis with one voice accept and affirm the opinion that the prophet is speaking of the King Messiah." A traditionalist himself, the rabbi therefore wrote, "We shall ourselves also adhere to the same view." But in order to avoid conceding that the passage speaks of Jesus, he quickly added, "The Messiah is of course David."[4]

For those who lived in the Old Testament era, some measure of confusion about how to interpret this passage was understandable. Like most of the Old Testament prophecies about the coming Messiah, Isaiah 53 was somewhat shrouded in mystery until the fulfillment of the prophecy made its meaning clear. The apostle Peter acknowledges that even "the prophets . . . searched and inquired carefully, inquiring what person or time the Spirit of [Messiah] in them was indicating when he predicted the sufferings of [Messiah] and the subsequent glories" (1 Pet. 1:10–11).

And make no mistake, the Old Testament is full of prophecies about Messiah that point only to Jesus. He is the central theme not only of

---

3. Believed to be composed by Eleazar ben Kalir. "Yinnon" was a rabbinical name for the Messiah. Cited in David Baron, *The Servant of Jehovah: The Sufferings of the Messiah and the Glory That Should Follow* (New York: Marshall, Morgan & Scott, 1922), 14.

4. Mosheh El-Sheikh (commonly known as Moses Alshech), in *The Fifty-third Chapter of Isaiah According to the Jewish Interpreters*, trans. S. R. Driver and A. Neubauer (Oxford, UK: Parker, 1877), 258.

New Testament preaching (Acts 5:42; 8:12; 9:27; 11:20; 17:18; Rom. 16:25; Titus 2:8), but also of Old Testament prophecy. After Jesus called Philip to follow him, Philip "found Nathanael and said to him, 'We have found him of whom Moses in the Law and also the prophets wrote, Jesus of Nazareth, the son of Joseph'" (John 1:45). Indeed, "the testimony of Jesus is the spirit of prophecy" (Rev. 19:10).

In John 5:39 Jesus said to the Jewish religious leaders, "You search the Scriptures because you think that in them you have eternal life; and it is they that bear witness about me." Later in that discussion the Lord added, "If you believed Moses, you would believe me; for he wrote of me" (v. 46). In Matthew 5:17 he said to those listening to the Sermon on the Mount, "Do not think that I have come to abolish the Law or the Prophets; I have not come to abolish them but to fulfill them"—a claim that he repeated throughout his earthly ministry (see Matt. 26:24, 31, 54, 56; Mark 9:12; 14:26–27; Luke 4:16–21; 18:31; 22:37; John 13:18; 15:25; 17:12; 19:28).

Messiah in the Old Testament

In fact, the Old Testament is so full of teaching about Messiah that when the disciples were confused about Jesus's death and unprepared for his resurrection, he rebuked them for their ignorance of the Scriptures. Remember that after his resurrection he said to those two disciples on the road to Emmaus, "'O foolish ones, and slow of heart to believe all that the prophets have spoken! Was it not necessary that the Christ should suffer these things and enter into his glory?' And beginning with Moses and all the Prophets, he interpreted to them in all the Scriptures the things concerning himself" (Luke 24:25–27). Later that same evening the Lord said to the eleven remaining apostles who were gathered in the upper room,

> "These are my words that I spoke to you while I was still with you, that everything written about me in the Law of Moses and the Prophets and the Psalms [the three divisions of the Old Testament] must be fulfilled." Then he opened their minds to understand the Scriptures, and said to them, "Thus it is written, that the Christ should suffer and on the third day rise from the dead, and that

repentance for the forgiveness of sins should be proclaimed in his name to all nations, beginning from Jerusalem." (Luke 24:44–47)

As we noted in the introduction, Scripture does not record the specific content of our Lord's teaching that afternoon on the road to Emmaus. But it would undoubtedly have included both direct, explicit predictions concerning him and many symbols that pictured him. The latter would include Noah's ark, which pictures him as the true ark into which sinners enter and are kept safe through the waters of divine judgment (cf. 1 Pet. 3:20–21); the ram Abraham offered as a substitute for his son Isaac (Gen. 22:13); the Passover lambs, which pointed to Jesus as the Lamb of God, the final sacrifice (Exodus 12; Num. 9:12; cf. 1 Cor. 5:7; John 1:29); the manna in the wilderness (Exodus 16), which pictured him as the true bread from heaven (John 6:32–35); the bronze serpent that was lifted up (Num. 21:4–9; cf. John 3:14), which symbolized his crucifixion; and the five major offerings in Leviticus (burnt offerings, grain offerings, peace offerings, sin offerings, and guilt offerings), of which he is the fulfillment. The Day of Atonement pictures him both in the sacrifice on the altar and in the scapegoat that bore away sin (Lev. 16:7–10). The rock that gave water in the wilderness (Ex. 17:5–6; Num. 20:8–11) prefigured him as the source of spiritual provision for his people (1 Cor. 10:4). And Jonah's emergence alive after three days and nights in the stomach of a large fish was a prophetic picture of Jesus's resurrection from the dead (Matt. 12:39–41).

Jesus is the rejected cornerstone (Ps. 118:22; cf. Matt. 21:42; Acts 4:11; Eph. 2:20); "the shepherd of the flock doomed to be slaughtered by the sheep traders" (Zech. 11:4–14); the stone cut out without human hands who will destroy Antichrist's empire at his second coming (Dan. 2:34–35, 44–45); and the Branch out of David's family tree—"a shoot from the stump of Jesse" (Isa. 11:1–5; Jer. 23:5; 33:15; Ezek. 17:22–23; Zech. 3:8; 6:12). Psalm 72 pictures Christ's millennial reign as King (see especially verses 7 and 17). In some of the messianic prophecies Jesus is referred to as "David," since he is the greatest of David's descendants, the ultimate fulfillment of God's promise to David in 2 Samuel 7, and the culmination of David's kingly line (Jer. 30:9; Ezek. 34:23–24; 37:24–25; and Hos. 3:5). Since all those prophecies that refer to Messiah as "David" came many years after David died, they clearly referred to someone yet to come, who would embody what David's throne was meant to signify.

Of course the Old Testament also contains many direct predictions concerning our Lord's first coming. In the protoevangelium (the "first gospel") recorded in Genesis 3:15, he is the seed of the woman (cf. Gal. 4:4) who will destroy Satan (1 John 3:8). He is the great prophet of whom Moses wrote (Deut. 18:15–22; cf. Num. 24:17–19; Acts 3:22–23). Daniel 7:13–14 describes him as the glorious Son of Man (a title Jesus used of himself more than eighty times in the Gospels). This is the Messiah, who will return on the clouds of heaven (Matt. 24:30; Mark 14:62; Rev. 1:7). As the Old Testament predicted Messiah would be, Jesus was of the line of Abraham (Gen. 12:1–3; cf. Gal. 3:16), from the tribe of Judah (Gen. 49:10; cf. Rev. 5:5), and a descendant of David (2 Sam. 7:12–16; 1 Chron. 17:11–13; cf. Matt. 1:1).

Isaiah 7:14 predicted that the Messiah would be born of a virgin. Micah 5:2 foretold that he would be born in Bethlehem (cf. Matt. 2:6). Jeremiah 31:15 foreshadowed the weeping that accompanied Herod's slaughter of the male children in the vicinity of Bethlehem (Matt. 2:16–18). Isaiah 40:3–4 and Malachi 3:1 and 4:5–6 predicted the coming of his forerunner, John the Baptist (cf. Matt. 3:1–3; 11:10, 14; 17:12–13; Luke 1:17; John 1:23). Psalm 69:8 prophesied his rejection by members of his own family (cf. Matt. 12:46–50; John 7:3–5).

The Old Testament is full of implicit clues about Israel's Messiah. These include references to him as God incarnate (Ps. 45:6–7; cf. Heb. 1:8–9) and as the sovereign King and eternal high priest (Ps. 110:1–7; cf. Matt. 22:43–44; Acts 2:33–34; Heb. 1:13; 5:6–10; 6:20). Other subtle references to Messiah appear in phrases that serve as word pictures depicting how he would be hated without a cause (Ps. 69:4), hanged on a tree, cursed by God, and taken down before sunset (Deut. 21:22–23).

Daniel's prophecy of the seventy weeks (Dan. 9:24–27) predicted the exact day of his Triumphal Entry into Jerusalem.[5] Zechariah 9:9

---

5. For a credible accounting of how Daniel's seventy weeks reveal the date of Jesus's Triumphal Entry, see Harold Hoehner, *Chronological Aspects of the Life of Christ* (Grand Rapids, MI: Zondervan, 1977), 139.

even described how he would ride on the colt of a donkey during that event (cf. Matt. 21:4–5).

The Old Testament foretold many major details (and some seemingly minor ones) about specific events that occurred in connection with his crucifixion. The prophets foretold the treachery of Judas (Ps. 41:9; 55:12–14), including the exact amount of money the betrayer received and what was eventually done with it (Zech. 11:12–13); the scattering of his disciples after his betrayal and arrest (Zech. 13:7; cf. Matt. 26:31, 56); the beatings and abuse he received (Mic. 5:1) in the court of the high priest (Matt. 26:67–68), from the temple guard (Mark 14:65), and at the hands of the Romans (Matt. 27:27–30); the scene at the cross (Psalm 22)—including the Roman soldiers' casting lots for his clothing (Ps. 22:18); his being given sour wine (Ps. 69:21); his legs remaining unbroken (Ex. 12:46; Num. 9:12; Ps. 34:20; cf. John 19:31–33, 36); and the piercing of his side by a Roman soldier (Zech. 12:10). Psalms 2:7 and 16:8–10 predicted his resurrection (cf. Acts 13:34–37). Psalm 109:8 foreshadowed the choice of Matthias to replace Judas as one of the apostles (cf. Acts 1:20). And Psalm 68:18 refers to Christ's ascension (cf. Eph. 4:8).

But nowhere in the Old Testament is the coming Messiah, the Lord Jesus Christ, more fully and clearly revealed than in the prophecies recorded by Isaiah. Isaiah reveals him as the incarnate Son of God, Immanuel (7:14; 8:8); the Wonderful Counselor, Mighty God, Everlasting Father, and Prince of Peace (9:6); the branch (4:2; 11:1); and most frequently the servant of the Lord (42:1; 49:5–7; 52:13; 53:11).

Isaiah predicted that he would be born of a virgin (7:14), and he was (Matt. 1:20–23); that this virgin-born child would be the one who will rule the nations of the world (9:6), and he will (Rev. 11:15; 19:11–21); that the Holy Spirit would rest upon him in a unique way (11:2), and he did (Matt. 3:16; cf. Isa. 61:1–2 with Luke 4:18–19). Isaiah also revealed that he would be rejected by the nation of Israel (8:14–15; cf. 28:16). Indeed, "he came to his own, and his own people did not receive him" (John 1:11; cf. Mark 12:10; Acts 4:11; Rom. 9:32–33).

Isaiah 9:1–2 foretold Jesus's Galilean ministry (cf. Matt. 4:14–16). Jesus himself cited Isaiah 29:18 (cf. 35:5–6; 42:6–7) as a prophecy about his healing of deaf and blind people (Matt. 11:5). Verses 1–4 of

Isaiah 42 describe Messiah's character, revealing that he was gentle and meek, and that he would establish justice even for the Gentiles (Matt. 12:18–21). Isaiah 50:6–7 describes his perfect obedience to the Father's will—even in the face of brutal treatment at the hands of his enemies—and his resolute determination to continue that obedience all the way to the cross. Through his death and resurrection, he would fulfill the new-covenant promise of salvation for his people (55:3; cf. 61:1–2 [quoted by Jesus in Luke 4:18–19]; 2 Cor. 3:6–18; Hebrews 8–10).

Isaiah also noted the servant's role as the chief cornerstone of God's plan of salvation (28:16); his freeing lost sinners from spiritual blindness and bondage (9:2; 42:7); and the physical abuse he suffered at the hands of the Jewish and Roman authorities (50:6).

But of all the marvelous prophecies in Isaiah, this passage in chapter 53 rises above all the rest. It is a majestic description of Christ's sacrifice for sins. Some commentators call it the most important text in the entire Old Testament. Isaiah 53 has received many such accolades throughout the history of the church. Polycarp, the second-century church father and disciple of the apostle John, referred to it as "the golden Passional of the Old Testament." Augustine called the entire book of Isaiah "the fifth gospel," and that name applies particularly to chapter 53. A collection of John Calvin's sermons on Isaiah 53 is titled *The Gospel According to Isaiah*.[6] Martin Luther declared that every Christian ought to have the whole of Isaiah 52:13–53:12 memorized. The noted nineteenth-century Old Testament commentator Franz Delitzsch famously wrote, "In how many an Israelite has it melted the crust of his heart! It looks as if it had been written beneath the cross upon Golgotha. . . . [It] is the most central, the deepest, and the loftiest thing that the Old Testament prophecy, outstripping itself, has ever achieved."[7]

Although it is part of the Old Testament, this vital chapter of Holy Scripture features truths that are cardinal points of Christian doctrine. Its phraseology has become part of our Christian vocabulary, and the passage has been used by more people who have preached and written

6. John Calvin, *The Gospel According to Isaiah*, trans. Leroy Nixon (Grand Rapids, MI: Eerdmans, 1953).

7. Carl Friedrich Keil and Franz Delitzsch, *Biblical Commentary on the Prophecies of Isaiah*, 2 vols. (Edinburgh: T&T Clark, 1873), 2:303.

and sung about the gospel of salvation than any other portion of the Old Testament. Many have called this chapter "the Mount Everest of the Old Testament." It is the choicest of all the messianic prophecies, the pinnacle of the book of Isaiah, and the crown jewel of the Prophets in general. It is, in fact, the heart of the Hebrew Scriptures.

Isaiah 53 is the precise passage the Ethiopian eunuch was reading in the Gaza desert when Philip encountered him. The eunuch read a portion of the passage aloud: "Like a sheep he was led to the slaughter . . ." (Acts 8:32). Then he posed a question to Philip—and it was exactly the right question. This is the key that unlocks the passage: "About whom, I ask you, does the prophet say this, about himself or about someone else?" (v. 34).

"Philip opened his mouth, and *beginning with this Scripture* [Isaiah 53] he told him the good news about *Jesus*" (Acts 8:35)—the gospel according to God!

Isaiah 53 has always intrigued the faithful. Old Testament believers who struggled to understand it knew it was a highly important prophecy. It gave hints about the answer to the great unanswered question of Old Testament soteriology—namely, the problem of how humanity's sin could one day be fully and effectually redressed apart from the wholesale condemnation of every sinner. How could any sacrifice ever be sufficient to make a full and final atonement? How could a just and holy God redeem sinners without compromising his own perfect righteousness?

The unshakable persistence of human guilt and the impossibly high cost of redemption were truths built into the Old Testament sacrificial system. It was obvious (or should have been to anyone exercising a modicum of common sense) that "it is impossible for the blood of bulls and goats to take away sins" (Heb. 10:4). After all, "every priest stands daily at his service, offering repeatedly the same sacrifices, which can never take away sins" (v. 11). The relentless repetition of those sacrifices made clear (for centuries on end) that the work of atonement was not yet finished. And the bloody reality of so many animal sacrifices made clear that the true cost of atonement was higher than any mortal soul could ever hope to pay.

At first glance, Isaiah 53 would seem an unlikely place to find a prophecy heralding the triumphant answer to sin's dilemma. On its surface, the tone of the passage is bleak. The servant is described as "despised and rejected . . . a man of sorrows . . . acquainted with grief . . . one from whom men hide their faces . . . and we esteemed him not" (v. 3). This was not a picture of the Messiah most people in Israel were expecting. They envisioned him as a conquering king who would deliver his people, overthrow their adversaries, and "execute vengeance on the nations and punishments on the peoples, to bind their kings with chains and their nobles with fetters of iron, to execute on them the judgment written!" (Ps. 149:7–9). But Isaiah 53 tells of an unpretentious, lamb-like servant, who would be sorely persecuted and put to death: "By oppression and judgment he was taken away; . . . he was cut off out of the land of the living" (v. 8).

Nevertheless, this prophecy did contain bright rays of hope for faithful readers who already felt the weight of their own sin. It clearly describes one who would suffer for others' sake: "He was pierced for our transgressions . . . crushed for our iniquities" (v. 5). His chastisement is what brings us peace. "His soul makes an offering for guilt" (v. 10). The climactic verse of the passage is verse 11: "Out of the anguish of his soul he shall see and be satisfied; by his knowledge shall the righteous one, my servant, make many to be accounted righteous, and he shall bear their iniquities" (v. 11).

For anyone familiar with the New Testament account of Christ's life, death, resurrection, and high priestly intercession, there should be no mystery about what Isaiah 53 signifies. It is the complete gospel in prophetic form, a surprisingly explicit foretelling of what the Messiah would do to put away the sins of his people forever. It is the gospel according to God, set forth in the Hebrew Scriptures.

In the chapters that follow we will delve more deeply into the details of this amazing prophecy. I trust this study will strengthen your faith, intensify your love for Christ, and deepen your understanding of what Jesus Christ accomplished for his people by his death.

2

About Whom Does the Prophet Say This?

No person that is not either blinded by prejudice, or intoxicated with the pride of human learning, can fail of applying the words of our text to him, "who died for our sins, and rose again for our justification." The prophet spake not as a matter of doubtful disputation, when he declared the cause of the Messiah's sufferings: but with the fullest confidence asserted, that "Surely he hath borne our griefs," yea, "he died, the just for the unjust, that he might bring us to God."

Charles Simeon[1]

Anyone reading Isaiah 53 who is even vaguely familiar with the New Testament record of Jesus's crucifixion will immediately recognize the significance of this amazing passage from the Old Testament. It vividly describes the dreadful brutality of the Roman executioner's scourge and the horrifying physical condition of someone dying on a cross: "His appearance was so marred, beyond human semblance" (Isa. 52:14). It accurately depicts the precise demeanor of Jesus as he faced a cruel death he did not deserve: "He was oppressed, and he was afflicted, yet he opened not his mouth; like a lamb that is led to the slaughter, and like a sheep that before its shearers is silent, so he opened not his

---

1. Charles Simeon, *Horae Homileticae*, 21 vols. (London: Holdsworth and Ball, 1832), 8:353.

mouth" (53:7). It moves from the mention of "our transgressions [and] our iniquities" to "the chastisement that brought us peace" (v. 5). It states that in his dying, the suffering servant "makes an offering for guilt" (v. 10). It declares the doctrine of justification by faith: "By his knowledge shall the righteous one . . . make many to be accounted righteous" (v. 11). Then the chapter closes by saying that this devoted servant of God "makes intercession for the transgressors" (v. 12).

Neither happenstance nor human intuition can account for the prophetic accuracy of Isaiah 53. Here is convincing proof that God is the author of Scripture (2 Tim. 3:16). Who but God could describe details of his redemption plan so perfectly, hundreds of years before anyone else had any idea how the Lamb of God would take away the sin of the world? Every painstaking detail of Isaiah's prophecy is precisely fulfilled in the life, death, burial, resurrection, ascension, intercession, and coronation of the Lord Jesus Christ. "They made his grave with the wicked and with a rich man in his death" (Isa. 53:9). And *after that*, Isaiah says, "He shall prolong his days; the will of the LORD shall prosper in his hand" (v. 10).

For anyone with the barest knowledge of the gospel account, there is no question whom Isaiah is pointing to. To deny that Jesus is the one of whom Isaiah speaks is to reject the clear testimony of both Scripture and history, since he alone fulfilled every one of the prophecy's predictions. As Revelation 19:10 says, "the testimony of Jesus is the spirit of prophecy." Jesus is the central figure in all the typology and prophecies of the Old Testament. But nowhere is that more obvious than right here in Isaiah 53.

Jesus himself first drew the connection in Luke 22, quoting Isaiah 53:12. He told his disciples, "I tell you that this Scripture must be fulfilled in me: '*And he was numbered with the transgressors.*' For what is written about me has its fulfillment." The New Testament writers went on to quote from Isaiah 52:13–53:12 six more times:

- Romans 15:21 quotes 52:15
- John 12:38 and Romans 10:16 quote 53:1
- Matthew 8:17 quotes 53:4
- Acts 8:32–33 quotes 53:7–8
- 1 Peter 2:22 quotes 53:9

Notice: there are fifteen verses in the extended prophecy. All told, the New Testament cites phrases directly from seven of them—almost half. Attentive Bible students will find more than fifty additional New Testament allusions to words or concepts found in Isaiah 53.

No wonder the apostolic writers go back to this chapter so frequently. It is unsurpassed in clarity and precision—not only as a description of Christ's crucifixion but, more importantly, as a thorough explanation of *how* our Lord's death on the cross purchased atonement for his people. Isaiah gives us the sum and substance of the gospel. Every essential gospel doctrine rests on some fact of history, thread of truth, or article of faith declared in Isaiah 53. No serious study of gospel themes could possibly omit this portion of Scripture.

Do You Understand What You Are Reading?

Isaiah 53 is so replete with gospel truth that those who see the passage for the first time might well think they are reading the New Testament. Jewish people whose exposure to the Scripture is limited to texts that are read aloud in their synagogues each week will be completely unfamiliar with Isaiah 53. The entire passage is always omitted from the scheduled public readings.

Every Sabbath in every synagogue worldwide, two portions of Scripture are prescribed to be read aloud—one from the Pentateuch (the Torah), and the other (the *haftarah*) a selection of texts drawn from the prophets. The same schedule of readings is followed in all synagogues, year after year. Over a year's time, the rotation covers every verse of the Torah in canonical order. But the *haftarah* readings are more selective. One of the featured *haftarah* excerpts is Isaiah 51:12–52:12. The next reading in the cycle is Isaiah 54:1–10. *Isaiah 52:13—53:12 is therefore never read publicly in the synagogues.*

As a result, Isaiah 53 is an unfamiliar passage for multitudes of devout Jewish people. In mid 2015, an Israeli-based messianic (Christian) community known as *Medabrim* released a video on the Internet titled "The 'Forbidden Chapter' in the *Tanakh*" (Hebrew Bible), featuring a number of Israelis reading Isaiah 53 from the original Hebrew text. All of them were seeing it for the first time. The astonishment is obvious on the faces of those dear people. Their surprise quickly gives way to thoughtful reflection. As an interviewer asks them to put into their own words the implications of the passage, it is obvious that every one of them sees the clear connection between the prophecy and the New Testament record of Jesus.

Christians would do well to reflect on Isaiah 53 more carefully as well. This prophecy is like a bottomless well of biblical truth. The more we look into it, the more we realize that no human preacher or commentator could ever fully plumb its astonishing depth. This passage first arrested my attention when I was a young man, and every time I return to it, I am amazed at the fresh richness of its truths.

The Prophet's Point of View

Before we begin a careful study of the words and phrases of the text, it is important that we have a precise understanding of the unique vantage point from which Isaiah writes. He was given a prophetic glimpse of the cross with more profound insight into the reason for Christ's death than any other mere mortal before the event actually took place. In fact, if the rest of the New Testament had been lost except for the historical record of Jesus's crucifixion, sinners could be led to salvation through Isaiah's explanation of the atonement in chapter 53 alone. It is quite simply the most profound revelation of the Savior's work ever given to any prophet.

Still, an essential feature of Isaiah's prophecy is often totally overlooked by commentators and Bible students. Don't miss this fact: *the prophet is describing the sacrifice of the suffering servant from a vantage point that looks back from a time still in the future even now.* He is seeing the cross from a prophetic perspective near the end of human history. He is prophesying the collective response of the Jewish people when they finally see, understand, and *believe* that the one they rejected truly is the promised Messiah.

Scripture clearly tells us that ethnic Israel will one day turn en masse to Jesus Christ. When "the fullness of the Gentiles has come in" then "all Israel will be saved, as it is written, 'The Deliverer will come from Zion, he will banish ungodliness from Jacob'" (Rom. 11:25–26).

That event will occur in connection with Christ's second coming, "when they look on . . . him whom they have pierced, [and] mourn for him, as one mourns for an only child, and weep bitterly over him, as one weeps over a firstborn" (Zech. 12:10). As a result, "On that day there shall be a fountain opened for the house of David and the inhabitants of Jerusalem, to cleanse them from sin and uncleanness" (13:1). "The children of Israel shall return and seek the LORD their God, and David their king, and they shall come in fear to the LORD and to his goodness *in the latter days*" (Hos. 3:5).

Isaiah is standing prophetically on that very day, near the end of human history, literally thousands of years *after* Jesus was crucified. He therefore speaks of Christ's death on the cross as a past event. That explains why all the verbs in chapter 53 from verse 1 through the first part of verse 10 are in the past tense.

In other words, we need to understand this passage not merely as a description of the crucifixion per se; it is literally the lament of repentant Israel at a future time when the Jewish people will look back on the Messiah whom they had for so long rejected, and they will finally embrace him as their Lord and King. Isaiah 53 gives voice prophetically to the dramatic confession of faith that the believing remnant of Israel will make at that time. Ezekiel wrote that the Lord declares, "I will purge out the rebels from among you, and those who transgress against me" (Ezek. 20:38). After that purge, every living Jewish person in that day will embrace Jesus as the true Messiah.

The rest of the world will see as well. "Kings shall shut their mouths because of him, for that which has not been told them they see, and that which they have not heard they understand" (Isa. 52:15). Many Gentile kings and nations who have set themselves against him will persist in their rebellion, and he will wage war against their unbelief. "From his mouth comes a sharp sword with which to strike down the nations, and he will rule them with a rod of iron. He will tread the winepress of the fury of the wrath of God the Almighty" (Rev. 19:15).

Of course, Isaiah is specifically describing the response of his own people, the Jews. He verbalizes the profound regret that will smite the hearts and consciences of those who finally recognize Jesus as the Messiah. Isaiah 53 is therefore a plaintive song, a lament. Yet this minor-key hymn constitutes the greatest, most triumphant confession of faith that will ever be made in human history.

It is a significant moment in the yet-future final act of the story of redemption. The only worldwide ethnic community that will ever turn to Christ in multitudes *together as a group* will be Israel. And when they do so, the words of Isaiah 53 will be their confession.

The Threefold Promise of Deliverance

That perspective is important, given the context in which Isaiah 53 is set. Bear in mind that from chapter 40 through the end of the book, the prophet gives an extended view of God's saving work. Those are the good-news chapters of Isaiah's prophecy (a sort of prophetic parallel to the New Testament in its structure and message). While those twenty-seven chapters have a single unifying theme—*deliverance*—they are filled with divine promises ranging from the Jews' deliverance out of Babylon in the sixth century BC to Christ's earthly reign during the future millennial kingdom, and even beyond that, to the new heavens and the new earth (65:17). Since Isaiah was looking backward, we might say that Isaiah's view of the prophetic landscape stretched from the end of human history back to his own time.

Now here's another important thing to notice about the literary structure of Isaiah: the good-news portion of Isaiah (chapters 40–66) is an extended triptych. That part of Isaiah's prophecy divides naturally into three sections of nine chapters each. Each subsection promises a different kind of salvation for God's people. The first nine chapters (40–48) foretell Judah's *deliverance from the Babylonian captivity*. The second nine chapters (49–57) focus on *redemption from sin*. The final section (chapters 58–66), looking forward to Christ's millennial and eternal reign, speaks of *full emancipation from the curse of Adam's fall*.

In stark contrast to the theme of deliverance, each subsection *ends* with a warning about damnation for the wicked. The first two divisions conclude with nearly identical maledictions: "'There is no peace,' says the LORD, 'for the wicked'" (48:22). "'There is no peace,' says my God, 'for the wicked'" (57:21). The third section then ends the book of Isaiah with an expression Jesus himself used as a description of hell, the eternal abode of the wicked: "Their worm shall not die, their fire shall not be quenched, and they shall be an abhorrence to all flesh" (66:24).

Nevertheless forgiveness, not damnation, is the dominant note of these chapters. The subject comes up immediately in the opening verses of chapter 40—right at the key turning point of Isaiah's message: "Comfort, comfort my people, says your God. Speak tenderly to Jerusalem, and cry to her that her warfare is ended, that *her iniquity is pardoned, that she has received from the* LORD's *hand double for all her sins*" (40:1–2). That mention of pardon for iniquity sets the stage for everything that follows—all the way to the end of Isaiah 66.

This is a classic instance where the arrangement of chapters and verses in Scripture helps us see the symmetry inherent in the text. Isaiah 53 is the middle chapter of the second movement in Isaiah's triptych about salvation. In other words, centered squarely between two divine curses declaring "*no peace* for the wicked" is the blessed story of how the servant of the Lord *brings peace* to the people of God. They have been wicked, too, of course. (The first thirty-nine chapters of Isaiah repeatedly made that clear.) But they are the ones who repent of their wickedness, and they receive full and free forgiveness, not as a reward for their repentance (or for anything they have done). They are blessed for the servant's sake. Everything necessary to bring them peace has been done by him on their behalf. This is their confession: "He was pierced for our transgressions; he was crushed for our iniquities; *upon him was the chastisement that brought us peace,* and with his wounds we are healed" (Isa. 53:5). Finally the nation sees that his death was for their salvation.

That verse is the nucleus of chapter 53 and the heart of the gospel according to God. It is the principle of *penal substitution* stated in unambiguous terms. It teaches that the Lord's servant (Christ) redeems his people by taking their place and suffering the devastating punishment for their guilt. "He shall bear their iniquities" (v. 11). The reality of substitutionary sacrifice was clearly pictured in the Old Testament sacrificial system, but Isaiah 53 gave the first clear hint that Messiah himself would be the true Lamb of God who would take away the sin of the world. Although he himself "committed no sin" (1 Pet. 2:22), he took the full wages of sin—the punitive equivalent of an eternity in hell—on behalf of his people.

If we take the entire fifteen-verse pericope—Isaiah 52:13 through 53:12—verse 5 is literally the central verse of the whole passage: "*But he was pierced for our transgressions; he was crushed for our iniquities; upon him was the chastisement that brought us peace, and with his wounds we are healed.*" In other words, the doctrine of penal substitutionary atonement is the crux of the core verse in the middle chapter of the center panel in Isaiah's triptych on deliverance. It is the heart and the focal point of everything the book of Isaiah has to say about the forgiveness of sin. That is fitting, because there is no more vital gospel truth.

The literary symmetry is perfect and the focus is sharp. You can see it from every possible vantage point. Whether we look at Isaiah 53 in isolation, consider the nine-chapter section where forgiveness is the main topic, or expand our perspective to include the entire good-news section of Isaiah, the cross is always literally at the center. And there it remains, with a bright spotlight on the doctrine of penal substitutionary atonement.

Of course there would be no deliverance for anyone, ever, if God never pardoned sin. Judah's deliverance from Babylon would be moot without forgiveness for the sins that brought judgment in the first place. In fact, the reign of Messiah in the new heavens and the new earth would be rather pointless without redeemed people who are loyal to him.

Furthermore, "without the shedding of blood there is no forgiveness of sins" (Heb. 9:22). Therefore, every promise of forgiveness and deliverance God has ever made depends on a full and efficacious atonement. That's why, even today, believers see the cross of Jesus Christ as the focal point of all human history.

He Will Abundantly Pardon

Here is how the theme of grace and forgiveness flows through that middle section of Isaiah's triptych: chapter 49 features the second of Isaiah's Servant Songs (vv. 1–13). It is both a promise of redemption and a call to faith—in the servant's own voice. He says, "The LORD . . . formed me from the womb to be his servant, to bring Jacob back to him" (v. 5). The song then goes on to describe the servant not only as Israel's deliverer but also as the rightful ruler over all the kings of the earth. God the Father speaks to him, saying:

"It is too light a thing that you should be my servant
  to raise up the tribes of Jacob
  and to bring back the preserved of Israel;
I will make you as *a light for the nations,*
  that my salvation may reach to the end of the earth."

Thus says the LORD,
  the Redeemer of Israel and his Holy One,
to one deeply despised, abhorred by the nation,
  the servant of rulers:
"Kings shall see and arise;
  princes, and they shall prostrate themselves;
because of the LORD, who is faithful,
  the Holy One of Israel, who has chosen you." (49:6–7)

Chapter 50 opens with a reminder that sin is the reason for Judah's captivity. "Behold, for your iniquities you were sold, and for your transgressions your mother was sent away" (v. 1). Yahweh is the one speaking here, and he goes on to point out that there is ample proof from the Jews' own history that he has full power not only to judge but also to deliver. Verse 2 contains a clear allusion to the exodus: "Is my hand shortened, that it cannot redeem? Or have I no power to deliver? Behold, by my rebuke I dry up the sea, I make the rivers a desert; their fish stink for lack of water and die of thirst."

Then the servant of the Lord speaks, giving testimony about his own perfect obedience: "The Lord GOD has given me the tongue of those who are taught" (50:4). "The Lord GOD has opened my ear, and I was not rebellious" (v. 5). Indeed, in his incarnation, he "*learned* obedience through what he suffered" (Heb. 5:8). "He humbled himself by becoming obedient to the point of death, even death on a cross" (Phil. 2:8). And here in Isaiah 50 we get a brief prophetic glimpse of that truth. It is a one-verse preview of what is coming in Isaiah 53. These are the servant's own words: "I gave my back to those who strike, and my cheeks to those who pull out the beard; I hid not my face from disgrace and spitting" (Isa. 50:6). That verse foretells exactly what the New Testament says about the mocking abuse Jesus bore while on trial for his life: "They spit in his face and struck him. And some slapped him" (Matt. 26:67). "And they were striking his head with a reed and spitting on him and kneeling down in homage to him" (Mark 15:19). But "for the joy that was set before him [He] endured the cross, despising the shame" (Heb. 12:2). He says so prophetically in Isaiah 50:7, "I have set my face like a flint, and I know that I shall not be put to shame."

Both the Lord God and the servant then alternate for two and a half chapters, rehearsing the faithfulness of God and calling the people of God to faith. Words of reassurance and promises of salvation are woven through the text: "Thus says your Lord, the LORD, your God who pleads the cause of his people: ' . . . the bowl of my wrath you shall drink no more'" (Isa. 51:22). "You shall be redeemed" (52:3). "How beautiful upon the mountains are the feet of him who brings good news, who publishes peace, who brings good news of happiness, who publishes salvation" (v. 7). "For the LORD has comforted his people; he has redeemed Jerusalem. The LORD has bared his holy arm before the eyes of all the nations, and all the ends of the earth shall see the salvation of our God" (vv. 9–10).

That is the immediate context where the prophecy of the suffering servant is found. Remember, the passage actually starts three verses before the end of chapter 52 and spans all of chapter 53. Its theme we know already. It is about the suffering of the Lord's servant and the triumphant result of his sin bearing: "By his knowledge shall the righteous one, my servant, make many to be accounted righteous" (53:11). In other words, sinners will be justified because he bore their iniquities and God punished him in their place.

Isaiah 54 is therefore full of celebratory praise: "Break forth into singing and cry aloud" (v. 1). "'For the mountains may depart and the hills be removed, but my steadfast love shall not depart from you, and my covenant of peace shall not be removed,' says the LORD, who has compassion on you" (v. 10). That chapter concludes with another triumphant affirmation of the doctrine of justification by faith: "'No weapon formed against you shall prosper, and every tongue which rises against you in judgment You shall condemn. This is the heritage of the servants of the LORD, and *their righteousness is from Me*,' says the LORD" (v. 17 NKJV).

Isaiah 55 features this famous call to faith and repentance, promising free salvation for everyone who turns from sin and embraces the Messiah by faith: "Come, everyone who thirsts, come to the waters. . . . Seek the LORD while he may be found; call upon him while he is near; let the wicked forsake his way, and the unrighteous man his thoughts; let him return to the LORD, that he may have compassion on him, and to our God, for he will abundantly pardon" (Isa 55:1, 6–7).

Chapter 56 makes clear that God's proposals of mercy extend beyond Judah, even to Gentiles and strangers—"foreigners who join themselves to the LORD, to minister to him, to love the name of the LORD, and to be his servants, everyone who keeps the Sabbath and does not profane it, and holds fast my covenant—these I will bring to my holy mountain, and make them joyful in my house of prayer; their burnt offerings and their sacrifices will be accepted on my altar; for my house shall be called a house of prayer for all peoples" (vv. 6–7). That prophecy is being fulfilled right now, as people from every tribe, tongue, and nation turn to Christ for salvation.

There is a sudden dramatic tone change in the final four verses of chapter 56. The rest of that chapter and the first thirteen verses of chapter 57 are a harsh condemnation of Judah's wayward leaders, "shepherds who have no understanding; they have all turned to their own way, each to his own gain, one and all" (56:11). The prophet addresses them harshly, as "sons of the sorceress, offspring of the adulterer and the loose woman" (57:3). Chapter 57 goes on to expose and condemn the folly of Judah's past idolatry. It has the tone of a stern reprimand: "When you cry out, let your collection of idols deliver you!" (57:13).

Though addressed specifically to the nation of Judah in its backslidden state, Isaiah 57 stands as a reminder to people of all ages that God does not tolerate sin—and yet he offers forgiveness to repentant sinners. All those harsh words about Judah's many transgressions are finally punctuated with another promise of salvation: "He who takes refuge in me shall possess the land and shall inherit my holy mountain" (57:13). Isaiah then draws his extended homily on the forgiveness of sins to a close with some final words of comfort and peace. The Lord will "revive the spirit of the lowly, and . . . revive the heart of the contrite" (v. 15).

The closing words of the chapter quote God's own promise to his people:

> "I will not contend forever,
>   nor will I always be angry;
> for the spirit would grow faint before me,
>   and the breath of life that I made.
> Because of the iniquity of his unjust gain I was angry,
>   I struck him; I hid my face and was angry,
>   but he went on backsliding in the way of his own heart.
> I have seen his ways, but I will heal him;
>   I will lead him and restore comfort to him and his mourners,
>   creating the fruit of the lips.
> Peace, peace, to the far and to the near," says the LORD,
>   "and I will heal him." (vv. 16–19)

The whole nine-chapter subsection then ends (like each major division of Isaiah's triptych) with an anathema for those who stubbornly persist in rebellion against the Almighty: "'But the wicked are like the tossing sea; for it cannot be quiet, and its waters toss up mire and dirt. There is no peace,' says my God, 'for the wicked'" (vv. 20–21).

Although the passage ends on that note, there can be no doubt about the main theme of those nine chapters (Isaiah 49–57). It is a prophetic discourse about pardon from personal guilt. Its singular theme is deliverance from *sin*—interspersed with repeated calls to repentance and faith. God himself is the one who proposes mercy and pays the price of atonement. "Everyone who thirsts" is assured that God "will abundantly pardon" (55:1, 7). Those nine chapters thus constitute the evangelistic heart of Isaiah's message to the Jewish people, and Isaiah 53 is the prophecy that explains what makes the forgiveness of sins possible.

Why Isaiah 53 Was So Misunderstood

From Isaiah 53 alone, it was not always clear *how* the Messiah would suffer. In fact, until Christ opened the minds of his disciples to understand the Scriptures (Luke 24:45), this and other Old Testament references to Messiah's suffering and rejection seemed mysterious (and sounded contrary to popular messianic expectations). People hardly knew what to make of them. Over the centuries prior to Christ's coming, Isaiah 53 seemed to fade more or less into the background of the collective Jewish consciousness, eclipsed by the triumphant kingdom promises.

One other major spiritual factor contributed to a widespread lack of understanding about Isaiah 53. Most Jews simply did not see the need for a sin-bearing savior. Even the backslidden people of Judah in Isaiah's time were not convinced they needed that kind of redeemer. They were hoping instead for a powerful political figure. They wanted a conquering messiah who would vindicate the Jewish people, liberate the nation from their earthly oppressors, and elevate Israel to world dominance politically and militarily. That expectation persisted across the centuries, and it was still the dominant hope in Jesus's time. The idea of a suffering and rejected savior didn't fit well into that scenario.

Neither did the repeated confessions of national and individual guilt: "*our* transgressions . . . *our* iniquities . . . the iniquity of *us all*" (Isa. 53:5–6). Those words clearly indict the nation collectively, and each individual in particular. They speak a truth that applies, of course, to Jews and Gentiles alike (Rom. 3:9–12). In our natural, carnal state, every human being is fallen, hopelessly in bondage to sin, alienated from God, and lost. "All we like sheep have gone astray" (Isa. 53:6). Left to ourselves without a savior we would all be damned. But no one finds it harder to embrace that truth than those who are fully committed to establishing their own righteousness by obedience to the minutiae of God's law (Rom. 10:3).

After the captivity ended and multitudes returned from exile, the Jewish people never again fell into the kind of widespread, wanton idolatry that characterized the nation during the reigns of Ahaz and Manasseh. The Jews came back from captivity with a new devotion to the law. Perhaps the chief distinctive of postexilic Judaism was an unprecedented stress on strict legal obedience, with particular attention given to the law's external and ceremonial features—dietary laws, dress, ritual washings, and visible symbols of piety like phylacteries and robe tassels (Matt. 23:5).

But a show of religious zeal is no solution to the sin problem that plagues the human race. Sinners cannot make themselves holy, even by the most exacting attempts at obedience to God's law. Rules and regulations—"Do not handle, Do not taste, Do not touch. . . . These . . . are of no value in stopping the indulgence of the flesh" (Col. 2:21–23). Nevertheless, an increasingly ascetic form of Judaism emerged, and it was perpetuated by an appeal to tradition rather than authentic faith. By the time of Christ, sheer legalism was the dominant religion in Israel.

Legalism is the idea that sinners can earn merit with God by their own works of righteousness. Legalists are also prone to treat their traditions as the supreme rule of piety, adding to and thereby nullifying the actual law of God. The Pharisaical system epitomized both tendencies. Because of their rigorous law keeping, the Pharisees "trusted in themselves that they were righteous, and treated others with contempt" (Luke 18:9). Furthermore, Jesus told them, "You have a fine way of rejecting the commandment of God in order to establish your tradition!" (Mark 7:9). Their religion was a legalistic, hypocritical substitute for real faith. All those characteristics (legalism, self-righteousness, and hypocrisy, and contempt for others) stemmed from the fact that they didn't really feel the weight of their own guilt.

People who think their own works can earn merit with God simply do not see the need for a savior. As Paul wrote to the Galatian churches, "If righteousness were through the law, then Christ died for no purpose" (Gal. 2:21). Works-based religion overlooks the hopelessness of human depravity. But Scripture is clear: fallen people are incapable of saving themselves. "We have all become like one who is unclean, and all our righteous deeds are like a polluted garment" (Isa. 64:6). Here, from the pen of Isaiah, is what God says about religious devotion based on the hope of self-atonement: "I will declare your righteousness and your deeds, *but they will not profit you*" (57:12).

Yet because the Jewish nation was chosen by God as the line through whom the deliverer would come, many believed that by virtue of their Abrahamic descent, they already had a claim on God's favor and blessing. After all, "the adoption, the glory, the covenants, the giving of the law, the worship, and the promises" were all theirs by birthright (Rom. 9:4). They took the goodness and mercy of God for granted—exactly like multitudes in Christendom today. The notion that they needed a Savior to expiate their guilt or deliver them from God's condemnation was as thoroughly offensive to the average Jew of Jesus's time as it is to today's cultured secularists, moral relativists, and people who think they became Christians by birth or baptism. Those who followed the Pharisees' doctrines happily acknowledged that Gentiles and other reprobates were sinners, but they thought of themselves as "righteous persons who need no repentance" (Luke 15:7). They were "clean in their own eyes but . . . not washed of their filth" (Prov. 30:12).

That is the deadly danger of works religion. That is the attitude Jesus was condemning when he said, "Those who are well have no need of a physician, but those who are sick. . . . I came not to call the righteous, but sinners" (Matt. 9:12–13).

And make no mistake: *all* false religions cultivate sinful self-confidence. That includes every brand of genteel "faith" and pseudo-Christianity that is stylish today. Self-righteous souls who don't see themselves as hopeless sinners in need of a savior can never truly appreciate the message of Isaiah 53.

That, I am convinced, remains the major reason (even today) why so many—Jews and Gentiles alike—remain unmoved by the account of the suffering servant of Isaiah 53.

And so, dear reader, my plea to you before you read on is that you will pause, carefully ponder, and embrace verse 6 of Isaiah's narrative. It is a solemn confession: "All we like sheep have gone astray; we have turned—every one—to his own way." We need a divine shepherd to save us.

Only those who make that confession will ever truly be able to say, "Upon him was the chastisement that brought us peace, and *with his wounds we are healed.*"

3

Astonishing!

This glorious King will be in such a form that many will be astonished at Him. I read it thus: Many are offended at Him. The Hebrew שָׁמֵם means to be startled, distorted. The word describes the posture of one about to vomit and of one full of revulsion, because His appearance will be so vile that many will be sick and offended.

Martin Luther[1]

Isaiah 52:13–53:12 comprises five stanzas that present different aspects of the servant's ministry not only to Israel but also to the whole world. The language and literary style Isaiah employs are typical of the uniquely poetic forms found everywhere in the Old Testament prophets.

Verses 13–15 of chapter 52 make up the first stanza. Those verses are a summary statement that introduces two contrasting ideas—themes that will loom large in chapter 53. Specifically, the three verses at the end of chapter 52 reveal that Israel's Messiah and King, the Lord Jesus Christ, will both suffer and be exalted. God himself is the speaker:

> Behold, my servant shall act wisely;
>> he shall be high and *lifted up*,
>> and shall be *exalted*.

---

1. Jaroslav Pelikan, ed., *Luther's Works: Lectures on Isaiah: Chapters 40–66* (St. Louis, MO: Concordia, 1972), 216.

As many were astonished at you—
> his appearance was so *marred*, beyond human semblance,
> and his form beyond that of the children of mankind—
so shall he sprinkle many nations.
> Kings shall shut their mouths because of him;
for that which has not been told them they see,
> and that which they have not heard they understand.

As always, suffering precedes glory. The order may seem to be reversed in those three verses, but notice how the prophecy about his exaltation is stated in the future tense. The verse about his suffering is in the past tense. Remember that Isaiah is looking backward from a prophetic viewpoint near the end of world history. So the prophet was seeing Christ's suffering as a past event, with his exaltation in glory still awaiting an imminent future.

Isaiah 53 spells out in detail both his suffering and his glory. It introduces him as "a man of sorrows and acquainted with grief" (v. 3). He was "stricken, smitten by God, and afflicted" (v. 4). "He was oppressed, and he was afflicted, yet he opened not his mouth; like a lamb that is led to the slaughter, and like a sheep that before its shearers is silent, so he opened not his mouth" (v. 7). "He was cut off out of the land of the living" (v. 8). That is a Hebrew expression for death. Verse 9 speaks of his being buried after his death. Verse 10 notes that he died as a guilt offering, and verse 12 that he "poured out his soul to death."

But then: "He shall see his offspring; he shall prolong his days; the will of the LORD shall prosper in his hand" (v. 10). "Out of the anguish of his soul he shall see and be satisfied" (v. 11). God "will divide him a portion with the many, and he shall divide the spoil with the strong" (v. 12). All those statements presuppose his resurrection.

The language of those three introductory verses in Isaiah 52 emphasizes that everything about the servant of the Lord is astonishing—his character, his death, his resurrection, and his exaltation. Verse 13 opens with the word "Behold" and then says, "many were astonished at [him]" (v. 14). Kings will "shut their mouths because of him," and he will open their eyes to see and understand things they never imagined (v. 15). So the servant's coming, his humiliation, and his exaltation—themes that are developed in Isaiah 53—are all introduced in the final verses of Isaiah 52.

The Servant's Astonishing Revelation

That opening exclamation, "Behold," translates a common Hebrew word used more than a thousand times in the Old Testament. The word demands attention and could be translated as an outcry ("Look!") or as a simple command ("Observe this carefully"). It is used by Old Testament prophets four other times in texts featuring important messianic promises. Zechariah 3:8 (like Isaiah 52:13) speaks with the voice of God, introducing his anointed one as "my *servant* the Branch." In Zechariah 6:12 the word "Behold" points to "the *man* whose name is the Branch," emphasizing the Messiah's humanity. Zechariah 9:9 uses the same word to highlight this famous prophecy: "Behold, your *king* is coming to you; righteous and having salvation is he, humble and mounted on a donkey, on a colt, the foal of a donkey." And Isaiah 40:9 says, "Go on up to a high mountain. . . . Say to the cities of Judah, 'Behold your *God!*'" Those four titles, servant, man, king, and God, find a unique parallel in the four Gospels. Mark portrays Jesus as a servant. Luke stresses his humanity. Matthew presents Jesus as King. And John emphasizes his deity.

The word translated "servant" refers to one who did hard work in obedience to his master. A true servant did not act independently to fulfill the desires of his own will; he sought only to please the one he served. The word describes someone who is duty bound to obey his master. It is an exact parallel of the English word *slave*.

But when Scripture employs the word to speak of someone who serves God, it is with lofty, not demeaning, connotations. In the Old Testament it is used of such luminaries as Abraham (Gen. 26:24), Isaac (Gen. 24:14), Jacob (Ezek. 28:25), Moses (Ex. 14:31), David (2 Sam. 3:18), Joshua (Josh. 24:29), Elijah (2 Kings 10:10), Isaiah (Isa. 20:3), Job (Job 1:8), Jonah (2 Kings 14:25), and the prophets in general (2 Kings 17:13).

Although he is absolutely equal to the Father in his eternal essence (Phil. 2:6; Col. 1:15; Heb. 1:3), the Lord Jesus Christ voluntarily "emptied himself, by taking the form of a servant"—the slave or servant of the Lord (Phil. 2:7). He *always* did what was pleasing to God (John 8:29). "For I have come down from heaven," he declared, "not to do my own will but the will of him who sent me" (John 6:38; cf. 4:32; 5:30; 14:31; 15:10).

Isaiah says the servant of the Lord will "act wisely" (Isa. 52:13). The Hebrew word speaks of someone who performs a task with skill and expertise. One modern translation says, "My servant will *prosper*" (NASB). Both translations are valid. The Hebrew word speaks of prudent action that gains prosperous results. Wisdom and success are often linked in Scripture (cf. Josh. 1:7–8; 1 Sam. 18:5, 30; 1 Kings 2:3 where the same verb appears). The language accents the fact that the servant's exaltation is not owing to accidental success or good fortune. His ultimate triumph is an accomplishment attained by adroit know-how. The servant's amazing wisdom will result in the attainment of his purpose. He will not fail to accomplish God's will, because he prudently employs righteous means to achieve the noblest results. Moreover, "the Servant's wisdom is deeply self-denying, for it means accepting ends determined by God and willingly shouldering a burden of untold suffering to make them possible. Here God's wisdom and humankind's decisively part company (cf. 1 Cor. 1:17–25)."[2]

Praise for the servant in verse 13 is stated in three parts. Because he *"shall act wisely;* he *shall be high and lifted up*, and *shall be exalted."* Those phrases are not redundant; rather, they are escalating statements, going from high to higher to highest. The ascending degrees parallel Christ's resurrection (high), his ascension (higher), and (culminating in the highest possible honor) his coronation (Phil. 2:9–11). No one else ever acted so wisely or as a result was so highly exalted.

One clear fact that cannot escape our notice is that Christ's sufferings were planned, purposeful, and successful. Skeptical critics sometimes try to write off Jesus as a failure. They view him as a promising but disappointing figure whose crucifixion made him a martyr instead of a messiah—as if the cross marked the sudden collapse of a grand plan. His death, they claim, was a tragic, unfortunate ending to a well-intended life. Some have even suggested that Jesus *un*wisely miscalculated people's willingness to tolerate his teaching, and when he went too far, it cost him his life. Others view him as a misguided nationalist whose efforts to start a revolution against Rome were

---

2. Geoffrey W. Grogan, *Isaiah*, Expositor's Bible Commentary, ed. Tremper Longman III and David E. Garland, 13 vols. (Grand Rapids, MI: Zondervan, 2008), 6:798.

hopelessly inept. He has even been portrayed as an ambitious, self-styled conqueror—despite the fact that he forcefully rebuffed the common people's attempt to make him their king (John 6:14–15). Agnostics, doubters, cynics, and scoffers of all kinds invariably try to categorize Jesus as just another religious fanatic, swept away by delusions of grandeur.

All such views of him are false and blasphemous. No one who comes to the Bible honestly would ever conclude that the events of Jesus's life did not go the way he intended—as if his dream about a better world ended instead in a personal nightmare.

In fact, nothing could be further from the truth. His death in all its horror and anguish was prophesied centuries earlier in Isaiah 53. This passage makes undeniably clear that Jesus was not some well-meaning victim of a plan that surprisingly went horribly wrong. He "act[ed] wisely." He knew exactly how his life would end, down to the minutest detail, and he had known it since before the foundation of the world, when the plan of salvation was formed.

Jesus understood every prophetic passage in the Old Testament. He rebuked the disciples for not understanding that the Old Testament foretold that he would die: "O foolish ones, and slow of heart to believe all that the prophets have spoken! Was it not necessary that the Christ should suffer these things and enter into his glory?" (Luke 24:25–27, 44). He himself had told them about his coming death again and again throughout the course of his ministry:

> Jesus said to them, "Can you make wedding guests fast while the bridegroom is with them? The days will come when the bridegroom is taken away from them, and then they will fast in those days." (Luke 5:34–35)

> He strictly charged and commanded them to tell this to no one, saying, "The Son of Man must suffer many things and be rejected by the elders and chief priests and scribes, and be killed, and on the third day be raised." (Luke 9:21–22)

> Jesus said to his disciples, "Let these words sink into your ears: The Son of Man is about to be delivered into the hands of men." (Luke 9:43–44)

I have a baptism to be baptized with, and how great is my distress until it is accomplished! (Luke 12:50)

He said to them, "Go and tell that fox [Herod], 'Behold, I cast out demons and perform cures today and tomorrow, and the third day I finish my course.'" (Luke 13:32)

O Jerusalem, Jerusalem, the city that kills the prophets and stones those who are sent to it! How often would I have gathered your children together as a hen gathers her brood under her wings, and you were not willing! Behold, your house is forsaken. And I tell you, you will not see me until you say, "Blessed is he who comes in the name of the Lord!" (Luke 13:34–35)

But first he must suffer many things and be rejected by this generation. (Luke 17:25)

Taking the twelve, he said to them, "See, we are going up to Jerusalem, and everything that is written about the Son of Man by the prophets will be accomplished. For he will be delivered over to the Gentiles and will be mocked and shamefully treated and spit upon. And after flogging him, they will kill him, and on the third day he will rise." (Luke 18:31–33)

Despite the many clear predictions that he would die, those closest to Jesus were caught totally off guard—astonished and confused—when he was finally crucified.

Indeed, the crucifixion of Christ is still an utterly staggering event that should be shocking to anyone who ponders it carefully. We stand amazed at how cruelly Christ was treated. We rightly tremble when we read the many statements Christ made during his lifetime about his impending death—realizing that he fully knew what lay ahead. The fact that these things were foretold in such careful detail does not mitigate the wonder of the cross; it magnifies it.

The Servant's Astonishing Humiliation

It *is* utterly astonishing that the faithful servant of the Lord, the promised deliverer of Israel, would be put on public display in a horrifying, humiliating fashion. That is the very word Isaiah uses: "Many were *astonished* at you—his appearance was so marred, beyond human semblance, and his form beyond that of the children of mankind" (Isa. 52:14).

That verse is an abrupt and startling interruption set between two verses that describe the servant's honor, influence, and exaltation. It is written in a way that purposely magnifies the reader's astonishment. The sudden shift in topics—from *exaltation* to *humiliation* with no warning or transition whatsoever—illustrates the reason "many were astonished." Putting it simply, as we keep stressing, the death of the promised Messiah was profoundly shocking. It seems no one besides Jesus himself was prepared for his death.

Incidentally, the Hebrew word translated "astonished" is a rich one. The English word is capable of being used in a very positive sense. It's used, for example, in Mark 7:37, where it describes the people's fascination and delight after Jesus healed a deaf man, and Scripture says "they were *astonished* beyond measure, saying, 'He has done all things well.'" When he taught the multitudes, "they were *astonished* at his teaching, for his word possessed authority" (Luke 4:32). And when he healed a boy with an unclean spirit, "all were *astonished* at the majesty of God" (Luke 9:43).

Isaiah 52:14 is speaking about a different kind of astonishment. Isaiah uses a Hebrew term (*shamem*) that is never used to describe a positive reaction. It's closer to the English word *appalled*. But it's even stronger than that. It speaks of being totally devastated. In fact it's a term that can describe the total defeat of an army or the utter desolation of a vast region that has fallen into ruins. (Isaiah used this word in 49:19 to describe the land of Judah after the Chaldean armies had demolished almost every trace of human habitation. He spoke of "your desolate [*shamem*] places and your devastated land.")

The same Hebrew word is used quite frequently in the Old Testament, and it is usually translated "left desolate" or "laid waste." But when used in a context such as Isaiah 52:14, the word has the connotation of horror. It speaks of a shock so staggering that one loses control of all rational faculties. It could be translated "numbed," "petrified," or "paralyzed."

So this is a very strong word with a broad range of uses but a very clear meaning. Leviticus 26:32 uses the word twice in a kind of play on words that shows its wide semantic range. God himself is speaking, and he says, "I myself will devastate [*shamem*] the land, so that your enemies who settle in it shall be appalled [*shamem*] at it."

Isaiah employs the term to describe the dismay of those who would witness the atrocious injuries inflicted on the suffering servant. They were devastated. But the damage done *to him* is indescribably worse: "His appearance was so marred, beyond human semblance, and his form beyond that of the children of mankind" (Isa. 52:14). In other words, he would be so disfigured from the sufferings inflicted on him that his face and body would not even appear to be human.

The marring and disfigurement in view here are of course a description of what took place immediately prior to our Lord's crucifixion, while he was on trial. Jesus's disfigurement actually began in Gethsemane on the night of his betrayal and arrest. Scripture describes the deep, inward anguish and utter physical exhaustion he experienced as the sinless Son of God contemplated sin bearing and separation from his Father. He was literally sweating blood at the thought of what he would suffer on behalf of sinners. So he would have been weak and haggard-looking even before he was dragged away and put on trial.

But what left him "so marred, beyond human semblance" were the many tortures inflicted on him by those who put him to death. We know from the Gospel accounts that Jesus was struck on the head, spat upon, mocked, and flogged. He was beaten and abused by the chief priests (Matt. 26:67–68), the temple guard (Mark 14:65), and the Romans (Matt. 27:27–30). Added to that was the terrible scourging he received on Pilate's orders (John 19:1).

To be flogged with a Roman scourge was a severe, even life-threatening punishment. The victim was lashed mercilessly with a *flagellum,* a short whip consisting of a wooden handle to which long leather thongs were attached. Each strip of leather had sharp pieces of bone, iron, and zinc held in place by knots spaced an inch or two apart (for a foot or more) along the business end of each thong. The victim would be tied to a post with his hands above his head and his feet suspended off the ground, stretching his body taught. As the biting strands of the flagellum tore into his back, muscles would be lacerated, veins cut, and internal organs exposed. So massive was the trauma inflicted that the scourging itself did sometimes prove fatal.

Of course, when the sentence called for crucifixion, death by the scourge was an undesirable outcome. A skilled *lictor* (the officer wielding the scourge) knew just how to apply the instrument in a way that would maximize the pain and injury, yet keep the victim alive so that the sentence of crucifixion could be carried out.

Crucifixion was the most brutal form of public execution ever devised. The injuries inflicted in the process were unspeakably savage. Nevertheless, the New Testament narrative makes very little mention of the actual wounds Christ suffered. After the resurrection, Jesus himself spoke of the wounds in his hands and side (John 20:27). But the New Testament doesn't attempt to describe in detail the severity of Jesus's injuries. Anyone within the realm of Roman influence would already be familiar with the awful damage done to a person's body by crucifixion.

Therefore, the Old Testament prophecies about Christ's death tell us more about the humiliating injuries he suffered than the New Testament does. Isaiah 52:14 is the Bible's most graphic one-verse description of our Lord's extreme disfigurement—his face so marred that he no longer appeared to be human. Psalm 22 provides even more insight into what Jesus endured on the cross. That psalm begins with the very words Christ uttered on the cross: "My God, my God, why have you forsaken me?" The psalm also quotes the words of those who mocked the Savior as he hung there: "He trusts in the LORD; let him deliver him; let him rescue him, for he delights in him!" (v. 8; cf. Matt. 27:42).

So there can be no doubt what Psalm 22 refers to. This is Christ's own testimony about the cross, given to us prophetically in a psalm that was written at least a thousand years before it was fulfilled. He says,

> I am poured out like water,
> and all my bones are out of joint;
> my heart is like wax;
> it is melted within my breast;
> my strength is dried up like a potsherd,
> and my tongue sticks to my jaws;
> you lay me in the dust of death.

For dogs encompass me;
    a company of evildoers encircles me;
they have pierced my hands and feet—
I can count all my bones—
they stare and gloat over me. (vv. 14–17)

That describes the crucifixion of Christ with uncanny accuracy, even though it was written centuries before anyone ever thought of executing criminals this way. The piercing of hands and feet refers, of course, to the nails used to fasten Jesus to the cross. Jesus's bones would be wrenched "out of joint" when (after nailing him to the cross) the executioners would lift the cross upright and let it drop into a post-hole that had been dug deep enough to allow the cross to stand upright. The bone-jarring impact would dislocate multiple joints throughout the body. The bones could be counted because extreme trauma and dehydration left him an almost skeletal figure. The surrounding "company of evildoers" is precisely what the Gospel accounts describe (Mark 15:27–32). The phrase "my heart . . . melted within my breast" is the very image one gets from John's description of the scene when "one of the soldiers pierced [Jesus's] side with a spear, and at once there came out blood and water" (John 19:34).

Again, Psalm 22 is a precise prophetic description of the results of crucifixion, more graphic than we get even from the New Testament eyewitness accounts. Yet the earliest mention of crucifixion in any historical record refers to an event that occurred five hundred years after David. When Darius I conquered Babylon for the second time in 519 BC, he had three thousand of the city's most prominent men impaled and left to die slowly.[3] The practice was subsequently adopted as a means of public execution because of the way it struck terror into the hearts of those who witnessed it. Various forms of impalement and crucifixion were employed by world empires for the next five hundred years. The Greeks generally scorned the practice and used it only sparingly. It was the Romans who perfected a method that would keep victims suffering in agony for three days or longer.

A nineteenth-century English church leader, Frederic Farrar, wrote this description of the horrors of crucifixion:

---

3. Herodotus, *Histories*, 3.159.

[On a cross], in tortures which grew ever more insupportable, ever more maddening as time flowed on, the unhappy victims might linger in a living death so cruelly intolerable, that often they were driven to entreat and implore the spectators, or the executioners, for dear pity's sake, to put an end to anguish too awful for man to bear—conscious to the last, and often, with tears of abject misery, beseeching from their enemies the priceless boon of death.

For indeed a death by crucifixion seems to include all that pain and death *can* have of horrible and ghastly—dizziness, cramp, thirst, starvation, sleeplessness, traumatic fever, tetanus, publicity of shame, long continuance of torment, horror of anticipation, mortification of untended wounds—all intensified just up to the point at which they can be endured at all, but all stopping just short of the point which would give to the sufferer the relief of unconsciousness. The unnatural position made every movement painful; the lacerated veins and crushed tendons throbbed with incessant anguish; the wounds, inflamed by exposure, gradually gangrened; the arteries—especially of the head and stomach—became swollen and oppressed with surcharged blood; and while each variety of misery went on gradually increasing, there was added to them the intolerable pang of a burning and raging thirst; and all these physical complications caused an internal excitement and anxiety, which made the prospect of death itself—of death, the awful unknown enemy, at whose approach man usually shudders most—bear the aspect of a delicious and exquisite release.[4]

Isaiah 52:14 must be understood in that light. The brutal treatment Jesus suffered left him so maimed and mangled that he hardly looked human.

The people's astonishment expressed their contempt. It reflects the profound shock they felt as they saw Jesus's humiliation. They found him repulsive, far from their conception of what the Messiah King should be like. His degradation was the deepest possible, the most severe, and the most horrible.

---

4. Frederic William Farrar, *The Sweet Story of Jesus: The Life of Christ* (New York: Commonwealth, 1891), 619. For an analysis of the medical aspects of crucifixion, see William D. Edwards, Wesley J. Gabel, and Floyd E. Hosmer, "On the Physical Death of Jesus Christ," *Journal of the American Medical Association* 255 (March 21, 1986): 1455–63.

But in contrast, his exaltation would be the highest, most profound, and most glorious.

The Servant's Astonishing Exaltation

The way Isaiah 52:12–15 shifts from scene to scene would be very difficult to follow for readers who know nothing about Christ. When he begins in 52:13, the servant of the Lord is "high and lifted up . . . exalted." Verse 14 gives us that shocking past-tense glimpse of the Savior "so marred, beyond human semblance." But then in verse 15 once more the scene, the verb tense, and the tone all change abruptly, and we are looking ahead to Christ's glorious, triumphant return, when "all kings [will] fall down before him, [and] all nations serve him!" (Ps. 72:11). Here the astonishment belongs to Gentile nations and kings, who are left speechless when they see him: "So shall he sprinkle many nations. Kings shall shut their mouths because of him, for that which has not been told them they see, and that which they have not heard they understand" (Isa. 52:15).

"Sprinkle" is one of the possible translations of the Hebrew word *nazah*, which literally means "to spurt" or "to spatter." The word can also mean "to cause to leap" or "to startle." Robert Lowth, an early nineteenth-century Anglican bishop (who published his own translation of Isaiah from the original Hebrew), cited "Bishop Chandler, *Defence*, p. 148, [who] says, 'that *to sprinkle* is used for *to surprise and astonish*, as people are that have much water thrown upon them. And this sense is followed by the LXX [the Septuagint].'"[5] Indeed, the ancient Greek translation of Isaiah that was used in Jesus's time employs a form of the Greek verb *thaumazō*, "to marvel," or "to admire." A literal translation of verse 15 from the Septuagint would therefore say, "Many nations will be amazed at him; kings will keep their mouths shut." That translation fits this context well. It maintains the theme of those final three verses in Isaiah 52: "Behold[!] . . . Many were astonished. . . . [Nations will be amazed]. . . . Kings shall shut their mouths because of him."

Just as many were astonished by the servant's humiliation, so

---

5. Robert Lowth, *Isaiah: A New Translation with a Preliminary Dissertation and Notes* (London: Thomas Tegg & Son, 1837), 363.

also will the nations and their kings be astonished by his exaltation. Kings—those who think they *always* have the right to speak—will be left speechless. And when that day comes, all the nations of the world will see it. "All the tribes of the earth will mourn, and they will see the Son of Man coming on the clouds of heaven with power and great glory" (Matt. 24:30). They will be dumbfounded at the terrifying but spectacular scene. Their silence will be the involuntary effect of extreme astonishment and intense emotion that will render them mute.

Here is how Scripture speaks of that day:

> The sun will be darkened, and the moon will not give its light, and the stars will fall from heaven, and the powers of the heavens will be shaken. Then will appear in heaven the sign of the Son of Man, and then all the tribes of the earth will mourn, and they will see the Son of Man coming on the clouds of heaven with power and great glory. (Matt. 24:29–30)

> But I tell you, from now on you will see the Son of Man seated at the right hand of Power and coming on the clouds of heaven. (Matt. 26:64)

> Men of Galilee, why do you stand looking into heaven? This Jesus, who was taken up from you into heaven, will come in the same way as you saw him go into heaven. (Acts 1:11)

> God considers it just to repay with affliction those who afflict you, and to grant relief to you who are afflicted as well as to us, when the Lord Jesus is revealed from heaven with his mighty angels in flaming fire, inflicting vengeance on those who do not know God and on those who do not obey the gospel of our Lord Jesus. (2 Thess. 1:6–8)

God will install his Son as King of the world. The kings of the earth will see it and be terrified:

> Why do the nations rage
> and the peoples plot in vain?
> The kings of the earth set themselves,
> and the rulers take counsel together,
> against the LORD and against his Anointed, saying,

"Let us burst their bonds apart
 and cast away their cords from us."

He who sits in the heavens laughs;
 the Lord holds them in derision.
Then he will speak to them in his wrath,
 and terrify them in his fury, saying,
"As for me, I have set my King
 on Zion, my holy hill." (Ps. 2:1–6)

Notice that most of those prophecies emphasize how the second coming of the Lord Jesus Christ will catch people completely unaware. It's easy to see why. Even today, despite the vast number of people worldwide who profess some kind of faith in Christ, most people in the world are not looking for Christ's return. But when he comes, "that which has not been told them they [will] see, and that which they have not heard they [will] understand." And they will be stunned into silence.

That final phrase in Isaiah 52:15 states an important principle with far-reaching implications. The prophet is declaring that people worldwide who have never heard the Word of God and have no earthly reason to grasp the truth about Israel's Messiah will suddenly see and understand who he is, because God himself will open their eyes to the truth. Paul cited that text to explain why he was so committed to the task of preaching the gospel to the Gentiles: "Those who have never been told of him will see, and those who have never heard will understand" (Rom. 15:21).

But the context here in Isaiah 52 suggests that the ultimate fulfillment of this promise will occur when he comes on the clouds "and every eye will see him, even those who pierced him, and all tribes of the earth will wail on account of him" (Rev. 1:7).

Now consider once more as a unit those final three verses of Isaiah 52. At first glance, they may have seemed like a series of non sequiturs. But they are bound together with a clear theme: the servant of the Lord is one astonishing person. His innate wisdom and splendor are wonders to behold (v. 13). That one so glorious could be subjected to such gross humiliation and disfigurement is utterly preposterous and staggering (v. 14). But the greatest wonder of all will occur at his glorious and victorious return, when every mouth will be stopped and the whole world will stand guilty before God (cf. Rom. 3:19).

Those three verses (uttered by God himself) about the servant's astonishing *revelation,* *humiliation,* and *exaltation* are only the introduction to the full message Isaiah is going to deliver in chapter 53. There we will come face-to-face with the most appalling fact of all—namely, the servant's astonishing *rejection.* Although he came at a time when hopeful messianic expectation was at its peak, he was met with the most vehement kind of scorn and refusal. His own people "despised and rejected" him (53:3). It is to that tragic reality that we turn in the second stanza of this marvelous prophecy.

4

What If Some Did Not Believe?

Every unprejudiced person might have seen from this passage that
the Messiah, when he came, was not to be surrounded with pomp,
but would come as "a man of sorrows, and acquainted with grief,"
to be "despised and rejected of men." Yet, though the truth was
written as with a sunbeam, and the Jewish people were pretty generally acquainted with their own Scriptures, so that they had the
opportunity of knowing it, yet when the Messiah came unto his
own, his own received him not, and though favoured with the clear-
est prophecies concerning him they rejected his claims, and cried,
"Let him be crucified!"

Charles Spurgeon[1]

If messianic expectation was so high when Jesus came, why was he
rejected by the vast majority of Jewish people? "Did Israel not understand?" (Rom. 10:19). "His own people did not receive him" (John
1:11). Does that in any way discredit the claim that Jesus is the true
Messiah?

Not at all. Isaiah clearly prophesied that the suffering servant of
Yahweh would be met with unbelief and rejection. From the opening verses of Isaiah 53 the point is made clear, repeatedly: "Who has
believed what he has heard from us? . . . He had no form or majesty

---

1. Charles Spurgeon, *The Metropolitan Tabernacle Pulpit* (London: Passmore & Alabaster, 1872), 18:565.

that we should look at him, and no beauty that we should desire him. He was despised and rejected by men. . . . He was despised, and we esteemed him not" (vv. 1–3). The rejection of the Messiah is one of the major features of Isaiah 53.

Saul of Tarsus was himself a Jewish scholar who once rejected the claims of Jesus Christ and hated Christianity with such extreme malice that he "not only locked up many of the saints in prison after receiving authority from the chief priests, but when they were put to death [he] cast [his] vote against them" (Acts 26:10). He basically oversaw the earliest attempts by the leading Jewish authorities to eradicate Christianity. But then he himself was miraculously converted, called by the risen Christ to serve, and appointed to be an apostle. He ultimately planted churches in Gentile regions from Antioch to Rome.

Occasionally someone will suggest that Paul ministered among the Gentiles because his own conversion caused him to develop a kind of self-loathing for his own ethnicity. But Paul was clearly no anti-Semite. He said his heart's desire and constant prayer to God for his brethren was that they might grasp the truth of Christ and be saved (Rom. 10:1). He even said he would accept being damned if that could be the means of saving his Jewish brethren: "I could wish that I myself were accursed and cut off from Christ for the sake of my brothers, my kinsmen according to the flesh. They are Israelites, and to them belong the adoption, the glory, the covenants, the giving of the law, the worship, and the promises" (Rom. 9:3–4).

Pondering the unbelief of so many people who knew the Old Testament promises and had every reason to embrace Jesus as Messiah but rejected him anyway, Paul pointed to Isaiah 53 to make the point that Israel's unbelief was foretold by the prophets right alongside the messianic prophecies. He wrote, "They have not all obeyed the gospel. For Isaiah says, 'Lord, who has believed what he has heard from us?'" (Rom. 10:16).

The verse he was quoting is Isaiah 53:1.

They Have Not All Obeyed the Gospel

The Old Testament messianic prophecies fulfilled by Jesus are amazingly detailed and specific. We listed many of those prophecies in chapter 1. Here it might be helpful to examine some of them carefully in context, because they often appear unexpectedly, in places where readers might not be looking for them. Collectively, however, they give too many specific details about the coming Messiah to brush aside his true identity as indefinite or ambiguous.

Micah 5:2, for example, is the verse that predicts where Messiah would be born: "But you, O Bethlehem Ephrathah, who are too little to be among the clans of Judah, from you shall come forth for me one who is to be ruler in Israel, whose coming forth is from of old, from ancient days." The verse appears in a context where Micah is speaking a prophecy against Zedekiah, whom Nebuchadnezzar had illegitimately appointed as vassal king over Judah. But Zedekiah tried to rebel, so Nebuchadnezzar gouged his eyes out (2 Kings 25:1–7).

In chapter 10 we will survey the succession of kings who ruled Judah after the death of Isaiah until the Babylonian captivity. Zedekiah fits into that era. But a little background on him here is necessary to understand the historical references in Micah 5:1–2.

Though he was not directly in the line of succession, Zedekiah was the last person to sit on the throne of David. His reign ended when Nebuchadnezzar lost patience with him, leveled Jerusalem, blinded Zedekiah, and carried him to Babylon, where he died (Ezek. 12:13). Micah 5:1 refers to Nebuchadnezzar's assault on Jerusalem: "Now muster your troops, O daughter of troops; siege is laid against us; with a rod they strike the judge of Israel on the cheek." The "daughter of troops" refers to the band of soldiers from the Chaldean army sent by Nebuchadnezzar to punish Zedekiah. Zedekiah is mentioned in verse 1 as "the judge of Israel." The rod that smites his cheek is the instrument used to put his eyes out.

Verse 2 is then addressed to the town of Bethlehem. Since no king ever took the throne of David after Zedekiah was deposed, the promise in verse 2 was given to assure the Israelites that their true ruler, the rightful heir to David's throne, would nevertheless come forth. The messianic implications of that prophecy were obvious even in Old Testament times. But like most of the Old Testament's messianic promises, Micah 5:2 would have been somewhat mysterious until it was finally fulfilled. Micah gives no clue about *when* or *how* Messiah would come, but he is very specific about *where* the promised ruler would come from.

Proof that people before the time of Christ clearly understood the messianic significance of Micah 5:2 is seen in the fact that when Magi from the east came seeking the newborn king in Herod's time, the chief priests and scribes cited this text without hesitation, and they directed the wise men to Bethlehem.

Various Old Testament prophecies about the messianic deliverer were full of specific details that fit Jesus precisely. They are scattered here and there across the entire Old Testament. In the earliest chapters of Genesis, for example, Adam and Eve were promised that the one who would ultimately defeat Satan and overthrow the curse of sin would be a man, the offspring of the woman (Gen. 3:15). He would be a descendant of Abraham (Gal. 3:16). He would come from the tribe of Judah (Gen. 49:10) in the bloodline of David (Jer. 23:5–6; Rom. 1:3).

There were also clues along the way that Messiah would be more than merely a man. He would be God incarnate. There's a hint of his deity even in Micah 5:2, for example: "[His] coming forth is *from of old, from ancient days.*" The King James Version quite properly translates it as "from of old, from everlasting." The Hebrew expression means "from eternity past," so the one who comes forth from Bethlehem, "who is to be ruler in Israel," would be someone who did not have his origins in the human realm; he existed before the beginning of time.

The evidences for Messiah's deity are subtle but undeniable. To cite another example, David called the Messiah his "Lord" (Ps. 110:1). Jesus himself asked rhetorically after his confrontation with some Jewish religious leaders, "If then David calls him Lord, how is he his son?" (Matt. 22:43–45). David was unquestionably referring to the Messiah as God, since no Middle Eastern father, least of all a king, would address his own son as "Lord." Add to those examples Isaiah's famous prophecy of the virgin birth in Isaiah 7:14. That prophecy also strongly suggested that Messiah would be God incarnate, because his name would be *Immanuel*, "which means, God with us" (Matt. 1:23). Isaiah 9:6 goes on to say, "His name shall be called Wonderful Counselor, *Mighty God*, Everlasting Father, Prince of Peace."

After centuries of waiting, the Lord Jesus Christ finally came, born of a virgin as Isaiah had predicted (cf. Luke 1:26–35), in Bethlehem (Matt. 2:1), a descendant of Abraham and David (Matt. 1:1), his deity confirmed by his unparalleled words and works (Luke 24:19; Acts 2:22; John 5:36; 7:46; Matt. 7:28–29). His messianic credentials were impeccable, which caused many who saw and heard him to wonder, "Can it be that the authorities really know that this is the Christ?" (John 7:26). And, "When the Christ appears, will he do more signs than this man has done?" (v. 31). After witnessing his miracle-working power, a mob consisting of thousands even attempted to "take him by force to make him king" (John 6:15). Frenzied crowds hailed him as Messiah when he made his final journey to Jerusalem (Matt. 21:9; John 12:13).

Yet most of the people of Israel, following their religious leaders (Matt. 27:20), ultimately rejected him as their Messiah. They "crucified and killed [him] by the hands of lawless men [the Roman authorities]" (Acts 2:23; cf. 3:13–15; 4:10–11; 5:30; 7:52; 13:27).

How could that have happened? How could Jesus's own people reject him despite overwhelming evidence that he was indeed Israel's long-awaited Messiah? We've suggested already that at least part of the answer lies in their mistaken expectations concerning the Messiah. They were looking for a conquering champion who would liberate them from their hated Roman oppressors, usher in his kingdom, and bestow blessings on Israel.

Emil Schürer, a famous nineteenth-century historian and German professor of theology, wrote a meticulously researched multivolume work on first-century Judaism. He described the messianic hope of that era in a lengthy section he referred to as "a systematic statement of Messianic doctrinal theology."[2] According to Schürer, Jewish theologians believed Messiah's coming would unfold in a nine-phase chain of closely linked events. Here's how Schürer summarized first-century Hebrew eschatology:

1. "*The last tribulation and perplexity.* . . . The appearance of redemption must be preceded by a period of special trouble and affliction."[3]

---

2. Emil Schürer, *A History of the Jewish People in the Time of Jesus Christ* (Edinburgh: T&T Clark, 1896), 2:154.
3. Ibid.

2. "*Elijah as the forerunner.* The return of the prophet Elijah to prepare the way of the Messiah was expected on the ground of Mal. [4:5–6]."[4]

3. "*The appearing of the Messiah.*"[5] Professor Schürer says the earliest messianic hope was not focused on a single individual but on the entire dynasty of theocratic kings in the Davidic line. Over time, however, "the hope was consolidated and raised more and more into the expectation of *a personal Messiah* as a ruler endowed by God with special gifts and powers."[6] Schürer acknowledges that it isn't entirely clear whether ancient Jewish writers in general understood Messiah to be simply human or a preexistent being of a higher order. But he cites several sources, including the Book of Enoch (an ancient Jewish apocryphal work), where Messiah is said to have been chosen, named, and hidden with God before the world was created. He also points out that by the first century, the Jews fully expected their Messiah to have power to work signs and wonders.[7] Clearly first-century Jewish hopes regarding Messiah were more robust and more in harmony with New Testament revelation than many Jewish leaders today would care to admit.

4. "*Last attack of the hostile powers.* After the appearing of the Messiah the heathen powers will assemble against him for a last attack."[8]

5. "*Destruction of the hostile powers.* . . . A great [apocalyptic] judgment, inflicted by God Himself upon His adversaries,"[9] would finally make possible the removal of sin's curse and the inauguration of the messianic age, a time of unprecedented peace and prosperity worldwide.

6. "*Renovation of Jerusalem.* Since the Messianic kingdom is to be set up in the Holy Land (comp *e.g.* Ezra ix. 9), Jerusalem itself must first of all be renovated."[10]

---

4. Ibid., 156.
5. Ibid., 158.
6. Ibid., 160; emphasis in original.
7. Ibid., 161.
8. Ibid., 164.
9. Ibid., 165.
10. Ibid., 168.

7. "*Gathering of the Dispersed.*" Professor Schürer says the expectation that the dispersed of Israel would return to their land "was so self-evident, that this hope would have been cherished even without the definite predictions of the Old Testament."[11]

8. "*The kingdom of glory in Palestine.*"[12] The setting up of Messiah's kingdom in Jerusalem meant Israel would become the center of world power, and all other nations would be subjugated to the Jewish Messiah. "*The Holy Land* forms the *central point* of this kingdom. Hence, to 'inherit the land' is equivalent to having a part in the Messianic Kingdom."[13]

9. "*Renovation of the world.* The hope of a renovation of heaven and earth is chiefly based on Isa. lxv. 17, lxvi. 22."[14]

That view of the last days obviously has a lot in common with Christian premillennialism (the belief that Christ will return to rule and reign the world in peace for a thousand years). The parallels are too numerous to ignore. Indeed, if we take the Old Testament promises about Messiah's kingdom at face value and employ the same rules of interpretation we would use to understand any other passage of Scripture, that is a suitable outline of what the Bible teaches about the ultimate reign of Israel's Messiah in the last days. In Matthew 24, Jesus himself foretold that the end of the age would begin with a time of "great tribulation, such as has not been from the beginning of the world until now, no, and never will be" (v. 21; cf. Rev. 7:14). Every detail of the ancient scholars' prophetic timeline is also echoed in the book of Revelation, culminating with the millennial reign of Christ (Rev. 20:4–5).

What the scholars of Jesus's time failed to take into account, however, was the theme of Isaiah 53. Before conquering the last of his enemies and establishing his throne in Jerusalem, Messiah would first shed his own blood in order to pay the redemption price for sin and thereby "[ransom] people for God from every tribe and language and people and nation" (Rev. 5:9). In short, there was no place in Jewish

---

11. Ibid., 169.
12. Ibid., 170.
13. Ibid., 172.
14. Ibid., 177.

messianic theology for a sacrificed, dead, or even a risen Messiah. In the words of one commentator,

> Death and resurrection formed no part of their concept of Messiah's office and programme. . . . They were hoping for a Messiah who would break the imperialist domination of the Romans by force of arms. A Messiah who managed to allow himself to be caught by the Jewish authorities, handed over to the Romans and crucified before he had even begun to organize any guerrilla operations, popular uprising or open warfare—what use was he? If the Old Testament prophesied a liberator who should not die, but be triumphant, Jesus was already disqualified: he had died. After that, it was almost irrelevant to talk of resurrection.[15]

Compared to those lofty expectations, the circumstances of Jesus's life and ministry did not seem to match what the Jewish people expected of the Messiah. He was born in the most humble of circumstances. After giving birth, Mary "wrapped him in swaddling cloths and laid him in a manger" (Luke 2:7). A manger, of course, is a feeding trough for animals—as nonregal a bed as any infant king was ever placed in. He was not attended in his birth by the wealthy and elite of society, but by shepherds—minimally skilled laborers who were near the bottom of the social ladder. Jesus himself grew up in the humblest of circumstances, raised in a working-class family in a poor village of no repute (John 1:46), in a region scorned by the rest of the nation (John 7:41, 52).

Unlike the haughty, proud, self-righteous Pharisees (John 7:49; 9:34), Jesus ministered to the outcasts of Jewish society—the tax collectors (Matt. 9:10–11; 11:19; Luke 15:1–2); gross sinners such as thieves, drunkards, and prostitutes (Matt. 21:31–32; Luke 7:37, 39); and even the despised Samaritans (John 4:4–43).

He didn't bother seeking status or affirmation from the nation's elite spiritual leaders, the chief priests, scribes, and Pharisees. Nor did he choose his closest followers from among the prominent, the wealthy, or the politically powerful. The twelve apostles were mostly fishermen. One was a tax collector. All but one were Galileans, viewed with con-

---

15. David Gooding, *According to Luke* (Grand Rapids, MI: Eerdmans, 1987), 351.

tempt by the more sophisticated people of Jerusalem and Judah. Worse yet, the one non-Galilean turned out to be a traitor who betrayed Jesus to his enemies.

Jesus was not educated in the rabbinic schools, had no political agenda, sought no office or position of power or influence, gathered no army, and presented no strategy to establish his rule. Furthermore, among the multitudes over the past twenty centuries who have acknowledged him as their Messiah with true, obedient faith, "not many . . . were wise according to worldly standards, not many were powerful, not many were of noble birth" (1 Cor. 1:26).

Yet on the other hand, his supernatural power over disease, death, and demons was obvious (cf. John 2:23; 3:2; 6:2; 7:31). Even his bitterest opponents, the chief priests and Pharisees, exclaimed in exasperation, "What are we to do? For this man performs many signs. If we let him go on like this, everyone will believe in him, and the Romans will come and take away both our place and our nation" (John 11:47–48).

Jesus's amazing power and wisdom did raise the common people's hopes that he would be the Messiah and deliverer they hoped for. It was during his Galilean ministry that they tried to force the issue, seeking to make him king by popular acclaim (John 6:14–15). Finally, when he approached Jerusalem for the last Passover, they hailed him as their King and Messiah in a massive display of popular optimism. Crowds of people who were there that day to witness his triumphal entry into the city were hoping, like the two men Jesus encountered on the road to Emmaus, "that he was the one to redeem Israel" (Luke 24:21).

But when he returned to Jerusalem the next day, Jesus did not assault the Romans, overthrow the enemies of God, or rally Israel to his cause. Instead, he shockingly assaulted the corrupt businesses run by the religious authorities in the temple—the very heart of Judaism. Throughout the rest of Passion Week, Jesus continued to confront the false teaching of the Jewish leaders and to teach the truth openly. By Friday the crowds, influenced by their leaders (Matt. 27:20), had turned against him. "Crucify, crucify him!" they demanded of a reluctant Pilate (Luke 23:21). "His blood be on us and on our children!" (Matt. 27:25). They decided he was not the king they wanted.

He *is*, however, the Savior we all need. Remember, first-century

Judaism had diminished the biblical emphasis on grace and injected the notion of human merit. People had come to believe that what set them apart from the rest of the world was their Abrahamic ancestry, boldly highlighted by the law's ceremonial features (mostly rites, rituals, and dietary restrictions that made their piety conspicuous). To those things the rabbis added many ostentatious customs of their own—additional ceremonial washings, rigid rules about tithing, the wearing of ornate phylacteries and tassels, restrictions against eating with sinners, and so on. Obedience to the law and its rabbinic accretions became a means by which they believed they could accumulate righteous merit. All those things combined surely gave them a standing before God. Or so they thought.

But legalism (including a public display of ceremonial religion—especially when used as a cover for evil) is an abominable substitute for real holiness. God condemns such behavior repeatedly (Isa. 1:11–16; 66:3–4; Jer. 6:20; Amos 5:21–25). Everything we do is corrupted with selfish motives, sinful desires, and a want of pure-hearted love for the Lord. Therefore Scripture says the works of righteousness we perform—even the very *best* things we do—are nothing more than a "polluted garment" (Isa. 64:6). Only God can clothe sinners "with the garments of salvation" or cover them "with the robe of righteousness" (Isa. 61:10).

Jesus is the true Messiah, and he will one day return to reign as King over all the earth. But he could not establish his kingdom (with all its promised blessings for Jews and Gentiles alike) until he had provided salvation. People cannot be delivered from their suffering until they are delivered from their sin. The countless millions of sacrificed animals offered under the sacrificial system did not atone for sin. "Otherwise, would they not have ceased to be offered?" (Heb. 10:2). The constant offering of those sacrifices was designed to *remind* people of their sin and the need for an adequate atonement. "In these sacrifices there is a reminder of sins every year" (v. 3). The sacrifices pointed to Jesus, "the Lamb of God, who takes away the sin of the world!" (John 1:29). Only the death of a perfect substitute would truly satisfy the demands of God's justice and pay the penalty for sin. Isaiah 53 is God's promise that he himself would provide a suitable Lamb (cf. Gen. 22:8).

Who Has Believed?

Isaiah 53 opens with two questions. The New American Standard Bible offers the most literal translation of verse 1: "Who has believed our message? And to whom has the arm of the LORD been revealed?" The sense of the question is, "Who among us has believed *the message we heard?*" This is not about a message others have "heard from us" (ESV); it is about a message that was *given* to the voices who are speaking. It is a reference to the gospel, and specifically the news that Israel's Messiah would die for the sins of his people. That is clear from the context, because that's what the rest of the chapter focuses on.

Who is "we"? Bear in mind that this passage represents the collective confession all Israel will make on that day yet future when the nation finally turns to Christ. The words, of course, would be a suitable expression of repentance for anyone who has known *about* Christ but spurned him for some time before embracing him as Lord and Savior. But in this context it is a remarkable confession of national repentance, and we need to understand it in that light.

The prophecy indicates that when "the children of Israel . . . return and seek the LORD their God, and . . . come in fear to the LORD and to his goodness in the latter days" (Hos. 3:5), they will acknowledge and confess their own culpability for having refused to believe. They of all people ought to have received him gladly. Remember how the apostle Paul outlined the many spiritual advantages the children of Israel enjoyed as the chosen people of God. "To begin with, the Jews were entrusted with the oracles of God" (Rom. 3:2). Moreover, "to them belong the adoption, the glory, the covenants, the giving of the law, the worship, and the promises. To them belong the patriarchs, and from their race, according to the flesh, is the Christ, who is God over all, blessed forever. Amen" (Rom. 9:4–5). The gospel itself was given "to the Jew first" (Rom. 1:16). When Christ came, "he came to his own" (John 1:11). Although he dealt graciously with every Gentile who ever sought his blessing, the main focus of his earthly ministry was to the Jewish people. He himself said, "I was sent only to the lost sheep of the house of Israel" (Matt. 15:24). He "became a servant to the circumcised to show God's truthfulness, in order to confirm the promises given to the patriarchs" (Rom. 15:8).

We've seen already how all the Old Testament prophecies concerning Messiah have been or will be perfectly fulfilled by Jesus. His many miracles, witnessed by thousands, gave further testimony that he was indeed the Anointed One of God. His teaching bore all the marks of divine authority (Matt. 7:28–29). So there was more than ample evidence confirming who he really was. Yet, as John says near the start of his Gospel, "his own people did not receive him" (John 1:11). The overwhelming majority of Jewish people from the time of Jesus until today have rejected his messianic claims and turned their backs on the gracious promise of forgiveness and full redemption.

They are not alone in that, of course. Most Gentiles also say no to the gospel. "The gate is wide and the way is easy that leads to destruction, and those who enter by it are many" (Matt. 7:13). Christ is "a living stone rejected by men but in the sight of God chosen and precious" (1 Pet. 2:4). It is to the eternal shame of all unbelievers that they would rebuff the Son of God, who is the perfect self-revelation of Yahweh (Col. 2:9). It is a matter of plain fact that unbelief is the dominant response to the gospel in virtually every culture worldwide. Proud yet fallen people refuse to confess their need for forgiveness. They will suppress or mock any mention of sin's guilt or God's wrath. They recklessly dismiss the good news of salvation as foolish and offensive.

It is of course appalling that *anyone* would scoff at the prospect of divine judgment. But it is especially disgraceful when people who have heard the tender pleas and promises of Christ turn away from him anyway—often even hating the mere mention of his name. Jesus told the eleven faithful disciples, "If the world hates you, know that it has hated me before it hated you" (John 15:18). The whole world—not just one nation or ethnic group—bears guilt for rejecting Christ.

Nevertheless, for the unbelieving majority in national Israel—beginning with the first-century religious leaders in Jerusalem who colluded with the Romans to put Jesus to death—the shame of their rejection is intensified by the fact that they had the messianic prophecies and promises. They enjoyed every possible spiritual advantage. The gospel literally did come to them first. As we have seen, Scripture indicates that the chief priests and religious authorities had every reason to believe that Jesus was who he claimed to be, yet their greatest fear was the loss of their own status: "If we let him go on . . . the Romans will come and take away both our place and our nation" (John 11:48). They purposely shut their minds to the possibility that Jesus's claims were true. Like every unbeliever, they were culpable for their own unbelief. They were without excuse (Rom. 1:20).

And their guilt was magnified by the fact that they had been given so many privileges. They saw and heard him firsthand, but they hardened their hearts anyway. Therefore, in Jesus's words, "they will receive the greater condemnation" (Mark 12:40). "Everyone to whom much was given, of him much will be required, and from him to whom they entrusted much, they will demand the more" (Luke 12:48).

Unbelief has a blinding effect. The Jewish leaders' fear that everyone would embrace Jesus as the promised Messiah might seem to indicate that they themselves knew he was who he claimed to be. But their vision was clouded by their own unbelief and their hatred for him. The apostle Paul was a rising star among the Pharisees at the time of the crucifixion. He must have known many of the most elite Jewish leaders personally. He was trained in Jerusalem at the feet of Gamaliel (Acts 22:3). Gamaliel was the most famous and highly respected rabbi of his time and a member of the Sanhedrin, the highest ruling council in all Judaism (Acts 5:34). According to Paul, "those who live[d] in Jerusalem and their rulers . . . *did not recognize* [*Christ or*] *understand the utterances of the prophets*" (Acts 13:27).

They were still culpable for their unbelief. They had no excuse for not recognizing him. They were blinded by willful sin. Paul goes on to say, "They did not recognize him nor understand the utterances of the prophets, which are read every Sabbath, [even though they themselves fulfilled those prophecies] by condemning him. And though they found in him no guilt worthy of death, they asked Pilate to have him executed" (vv. 27–28). It was a wicked breach of their duty as spiritual leaders in Israel. They led their nation into apostasy.

Paul says the entire nation has been subject to a similar blindness from that time on. "A partial hardening has come upon Israel, until the fullness of the Gentiles has come in" (Rom. 11:25). "Israel failed to obtain what it was seeking. The elect obtained it, but the rest were hardened, as it is written, 'God gave them a spirit of stupor, eyes that would not see and ears that would not hear, down to this very day'" (vv. 7–8). "Their minds were hardened. For to this day, when they read the old covenant, that same veil remains unlifted, because only through Christ is it taken away" (2 Cor. 3:14).

In other words, it is a judicial hardening, prophesied by the Old Testament and imposed by God in response to willful apostasy. The apostle compares Israel to an olive-tree branch that has been cut off ("broken off because of their unbelief") so that Gentiles can be grafted in (Rom. 11:17–20). Paul makes this point as an encouragement for Gentiles to "stand fast through faith. . . . Do not become proud, but fear" (v. 20).

It also underscores the sovereignty of God. The elect (including many Jewish people) *are* even now being saved. "Israel failed to obtain what it was seeking. The elect obtained it, but the rest were hardened, as it is written, 'God gave them a spirit of stupor, eyes that would not see and ears that would not hear, down to this very day'" (vv. 7–8). In other words, the corporate and national blindness of Israel was no accident, and it does not signify God's final abandonment of his people. It is a purposeful judgment, imposed by God after centuries of Israel's unbelief, disobedience, and half-heartedness. Its ultimate design is not to destroy the Jewish nation but to spur them to repentance: "Did they stumble in order that they might fall? By no means! Rather, through their trespass salvation has come to the Gentiles, so as to make Israel jealous" (Rom. 11:11).

With all of that on his heart and mind, Paul wrote, "They have not all obeyed the gospel" (Rom. 10:16). But he points out that even Israel's rejection fulfills the plan and prophecies of God. To make the point, he quotes Isaiah 53:1: "For Isaiah says, 'LORD, WHO HAS BE-LIEVED OUR REPORT?'" (Rom. 10:16 NASB).

In short, the underlying reason so many from Israel rejected and continue to reject the gospel message about Jesus Christ is not merely ignorance, but stubbornness: "But of Israel [God] says, 'All day long I have held out my hands to a disobedient and contrary people'" (v. 21; cf. Isa. 65:2).

The Power of God for Salvation to Everyone Who Believes

The second question Isaiah 53:1 asks is, "To whom has the arm of the LORD been revealed?" The "arm of the LORD" is a symbol of his divine power (cf. Isa. 51:9; 52:10; 59:16; 62:8; Luke 1:51; John 12:38). Here it refers to God's power demonstrated in the miracles of Jesus and ultimately revealed in his power to save through the good news about Messiah. Isaiah's focus is still firmly fixed on the gospel message. "It *is* the power of God ['the arm of the Lord'] for salvation to everyone who believes, to the Jew first and also to the Greek" (Rom. 1:16).

Even though the people of Israel collectively and overwhelmingly rejected their Messiah, his work carries on. Paul sorrowfully says that his "kinsmen according to the flesh" (Rom. 9:3) were "ignorant of the righteousness of God, and seeking to establish their own, they did not submit to God's righteousness" (10:3). They failed to grasp the truth that "Christ is the end of the law for righteousness to everyone who believes" (v. 4). In other words, they did not understand that they had no ground on which to stand before God and no possibility of earning his favor with their own good works. They therefore did not see their need for the servant's sacrifice on their behalf. Had they believed, the perfect righteousness of their sinless Messiah would have been imputed to them (cf. 2 Cor. 5:21; 1 Pet. 2:24). Instead, they chose to clothe themselves with their own self-righteousness. By refusing God's righteousness and trusting their own, they made themselves supremely offensive to God.

In fact, Isaiah casts off all the normal rules of genteel discourse in the way he describes the guilt of those who trusted their own good works. He says it was as if they were dressed in used menstrual rags. That is the literal meaning of the Hebrew expression in Isaiah 64:6: "We have all become like one who is unclean, and all our righteous deeds are like a *polluted garment.*"

Like all self-righteous sinners, they imagined that God was less holy than he is and that they were more virtuous than they were. So they came to God on their terms, not his. An inadequate view of the sinfulness of sin kept them from understanding why the Savior died.

Those who don't understand the glory of divine righteousness will never see the necessity of atonement.

That, again, is the plight of all unbelievers. It's an error that is in no way unique to Israel. As John the Baptist said of Christ, "He bears witness to what he has seen and heard, yet *no one* receives his testimony"

(John 3:32). But it was uniquely tragic and significant that the majority in Israel turned away in unbelief. They were, after all, the nation chosen to bring Messiah into the world.

John's Gospel gives us a clear snapshot of what the people who actually heard Jesus teach and saw his miracles were thinking. In John 12:32 the Lord said to them, "And I, when I am lifted up from the earth, will draw all people to myself." He was referring to his crucifixion (v. 33). Incredulous, "the crowd answered him, 'We have heard from the Law that the Christ remains forever. How can you say that the Son of Man must be lifted up? Who is this Son of Man?'" (v. 34). A dying Messiah was incomprehensible to them, since they saw no need for his death to atone for their sins.

Jesus went on to warn them about the dire consequences of such persistent unbelief:

The light is among you for a little while longer. Walk while you have the light, lest darkness overtake you. The one who walks in the darkness does not know where he is going. While you have the light, believe in the light, that you may become sons of light." When Jesus had said these things, he departed and hid himself from them. (John 12:35–36)

The apostle John then explained the significance of Jesus's warning and punctuated it with a quotation from Isaiah 53:

Though he had done so many signs before them, they still did not believe in him, so that the word spoken by the prophet Isaiah might be fulfilled: "Lord, who has believed what he heard from us, and to whom has the arm of the Lord been revealed?" Therefore they *could not* believe. For again Isaiah said, "He has blinded their eyes and hardened their heart, lest they see with their eyes, and understand with their heart, and turn, and I would heal them." Isaiah said these things because he saw his glory and spoke of him. (John 12:37–41)

The unbelieving majority of Israel rejected Jesus first of all because their theology was fatally deficient. They wrongly believed they could earn salvation through their own efforts. They had faith in themselves, not in God. So they rejected the gospel, which is, after all, "the arm of the Lord"—the power of God for salvation to everyone who believes.

God therefore judicially sealed their unbelief by blinding their eyes and hardening their hearts.

Don't read that and imagine that God is to blame for their unbelief. The fault is theirs because of their persistent, stiff-necked rejection of his Son.

He Was Despised, and We Esteemed Him Not

In Isaiah 53:2–3, Isaiah gives three reasons for the unbelief Israel will confess. All three express the unbelieving Israelites' contempt for the servant of the Lord.

First, from their perspective, the servant had a contemptible beginning. "He grew up before [Yahweh] like a young plant, and like a root out of dry ground" (v. 2a). At his birth, only a few in Israel recognized him for who he truly was. They were the shepherds (Luke 2:8–18), Simeon (Luke 2:25–32), Anna (Luke 2:36–38), and some others "who were waiting for the redemption of Jerusalem" (Luke 2:38). But he grew up in full view of God the Father, who watched approvingly as his incarnate Son "increased in wisdom and in stature and in favor with God and man" (Luke 2:52). At Jesus's baptism (and again at the transfiguration) God declared of him, "You are my beloved Son; with you I am well pleased" (Mark 1:11; cf. 9:7).

From the point of view of most in Israel—including those in his hometown of Nazareth (Matt. 13:53–58)—Jesus was merely a "young plant . . . a root out of dry ground." Israel was largely agrarian, so the illustration is one that would have been familiar to most people. The Hebrew word translated "young plant" refers to a sucker branch, a useless, uncultivated, unwanted parasitic shoot off the main plant, which is removed so it can't drain resources from the main branches. These shoots (called water sprouts) tend to be prolific on olive trees. They grow from the base of the tree trunk, where they siphon off moisture and nutrients. They also make the tree more susceptible to harmful insects and disease, so they must be removed.

The metaphorical reference to the servant as a sucker branch here reflects the fact that Jesus's beginning seemed irrelevant, insignificant, and totally unpromising. He was not someone whom the typical observer might expect to grow into the role of Messiah. His parents were common people, without any social status. As we've already noted, his first cradle was an animal's feed trough nearly a hundred miles from home, in some place that must have seemed like a squatter's habitation (Luke 2:7). He grew up in the small village of Nazareth, off the beaten track in Galilee, far from the centers of Jewish culture and religion. So insignificant was Nazareth that it is not even mentioned in the Old Testament, the Talmud, or the writings of Josephus. The town was so obscure that some skeptics used to claim that Nazareth could not have actually existed in Jesus's time. (Ample archaeological evidence has since debunked that claim.[16]) Nazareth was a place from which nothing good could be expected to come (John 1:46). Christ lived there in complete obscurity for thirty years, working as a carpenter until the start of his public ministry.

Second, Jesus's whole character was antithetical to what they expected of a triumphant, conquering, messianic deliverer. The phrase "a root out of dry ground" is obviously a close parallel to the expression "a young plant." But the connotation is slightly different. Here Isaiah uses a four-word phrase that literally means "a root in a parched wilderness portion of the earth." It describes a sapling no one purposely planted and no one cares about. (Had they cared, they would have watered it.) It could also refer to a parched root jutting up out of the ground that may trip someone. It's another way of saying that he was unwanted, unimpressive—even feeble and fragile in appearance, uncared for by people, and someone to be avoided. He gained nothing in their eyes from his family origin, social status, or education, since he was not trained in the rabbinic schools. And as we have emphasized already, even his closest followers were largely unrefined, uneducated working men, lacking any kind of social prestige or influence.

To think that the Messiah could be a nobody, as they thought Jesus was, seemed ludicrous to the typical Israelite. When he taught in the

---

16. Archaeologists have long known the location of the city well, and over the years they have discovered first-century pottery fragments, rock tombs, cisterns, storage pits, and defensive bunkers (used, apparently, by people seeking refuge during the Jewish revolt in AD 67). In 2009, archaeologists announced that they had uncovered a first-century dwelling place—the first house found in Nazareth that belonged to the time of Christ. http://www.bible-archaeology.info/nazareth.htm.

synagogue of his hometown of Nazareth, the people who had watched him grow up in their midst were astonished and exclaimed, "Where did this man get these things? What is the wisdom given to him? How are such mighty works done by his hands? Is not this the carpenter, the son of Mary and brother of James and Joses and Judas and Simon? And are not his sisters here with us?" (Mark 6:2–3). Or to paraphrase: *Where did this nobody, this sucker branch, this unpromising, useless root out of dry ground get these things?*

And they were not impressed. Mark says, "They took offense at him" (v. 3). Luke's account is even more chilling: "They rose up and drove him out of the town and brought him to the brow of the hill on which their town was built, so that they could throw him down the cliff. But passing through their midst, he went away" (Luke 4:29–30). In other words, he escaped the mob by miraculous means. Somehow—in a way that perfectly befits their spiritual blindness—he was able to pass "through their midst" unseen and simply depart the scene. The incident is reminiscent of when the angels struck the men of Sodom with blindness to protect Lot on the eve of Sodom's destruction (Gen. 19:11).

Two years after being rejected in Nazareth, Jesus seems to have employed a similar miracle to escape another murderous mob who wanted to stone him to death in John 8:59. On that occasion the Jewish leaders cynically dismissed him as a demon-possessed Samaritan (John 8:48) and "picked up stones to throw at him, but Jesus hid himself and went out of the temple" (v. 59).

Despite his miracles, which demonstrated his power over disease, demons, death, and the natural world, and in defiance of his gracious teaching ("No one ever spoke like this man!"—John 7:46), they saw him as having "no form or majesty that [they] should look at him, and no beauty that [they] should desire him" (v. 2).

They were obsessed with the outward appearance of things (cf. 1 Sam. 16:7). Jesus's physical presence provoked no fear and evoked no sense of grandeur. He was (by his own confession) "gentle and lowly in heart" (Matt. 11:29). It was inconceivable to them that someone so gracious and humble could be their Messiah. How could he possibly be the majestic conqueror they hoped for? So profoundly

bizarre and distasteful was the whole notion that when Pilate mock-
ingly put a placard on the cross declaring Jesus to be the king of the
Jews, the outraged religious leaders angrily said to him, "Do not write,
'The King of the Jews,' but rather, *'This man said,* I am King of the
Jews'" (John 19:21).

That points to the third reason they rejected the servant: his life
had a contemptible end. "He was despised and rejected by men, a
man of sorrows and acquainted with grief; and as one from whom
men hide their faces he was despised, and we esteemed him not" (v. 3).
The Hebrew word translated "despised" is used frequently in the Old
Testament as an expression of disdain and contempt. It is also used of
the servant of the Lord in Isaiah 49:7, describing him as "one deeply
despised, abhorred by the nation, the servant of rulers."

The same word is used where Esau despised his birthright (Gen.
25:34). Some of the men of Israel despised Saul when he was chosen to
be king (1 Sam. 10:27). David's wife Michal (2 Sam. 6:16) and Goliath
(1 Sam. 17:42) despised David. In Jeremiah 22:28 and Daniel 11:21
the word describes vile, contemptible kings.

Isaiah 53:3 applies that word to Israel's general impression of the
Lord's servant, and it has all those connotations. They deemed him vile,
contemptible, worthy of shame and derision—mainly because instead
of leading the nation to triumph over the Romans, he died. Worse yet,
his earthly life ended in sorrow, disappointment, and execution by
Roman officials.

The people of Israel could have looked at the death of Jesus with
all its horrors and recognized it for what it was—God's sacrifice of
his Son as "the Lamb of God, who takes away the sin of the world!"
(John 1:29). They could have viewed it as the sacrifice pictured when
God provided Abraham with a ram to offer as a substitute in place of
Isaac. They could have seen Christ's death foreshadowed in the Passover lamb whose blood on the doorpost delivered the people from
God's wrath. They ought to have been able to understand that he was
offering the final and only true sacrifice that takes away sin—something the countless millions of animals sacrificed over the centuries
could never do (Heb. 10:4). Jesus had, after all, repeatedly spoken of
his death as a ransom for sinners: "The Son of Man came not to be

served but to serve, and to give his life as a ransom for many" (Matt. 20:28).

But because they didn't really see themselves as sinners, they evidently thought the endless offerings of the Old Testament sacrificial system were sufficient means of dealing with their transgressions (rather than symbols of something better). They did not appreciate their need for any greater atonement than the blood of bulls and goats. Again, they were not looking for a Savior; they were hoping for a political and military hero. So when the Messiah turned out to be a man of sorrows, they held him in contempt—as many still do. The rabbinic writings contain numerous scornful, derogatory terms, and nicknames for Jesus, as well as appallingly blasphemous false allegations about him.[17] That is consistent with the double use of "despised" in Isaiah 53:3.

He was not only despised by his adversaries but also "rejected by men" of all kinds and classes. The idea is that he was rejected by mankind in general—symbolically excommunicated from the human race by public crucifixion. The New American Standard Bible renders the Hebrew literally: "He was despised and *forsaken* of men." It is a reminder that on the night of his betrayal, even "all the disciples left him and fled" (Matt. 26:56). No one stood by him.

As Jesus hung on the cross, the scene was the very opposite of what most people in Israel expected of their Messiah. Here was a man "so marred, beyond human semblance" (Isa. 52:14); despised, rejected, forsaken even by his closest followers. Instead of inflicting suffering and grief on Israel's enemies, the servant himself was a "man of sorrows" (53:3). The Hebrew word translated "sorrows" in most English translations has a broad range of meanings, including suffering, pain,

---

17. The Talmud, for example, claims "Jesus the Nazarene was hanged" because he "practiced sorcery and instigated and seduced Israel to idolatry" (Sanhedrin 43a); that he "[paid] too much attention to [an] inn-keeper's wife" and turned to idolatry (worshiping a fish) when his rabbi was slow to forgive him after he pointed out that the innkeeper's wife's eyes were "narrow" (Sanhedrin 107b); and that his mother was an adulteress (Sanhedrin 67a). Those of course echo charges the Pharisees had made against Jesus during his earthly ministry. When they said in Matt. 12:24, "It is only by Beelzebul, the prince of demons, that this man casts out demons," they were accusing him of using the dark arts—magic—to perform miracles. Elsewhere, they said he was possessed by Satan (Mark 3:22), and even called him "Beelzebul" (Matt. 10:25). The Pharisees also questioned Jesus's parentage. When they said in John 8:48, "You are a Samaritan and have a demon," right after saying, "*We* were not born of sexual immorality" (v. 41), they seemed to be implying that Jesus's birth was illegitimate. Interestingly, though, the Talmudic denunciations of Jesus do not expressly question his descent from David. See chap. 6, note 6.

and affliction. Sorrow of heart in all its forms is indeed in view here, not physical pain. But the expression speaks of extreme anguish that was inflicted on him through unspeakable torment, not merely a sad feeling that welled up spontaneously from within.

Here is someone truly well acquainted with grief. It is an intriguing fact that the New Testament records that Jesus wept, but it never says that he laughed. Of course, he was fully human in every respect ("yet without sin"—Heb. 4:15). So it would be an unwarranted conclusion to imagine that he never laughed. But when Scripture mentions his human emotions, it is always to tell us about his sorrow. When Lazarus died and Jesus saw the mourners weeping, "he was deeply moved in his spirit and greatly troubled" (John 11:33). At Lazarus's grave, he wept (v. 35). As he drew near Jerusalem, he wept over the city (Luke 19:41). Shortly before that last Passover, as he contemplated what lay ahead, he said, "Now is my soul troubled" (John 12:27). Notes of sorrow permeate his Upper Room Discourse and High Priestly Prayer (John 13–17). In the garden on the night of his betrayal, he "began to be greatly distressed and troubled" (Mark 14:33), and he told Peter, James, and John, "My soul is very sorrowful, even to death" (v. 34).

So the expression "man of sorrows" certainly fits what we know of Jesus's temperament. But Isaiah is writing this prophecy with an eye to the cross, and his focus is on the profound agony—both the physical pain and the soul-shattering grief—that Jesus endured. The torment of his body and soul was so appalling that he literally became "one from whom men hide their faces."

Remember, Isaiah started this prophecy by saying that "his appearance was so marred, beyond human semblance, and his form beyond that of the children of mankind." It would certainly have been hard to look at him, suffering in extreme agony and sickening disfigurement during those final hours before he died. Such misery simply did not fit their expectation of how their Messiah would come, so they "esteemed him not."

By the way, the Hebrew word translated "esteemed" is an accounting term—the Hebrew equivalent of the Greek word *logizomai,* meaning "imputed" or "reckoned." It's a vital word in the biblical doctrine of justification. Here it simply means that they wrongly reckoned that

God's faithful servant was a nobody. From their perspective, the view that Jesus was the Messiah just didn't add up.

It was the ultimate expression of scorn: he was a nothing, a nonentity. That was the attitude of those who called for his death. It is essentially the perspective of everyone who hears the gospel and turns away—including most of the Jewish nation.

Someday, however, the nation will turn, embrace him as Messiah and Savior, and make the confession in Isaiah 53. Until that time, the gospel *still* "is the power of God for salvation to everyone who believes, to the Jew first and also to the Greek" (Rom. 1:16).

5

The Substituted Servant

Scourging was such a punishment that it was generally regarded as worse than death itself, and indeed, many perished while enduring it, or soon afterwards. Our blessed Redeemer gave His back to the smiters, and the plowers made deep furrows there. O spectacle of misery! How can we bear to look thereon?

Charles Spurgeon[1]

As we noted in chapter 2, Isaiah's prophecy about the suffering servant is structured so that the most important point comes at the very center of the passage. Isaiah 53:4–6 is the third of five stanzas in the extended prophecy, and it is fittingly situated. This is a succinct and eloquent expression of the entire passage's central theme:

Surely he has borne our griefs
    and carried our sorrows;
yet we esteemed him stricken,
    smitten by God, and afflicted.
But he was pierced for our transgressions;
    he was crushed for our iniquities;
upon him was the chastisement that brought us peace,
    and with his wounds we are healed.
All we like sheep have gone astray;
    we have turned—every one—to his own way;

1. Charles Spurgeon, *The Metropolitan Tabernacle Pulpit*, 63 vols. (London: Passmore & Alabaster, 1879), 25:422.

and the Lord has laid on him
the iniquity of us all.

Those three verses may well be the most magnificent verses in the entire Old Testament.

The logical flow of Isaiah's prophecy is easy to follow if we trace the themes from stanza to stanza. The first stanza (52:13–15) describes the astonishment Jesus's contemporaries felt at his humiliation—particularly the inhuman suffering he endured in connection with his trials and crucifixion. The second stanza (53:1–3) records the beginning of repentant Israel's future confession, in which they acknowledge that they were unimpressed with how their Messiah was born, where he grew up, what he looked like, and (most of all) how he died.

This third stanza (53:4–6) reflects a staggering awakening—a sudden realization of *why* God's servant had to suffer such humiliating agony. It is not only the vital theological key to Isaiah 53; it is also the vital marrow of everything Scripture teaches about how sin is ultimately atoned for.

The word that opens this stanza is "Surely," used here as an exclamation. The word in the Hebrew text means both "nevertheless" and "without a doubt." It's a word that is used at least fifteen times in the Old Testament—translated most often as "surely" or "truly," but sometimes as "nevertheless." Both ideas are generally inherent in the expression. It is the word Jacob used after his dream about the ladder that reached to heaven with angels ascending and descending on it. "Then Jacob awoke from his sleep and said, '*Surely* the Lord is in this place, and I did not know it'" (Gen. 28:16). Used in that exclamatory sense, the word conveys the idea of great surprise—often with an element of dismay. Moses used the same word when he learned there were witnesses who saw him kill an Egyptian and hide the body in the sand: "Then Moses was afraid, and thought, '*Surely* the thing is known'"(Ex. 2:14).

Isaiah 53:4 employs the expression in much the same fashion. It indicates a sudden recognition of something totally unexpected; a dramatic change from a previous perception; a realization that the persons speaking have been egregiously wrong. Here it signals the total reversal of repentant Israel's attitude toward Jesus. It is a stunning and abrupt revelation—a complete reversal of how Israel had previously viewed him. For all the generations since he came, they had assumed his death on the cross proved he was a nobody, a fraud, whose once-promising career ended in humiliation and failure. But on that future day they will confess that he is indeed their true Messiah. Moreover, he came to deliver them not from earthly political oppression, but from the eternal guilt and condemnation of their sin.

Surprise mingled with dismay is exactly the mood here. This is the confession of people who have suddenly seen a truth they had long denied or neglected. They confess that the suffering servant of God died, but not because he failed. Much less was he put to death for his own sins. Rather, he was the perfectly sinless Lamb of God who died for the sins of his people.

And the most profoundly surprising element of this confession is the way verse 5 explains what that means: the righteous servant of the Lord dies like a sacrificial lamb, suffering for sins he did not commit, but bearing away the guilt of his people. "The LORD has laid on him the iniquity of us all" (v. 6).

Most shockingly, the sufferings described in this passage include the outpouring of God's wrath in righteous retribution for the sins of those who rebel against him. He was indeed "stricken, smitten *by God*, and afflicted" (v. 4). In other words, the servant's wounding and crushing were not merely unintended side effects of our sin. He was no martyr. He was not an accidental victim. His sufferings are not collateral damage somehow caused by a chain of events set in motion by mistake. Isaiah is describing a purposeful act of penal substitution carried out by the sovereign will of his Father, God.

"He was pierced for our transgressions; he was crushed for our iniquities." Both expressions mean his suffering made *an atonement for our sins*. The language is categorically punitive. "Upon him was the *chastisement* that brought us peace." That clearly means he bore the punishment sinners deserve—the full measure of God's wrath "against all ungodliness and unrighteousness of men" (Rom. 1:18). The griefs and sorrows he bore for his people are not merely sin's temporal consequences or side effects. The servant of Yahweh dies as a substitute and sin bearer for his people, shouldering their guilt and taking the punishment that was due them. This passage cannot be made to mean anything else.

I recently read some comments on Isaiah 53:4–6 in a popular Bible study resource by an author who claims the Bible nowhere teaches that Christ was punished for others' sins. Rather than dealing with the actual words of the text, he tried to make his argument by falling back on an appeal to human sentiment. If the cross was a punishment for sins, he asked, who administered the punishment? *Surely not our heavenly Father.* That writer was expressly arguing against the principle of penal substitution. To bolster his failed argument, he searched an English concordance for the words *punish*, *payment*, and *penalty*. He said that since the King James Version of the Bible never uses those words in reference to the atonement, the doctrine of penal substitutionary atonement must be rejected.

But there is no mistaking the message of Isaiah 53:5. The Hebrew word translated "chastisement" has the inescapable connotation of divine punishment. Verse 10 affirms it, with emphasis: "It was the will of the LORD to crush him; *he* [Yahweh] has put him to grief; . . . his soul makes an offering for guilt." Isaiah 53 is simply not a passage from which any credible attack against the doctrine of penal substitution can possibly be launched.

It is especially fatuous to write off the principle of penal substitution after a concordance search that fails to turn up the word *payment*. Jesus himself said, "the Son of Man came . . . to give his life as a ransom for many" (Matt. 20:28; Mark 10:45). A *ransom* by definition is the payment of a price to obtain pardon. Scripture also says Christ "is the propitiation for our sins" (1 John 2:2; cf. Rom. 3:25). *Propitiation* is a sacrifice offered (or a price paid) to appease an offended deity.

If you find such ideas shocking, that is precisely Isaiah's point. The price our Savior paid to redeem his people from the guilt and bondage of sin was horrific, and Scripture never tries to soften the dreadful aspects of the truth—especially if it means toning down the awful reality of the righteous wrath of God. Unless we understand

and embrace the truth that "it is a fearful thing to fall into the hands of the living God" (Heb. 10:31), we cannot truly appreciate the Father's great mercy and love toward us in sending his own Son to die in the place of sinners.

In fact, God's love (not his wrath) is the central point of the cross. Jesus Christ willingly drank the full cup of God's wrath so that his people could escape that judgment. It was an act of unspeakable love. "Greater love has no one than this, that someone lay down his life for his friends" (John 15:13).

And his death accomplished precisely what he intended. Because he bore the full outpouring of divine vengeance against sin, those who trust him as Savior will never have to face God's condemnation.[2] Jesus told his followers, "Whoever hears my word and believes him who sent me has eternal life. He does not come into judgment" (John 5:24). The apostle John, overwhelmed with how the sacrifice of Christ demonstrates the love of God, wrote:

> In this the love of God was made manifest among us, that God sent his only Son into the world, so that we might live through him. In this is love, not that we have loved God but that he loved us and sent his Son to be the propitiation for our sins. (1 John 4:9–10)

> God so loved the world, that he gave his only Son, that whoever believes in him should not perish but have eternal life. For God did not send his Son into the world to condemn the world, but in order that the world might be saved through him. (John 3:16–17)

The three verses in this central stanza of Isaiah's suffering-servant prophecy are fittingly tied together by a common theme—confession of sin. Each one expands the scope of what is being confessed, so they are like concentric circles. Each verse presents an aspect of Israel's sin and the servant's atonement. According to Isaiah's prophecy, the repentant remnant of Israel will one day confess that they rejected Jesus because they had a sinful attitude, manifested in wicked behavior, which flowed from a depraved nature.

---

2. Conversely, "whoever does not obey the Son shall not see life, but the wrath of God remains on him" (John 3:36).

They Confess Their Sinful Attitude

Isaiah 53:4 begins the confession: "Surely he has borne our griefs and carried our sorrows; yet we esteemed him stricken, smitten by God, and afflicted." They despised him because he did not meet their expectation of what the Messiah was supposed to be like. Yet what he was actually doing for his people was infinitely greater than anything they had expected. At the return of Christ, their spiritual heirs will see their error and confess that their attitude toward Jesus has been sinfully wrong.

The word translated "griefs" in that verse is a broad term that can also mean "sickness," "infirmity," or "calamity." Here, because the context is all about human iniquity and divine propitiation, it is clear that Isaiah is talking about "griefs and . . . sorrows" that are brought on by sin. He is considering the problem of human fallenness in terms of the objective, external effects our sin produces. Sin causes our lives to be a constant struggle with sickness, disease, and calamity of every kind.

The point here is not merely that Messiah shares our infirmities and feels our heartaches. He *does* do that, of course. He is "a merciful and faithful high priest" (Heb. 2:17) who can sympathize with our weaknesses (Heb. 4:15). But the point of Isaiah 53:4 is not that Jesus has compassion and understanding for all the pains of humanity, but rather that he "has *borne* our griefs and carried our sorrows." In other words, he took our sin and all its effects on himself—though he himself was perfectly innocent of any wrongdoing (Heb. 7:26; 1 Pet. 2:22). The parallel terms in verse 5 ("transgressions," "iniquities") make clear that this is not about undeserved griefs or sorrows that we endure as victims. This is speaking of the anguish that always accompanies sin— starting with guilt (Ps. 51:3) and ending in death (James 1:15). He bore all of that for his people.

The word translated "borne" literally means, "to lift or take up." It's an active verb. The servant of Isaiah 53 is suffering because he has taken on himself the full burden of his people's sin and guilt, with all its consequences—up to and including the wages of sin: death. That is precisely what the New Testament says Jesus did for sinners. He was "offered . . . to bear the sins of many" (Heb. 9:28). "He himself bore our sins in his body on the tree, that we might die to sin and live to righteousness" (1 Pet. 2:24). In fact, he *"offered himself without blemish to God"* (Heb. 9:14)—a perfect sacrifice to satisfy the demands of God's justice. He "redeemed us from the curse of the law by becoming a curse for us" (Gal. 3:13). In technical terms, he fully *expiated* his people's sin, meaning he put an end to it by death. He stood in their place and paid in full the penalty of their sin, thus carrying away their guilt and ending sin's total mastery over them (Rom. 6:14).[3]

An illustration of the Lord's carrying away believers' sins comes from the Day of Atonement. God commanded that on that day:

> Aaron shall cast lots over the two goats, one lot for the LORD and the other lot for [the scapegoat]. And Aaron shall present the goat on which the lot fell for the LORD and use it as a sin offering, but the goat on which the lot fell for [the scapegoat] shall be presented alive before the LORD to make atonement over it, that it may be sent away into the wilderness [as the scapegoat]. (Lev. 16:8–10; cf. vv. 20–22)

Again we see that this faithful servant of the Lord, the one who "was cut off out of the land of the living, stricken for the transgression of [his] people" (Isa. 53:8), can only be the Lord Jesus Christ. There is no escaping the obvious connection (confirmed by multiple links) between Isaiah's prophecy and the cross of Jesus Christ. As the apostle Peter wrote (in a direct allusion to Isaiah 53), "Christ also suffered for you. . . . He himself bore our sins in his body on the tree, that we might die to sin and live to righteousness. By his wounds you have been healed" (1 Pet. 2:21, 24).

Still, we are reminded once again that it is a simple—and persistent—matter of fact that even though Isaiah's prophecy was written down and canonized in the Hebrew Scriptures several centuries before Jesus was crucified, and even though Jesus perfectly fit Isaiah's descrip-

---

3. Sin is still present in principle, fighting to regain mastery (Rom. 7:17–24), and it is our duty to "mortify," or put to death, its evil influence over us (see 8:13). But the person who is truly born again is no longer in abject bondage to evil (enslaved to sin and devoid of righteousness) the way we were as unbelievers. Every true believer can be assured that "sin will have no dominion . . . since [we] are not under law but under grace" (6:14).

tion of the suffering servant, "his own people did not receive him" (John 1:11).

The New Testament repeatedly acknowledges and openly faces the problem of Jewish unbelief. "What then? If some did not believe, their unbelief will not nullify the faithfulness of God, will it?" (Rom. 3:3 NASB). "It is not as though the word of God has failed. For not all who are descended from Israel belong to Israel" (Rom. 9:6). "Isaiah is so bold as to say, 'I have been found by those who did not seek me; I have shown myself to those who did not ask for me.' But of Israel he says, 'All day long I have held out my hands to a disobedient and contrary people'" (Rom. 10:20–21).

Of course, while Jesus was teaching, feeding the multitudes, and doing miracles in their midst, "The great throng heard him gladly" (Mark 12:37). "They said, 'This is indeed the Prophet who is to come into the world!'" (John 6:14). Remember that they even tried "to come and take him by force to make him king" (v. 15). At his Triumphal Entry, a large crowd "took branches of palm trees and went out to meet him, crying out, 'Hosanna! Blessed is he who comes in the name of the Lord, even the King of Israel!'" (John 12:13).

But because of the way his earthly ministry ended, the Jewish nation wrongly concluded that he could not be the long-awaited Messiah after all. They "esteemed him stricken, smitten by God, and afflicted" (Isa. 53:4) and therefore unfit to be the king they hoped for. Most Jewish people throughout history have likewise rejected Jesus's messianic claims,[4] giving reasons that echo what Isaiah describes here.

A popular Jewish website includes a page titled, "Why Jews Don't Believe in Jesus." The first two reasons they give are that "Jesus did not fulfill the messianic prophecies," and "Jesus did not embody the personal qualifications of the Messiah."[5] The page goes on to cite several Old Testament prophecies relating to Messiah's millennial reign. For example, he will build the third temple (Ezek. 37:26–28), gather all Jews back to the land (Isa. 43:5–6), usher in an era of world peace

---

4. There are, of course, many blessed exceptions. "Israel failed to obtain what it was seeking. *The elect obtained it*, but the rest were hardened" (Rom. 11:7). Literally tens of thousands of Jews *do* believe in Jesus as the true Messiah. But they constitute a relatively small minority of the nearly sixteen million Jews worldwide.

5. http://www.aish.com/jw/s/48892792.html.

(Isa. 2:4), and so on. The fundamental argument is that a victim of crucifixion cannot be Messiah, much less God in human form. "Saying that God assumes human form makes God small, diminishing both his unity and his divinity," they argue.[6]

The extreme humiliation of Christ is, of course, the chief wonder of the incarnation and the main backdrop against which his eternal glory shines so brightly. "The Son of Man came not to be served but to serve, and to give his life as a ransom for many" (Matt. 20:28). "Christ became a servant to the circumcised to show God's truthfulness, in order to confirm the promises given to the patriarchs, and in order that the Gentiles might glorify God for his mercy" (Rom. 15:8–9).

The humble condescension of Jesus Christ is also the very highest expression of divine love. The New Testament faces the issue squarely and explains it:

> Have this mind among yourselves, which is yours in Christ Jesus, who, though he was in the form of God, did not count equality with God a thing to be grasped, but emptied himself, by taking the form of a servant, being born in the likeness of men. And being found in human form, he humbled himself by becoming obedient to the point of death, even death on a cross. Therefore God has highly exalted him and bestowed on him the name that is above every name, so that at the name of Jesus every knee should bow, in heaven and on earth and under the earth, and every tongue confess that Jesus Christ is Lord, to the glory of God the Father. (Phil. 2:5–11)

He is, after all, revealed throughout the book of Isaiah as the *servant* of Yahweh—literally, a willing slave to the will of his Father.

But there is no place in the standard rabbinical traditions for the idea that Messiah would serve, suffer, or succumb to the humiliation of death by crucifixion. The people of Jerusalem that day who watched him die "esteemed him stricken, smitten by God, and afflicted"—and they mocked:

> Those who passed by derided him, wagging their heads and saying, "Aha! You who would destroy the temple and rebuild it in three

---

6. Ibid.

days, save yourself, and come down from the cross!" So also the chief priests with the scribes mocked him to one another, saying, "He saved others; he cannot save himself. Let the Christ, the King of Israel, come down now from the cross that we may see and believe." (Mark 15:29–32)

That same sinful attitude is implicit in the heart of everyone—Jew and Gentile alike—who reads or listens to the Gospel accounts and rejects Christ anyway.

Remember, Isaiah is prophetically expressing the heartfelt remorse of the Jewish remnant when they suddenly see and believe what the nation has so long denied. As all genuine confessors must, they accept full responsibility for their sinful rejection. The New American Standard Bible correctly conveys the personal aspect in the way they confess their guilt: "*We ourselves* esteemed Him stricken, smitten of God, and afflicted." (The Hebrew pronoun is an intensified version of the first-person plural. There's much genuine humility and true remorse in the expression.)

The implication is that they assumed his public shame was fully justified—that Yahweh was striking and smiting him because he was a blasphemer. The word "stricken" in our text is not a reference to the mocking blows of Roman soldiers who struck him on the head with a reed (Matt. 27:30). The word refers to a brutal blow—but not necessarily a physical buffeting. In Genesis 12:17 the same Hebrew word is used to say that God struck the house of Pharaoh with plagues when he unknowingly attempted to add Abraham's wife, Sarah, to his harem. And in Exodus 11:1 a related word meaning "stroke" or "plague" is used to describe the plagues God brought on Egypt. "Smitten" can mean to beat, strike down, or even kill. "Afflicted" is a general term that can refer to being humiliated, degraded, mistreated, oppressed, or destroyed.

All three words are connected with the proposition "by God." To paraphrase: *We regarded him as a sinner being stricken, smitten, and afflicted by the very hand of God.* Thus the repentant remnant will confess that they regarded Jesus's suffering as a punishment from God that he justly deserved. Their attitude toward him was wrong. They falsely impugned his character.

They Confess Their Sinful Behavior

One day they will see clearly that the guilt that caused his suffering was theirs, not his. "But he was pierced for *our* transgressions; he was crushed for *our* iniquities; upon him was the chastisement that brought us peace, and with his wounds we are healed" (Isa. 53:5). This second aspect of Israel's confession acknowledges that the punishment that the servant suffered was actually due them for their own sinful behavior.

Again, there's no reasonable way to sidestep or deny the punitive aspect of the suffering and anguish described in verse 5. The graphic words "wounded," "crushed," "chastisement," and "wounds," are all very strong terms describing injuries that have been inflicted by punishment.

Remember, stoning was the usual method of execution in Old Testament Israel. Unaided by anything other than his own imagination, Isaiah could hardly have envisioned crucifixion as a method of capital punishment. Much less could he correctly anticipate and describe the specific details of a Roman-style crucifixion. The Holy Spirit led him to choose these specific words to express the extreme suffering the servant endured.

The words translated "pierced" and "crushed," according to some Hebrew scholars, are

> two of the strongest words in the Hebrew language to describe a violent and painful death. "Pierced" conveys the idea of "pierced through, or wounded to death" (cf. Deut. 21:1; Isa. 51:9; see also Psa. 22:16; Zech. 12:10; John 19:34). The related adjective *chalal* usually means "slain" (Isa. 22:2; 34:3; 66:16). "Crushed" conveys the sense of "beaten in pieces, destroyed." The servant is thus crushed to death by the burden of the sin of others which He took on himself, further weighted by the wrath of God due that sin.[7]

"Chastisement" is a general term used to express punishment. "Stripes (NKJV)" is from a Hebrew word that speaks of bruises, welts, and the raw wounds from the strokes of a whip. Isaiah uses the same word in his opening chapter:

---

7. Duane F. Lindsey, "The Career of the Servant in Isaiah 52:13–53:12," *Bibliotheca Sacra* 140, no. 557 (Jan–Mar 1983): 24.

From the sole of the foot even to the head,
    there is no soundness in it,
but bruises and sores
    and *raw wounds*;
they are not pressed out or bound up
    or softened with oil. (1:6)

All four terms describe things that happened to Jesus. He was *pierced* in his wrists, feet, and side (Ps. 22:16; Zech. 12:10; John 19:34, 37). He was *crushed* by the beatings he endured at the hands of the Sanhedrin (Matt. 26:67) and the Romans (Matt. 27:29–30; John 19:3). He was formally but illegally *punished* (Luke 23:16, 22) as the result of an unjust indictment, trial, verdict, and sentence. And he was severely *marked with stripes and raw wounds* as a result of the brutal scourging he received at the hands of the Roman lictors (Mark 15:15). Those were merely the visible wounds inflicted on him "by the hands of lawless men" (Acts 2:23b).

But we also know that he was "delivered up according to the definite plan and foreknowledge of God" (Acts 2:23a). Isaiah likewise underscores the fact that Christ's death was sovereignly ordained by God as the means of atonement for sin. "*The LORD* has laid on him the iniquity of us all" (Isa. 53:6). "It was *the will of the LORD* to crush him; *he* has put him to grief; . . . his soul makes an offering for guilt" (v. 10). So the servant was indeed "stricken, smitten *by God,* and afflicted" (v. 4)—not for his own sin, but because he took on himself the punishment for his people's guilt.

He "endured the cross, despising the shame" (Heb. 12:2) so that his people could be at peace with God. "Upon him was the chastisement that brought us peace." The Hebrew word for "peace" in Isaiah 53:5 is familiar, even in English: *shalom.* It refers here to the removal of enmity between God and sinners. "While we were enemies we were reconciled to God by the death of his Son" (Rom. 5:10). And now, "since we have been justified by faith, we have peace with God through our Lord Jesus Christ" (v. 1).

Likewise, the healing spoken of in Isaiah 53:5 ("with his wounds we are healed") is not immediate physical healing. The context, as we have seen, is all about "our transgressions," "our iniquities"—the moral and spiritual effects of sin, guilt, and alienation from God. Those who believe are "healed" in the sense of being restored to spiritual wholeness and released from the absolute bondage of sin. It's actually a more radical kind of healing (and a much greater manifestation of divine power) than the temporary healing of our physical infirmities. It is a divinely wrought miracle of spiritual resurrection: "When we were dead in our trespasses, [God] made us alive together with Christ" (Eph. 2:5)—thus guaranteeing eternal life and the future glorification of even our physical bodies (a greater physical healing than any earthly physician has ever seen).

Conversely, the sickness the prophet has in mind here is more deeply ingrained and more malignant than the worst kind of cancer. It is an utter depravity of soul, and we'll have much more to say about it shortly, when we consider verse 6. But here the point is simple: the heal-ing in view is a powerful remedy for an otherwise incurable spiritual infirmity: our fallenness and the resulting enslavement to sin. That is the underlying cause of our unrighteous deeds—"our transgressions" and "our iniquities."

So verse 5 is an explicit confession of sinful behavior. Although Isaiah is recording the confession that will be made by repentant Israel, it is also a fitting confession for anyone coming to faith in Christ, be-cause "all have sinned and fall short of the glory of God" (Rom. 3:23). All of us are sinful, guilty of perverting and violating God's law, and thus (in our fallen state) separated from him, spiritually sick, full of grief, and sorrowful. But Jesus took on himself his people's sin, guilt, grief, sorrow—and every other sinister expression of our fallenness. He voluntarily endured God's punishment for those evils. And he thereby purchased peace and blessing from God for us. The death of the physi-cian made the patient well.

They Confess Their Sinful Nature

The final stage in Israel's confession recognizes sin at its deepest level: "All we like sheep have gone astray; we have turned—every one— to his own way; and the LORD has laid on him the iniquity of us all" (Isa. 53:6). That verse completes the three-part confession. The newly awakened remnant of Israel have just acknowledged that their thinking about the Messiah was corrupt and wrongheaded. They have confessed their sinful behavior, admitting that *their* guilt and *their* transgressions are the true cause of the servant's suffering. In effect, they are pleading guilty to the same charges Isaiah leveled against their unfaithful ancestors in his opening prophecy:

Ah, sinful nation,
a people laden with iniquity,
offspring of evildoers,
children who deal corruptly!
They have forsaken the LORD,
they have despised the Holy One of Israel,
they are utterly estranged.

Why will you still be struck down?
Why will you continue to rebel?
The whole head is sick,
and the whole heart faint.
From the sole of the foot even to the head,
there is no soundness in it,
but bruises and sores
and raw wounds;
they are not pressed out or bound up
or softened with oil. (Isa. 1:4–6)

That is not merely a list of discrete offenses. Nor is it applicable only to the Jewish nation. It is an indictment of fallen human nature. It describes a sickness that infects the entire human race: total depravity. Sin has infected every aspect of human nature. This is the malady referred to in verse 5 that is healed by the suffering servant's stripes. But verse 6 uses a completely different metaphor, comparing the human race to sheep—spiritually helpless, hopeless, and condemned to wander and die, unless the Great Shepherd intervenes to save us.

The fault lies in our very nature, not merely our thoughts or our behavior. Wrong thinking and wrong actions flow ultimately from a sinful disposition. True confession of sin must therefore ultimately deal with sin at its origin (the human heart), not merely in its manifestations. "The heart is deceitful above all things, and desperately sick;

who can understand it?" (Jer. 17:9). Jesus declared that "out of the heart come evil thoughts, murder, adultery, sexual immorality, theft, false witness, slander" (Matt. 15:19; cf. Gen. 6:5; 8:21; Rom. 7:18). This is a truth that every sinner must come to grips with. Our problem is not just a matter of how we think or what we do. The real problem is *who we are*. We are not sinners because we sin; we sin because we are sinners.

Israel's likening of themselves (and all sinners) to sheep is an apt analogy. Phillip Keller wrote:

> Sheep do not "just take care of themselves" as some might suppose. They require, more than any other class of livestock, endless attention and meticulous care. It is no accident that God has chosen to call us sheep. The behavior of sheep and human beings is similar in many ways. . . . Our stubbornness and stupidity [and] our perverse habits are all parallels of profound importance.[8]

Sheep by nature *are* stupid animals, prone to wander off on their own and thereby place themselves in mortal danger. They are defenseless against predators and can't take care of themselves. For example, sometimes they roll over onto their backs and are unable to right themselves. This is a potentially life-threatening situation:

> The way it happens is this. A heavy, fat, or long-fleeced sheep will lie down comfortably in some little hollow or depression in the ground. It may roll on its side slightly to stretch out or relax. Suddenly the center of gravity in the body shifts so that it turns on its back far enough that the feet no longer touch the ground. It may feel a sense of panic and start to paw frantically. Frequently this only makes things worse. It rolls over even further. Now it is quite impossible for it to regain its feet.
>
> As it lies there struggling, gases begin to build up in the rumen. As these expand they tend to retard and cut off blood circulation to the extremities of the body, especially the legs. If the weather is very hot and sunny a cast sheep can die in a few hours. If it is cool and cloudy and rainy it may survive in this position for several days.[9]

---

8. W. Phillip Keller, *A Shepherd Looks at Psalm 23* (Grand Rapids, MI: Zondervan, 1970), 19.
9. Ibid., 55.

In a similar way, people are prone by nature to go astray from God, turn to their own way, and become lost or morally capsized. The psalmist had this in mind when he cried out, "I have gone astray like a lost sheep; seek your servant" (Ps. 119:176; cf. Matt. 18:12; Luke 15:4–6; 1 Pet. 2:25).

But unlike the parable Jesus told about the lost sheep, which focused on individual sinners, Israel's confession views the entire human race as sheep who have *all* gone astray from the Good Shepherd. Spurning his guidance and care, choosing instead to follow the natural path of sin, "we have turned—*every one*—to his own way." We have all become "harassed and helpless, like sheep without a shepherd" (Matt. 9:36), because that is our "own way."

It is important to confess our known sins, enumerating precisely where we have wronged God and broken his law. "If we confess our sins, he is faithful and just to forgive us our sins and to cleanse us from all unrighteousness" (1 John 1:9). But true repentance goes deeper yet. In fact, there can be no genuine repentance apart from the recognition that we are inveterate sinners *by nature*, helpless lost sheep desperately in need of the "Shepherd and Overseer of [our] souls" (1 Pet. 2:25) to rescue us. David modeled this principle in Psalm 51. He does not use generalities or euphemistic words such as "mistake" or "miscalculation" to gloss over the evil acts he has done: "I know my transgressions, and my sin is ever before me. Against you, you only, have I sinned and done what is evil" (vv. 3–4). But he also confesses the underlying problem: his inherent, pervasive depravity. Sin lies at the very core of his character. He is a fallen and utterly depraved individual. "Behold, I was brought forth in iniquity, and in sin did my mother conceive me" (v. 5).

The good news of the gospel is that "the LORD has laid on [Christ] the iniquity of us all." The expression "laid on him" is translated from a Hebrew word meaning "to fall on"—in the sense of a violent attack. The same word is used, for example, in 2 Samuel 1:15, where David instructs one of his warriors to execute the Amalekite who boasted that he had killed Saul: "Go near, and *fall upon him*" (KJV). The violence of the idea is perhaps better expressed in the way the New American Standard Bible translates the expression: "Go, *cut him down*." The same word is used several times in 1 Kings 2, describing Solomon's orders to execute men who had been disloyal or brought harm to his father: "So King Solomon sent Benaiah the son of Jehoiada, and he *struck [Adonijah] down,* and he died" (v. 25; cf. vv. 29, 31–32, 34, 46). The expression literally means "fell upon him," and the intent to kill is clearly implied.

The same word is used, with similar implications, in Isaiah 53:6: "The LORD has caused the iniquity of us all to *fall on Him*" (NASB). The idea of violence is implicit in the expression. One commentator fittingly put it like this: "The iniquity of which we are guilty does not come back to us to meet and strike us as we might rightly expect, but rather strikes [the servant of Yahweh] in our stead. . . . The guilt that belonged to us God caused to strike him, i.e. he as our substitute bore the punishment that the guilt of our sin required. . . . The shepherd has given his life for the sheep."[10]

Or, as the apostle Paul wrote, "God has done what the law, weakened by the flesh, could not do. By sending his own Son in the likeness of sinful flesh and for sin, he condemned sin in the flesh" (Rom. 8:3). The reality of Christ's vicarious, substitutionary death on our behalf is the heart of the gospel according to God—the central theme of Isaiah 53.

We must remember, however, that sin did not kill Jesus; God did. The suffering servant's death was nothing less than a punishment administered by God for sins others had committed. That is what we mean when we speak of penal substitutionary atonement. Again, if the idea seems shocking and disturbing, it is meant to be. Unless you recoil from the thought, you probably haven't grasped it yet. "Our God is a consuming fire" (Heb. 12:29). This is one of the major reasons the gospel is a stumbling block to Jews, and it's sheer foolishness as far as Gentiles are concerned (1 Cor. 1:23). "But to those who are called, both Jews and Greeks, [the message of Christ crucified embodies both] the power of God and the wisdom of God" (v. 24).

There's no way to sidestep the fact that the doctrine of penal substitution is unequivocally affirmed in the plain message of Isaiah 53. It is also confirmed and reiterated by many other passages throughout

---

10. Edward J. Young, *The Book of Isaiah,* 3 vols. (Grand Rapids, MI: Eerdmans, 1972), 3:350.

Scripture (cf. 2 Cor. 5:21; Gal. 3:13; Heb. 9:28; 1 Pet. 2:24). The servant of Yahweh, though perfectly innocent, bore the guilt of others and suffered unspeakable anguish to atone for their sins.

Despite the unsettling overtones in that message, it is good news. In fact, there is no more glorious good news. It explains why God "does not deal with us according to our sins, nor repay us according to our iniquities" (Ps. 103:10). He has not compromised his own righteousness. He does not merely overlook our transgressions. Rather, he fully satisfied justice and put away our sin forever through the death of his Son. "As far as the east is from the west, so far does he remove our transgressions from us" (Ps. 103:12). Now grace can truly reign through righteousness (Rom. 5:21). And God can be *both* "just and the justifier of the one who has faith in Jesus" (Rom. 3:26).

Israel's national salvation is still in the future. But no one (neither Jew nor Gentile) need wait for some future event in order to turn from sin and trust Christ. You can be saved "today, if you hear his voice" (Heb. 3:7). The righteousness of God is available even now "through faith in Jesus Christ for all who believe" (Rom. 3:22). And "everyone who calls on the name of the Lord will be saved" (Rom. 10:13).

"Behold, now is the favorable time; behold, now is the day of salvation" (2 Cor. 6:2).

6

The Silent Servant

Nothing can exceed the beauty and propriety of the images, by which our Lord's patience is here illustrated. As a sheep, when the shearer is stripping it of its clothing, makes neither noise, nor resistance; and as a lamb sports about even while being driven to the slaughter, yea, and licks the very hand that is lifted up to slay it, so our blessed Lord endured all his sufferings *silently, willingly*, and *with expressions of love to his very murderers*.

Twice is *his silence* noticed in the text, because it indicated a self-government, which, under his circumstances, no created being could have exercised. The most eminent saints have opened their mouths in complaints both against God and man. Job, that distinguished pattern of patience, even cursed the day of his birth. Moses, the meekest of the sons of men, who had withstood numberless provocations, yet, at last, spake so unadvisedly with his lips, that he was excluded, on account of it, from the earthly Canaan. And even the Apostle Paul, than whom no human being ever attained a higher eminence in any grace, broke forth into "revilings against God's high-priest," who had ordered him to be smitten contrary to the law. But "there was no guile in the lips of Jesus;" nor did he ever once open his mouth in a sinful or unbecoming manner.

Charles Simeon[1]

---

1. Charles Simeon, *Horae Homileticae*, 21 vols. (London: Holdsworth and Ball, 1832), 8:370; emphasis original.

Verse 7 of Isaiah 53 reveals (not in vague, uncertain terms but in a direct statement) that the servant of Yahweh will be put to death like a lamb that is slaughtered.

The imagery was unmistakable for Isaiah's readers, who lived in a largely agrarian society. They were very familiar with raising and harvesting crops and with animal husbandry. Sheep in particular were an important staple in their lives. The animals provided food, and their wool was used to make clothes. Having seen sheep killed both for food and as sacrifices, the people of Israel were well aware of the animal's docile nature.

In Isaiah 53 the image of a sacrificial lamb is used to introduce the startling concept that the servant of Yahweh—the Messiah, whom the Jewish people envisioned as a powerful military conqueror and political ruler—would be led passively and silently to slaughter like one of their sheep. Of course sheep do not know when they are being led to slaughter. But the servant, knowing full well what fate awaited him, would go meekly to his death in voluntary submission to the will of Yahweh.

Israel's future confession will acknowledge that their Messiah, Jesus, is the true "Lamb of God, who takes away the sin of the world!" (John 1:29). That is just what *all* who believe in the Lord Jesus Christ have always confessed—Gentiles as well as Jews. It is the essential message of the gospel. To be sure, Jesus is our teacher, Lord, Great High Priest, example, deliverer, and coming King. But we cannot rightly know him in any of those roles unless we first confess that he is "the propitiation for our sins" (1 John 2:2). That is the lesson of Isaiah 53. "There is salvation in no one else, for there is no other name under heaven given among men by which we must be saved" (Acts 4:12).

No one (including the genetic descendants of Abraham, Isaac, and Jacob)—*no one* can be saved who is unwilling to confess that Jesus was "pierced for our transgressions [and] crushed for our iniquities"; that the punishment he endured is what made peace with God possible; and that the wounds he suffered were the price he paid to free his people from sin's bondage and heal them spiritually (v. 5). We further confess that God caused our iniquity to fall on Jesus (v. 6); that he was cut off out of the land of the living, stricken for our transgressions (v. 8); that he gave his life as a guilt offering for our sins (v. 10); and that by bearing our sins he earned our justification (vv. 11, 12).

All those truths are implicit in any sound confession of faith. That is what it means to "believe in the Lord Jesus" (Acts 16:31). The apostle Paul summarized and comprised those same truths in shorthand fashion when he gave his famous abridged statement of gospel essentials in 1 Corinthians 15:3–4: "That Christ died for our sins *in accordance with the Scriptures*, that he was buried, that he was raised on the third day *in accordance with the Scriptures*." (Isaiah 53 was surely one of the main Old Testament texts the apostle had in mind when he penned that phrase twice in close succession.) The very essence of true faith in Christ is trusting that the vicarious, substitutionary sacrifice Jesus offered to God through the cross is a full and sufficient payment for all our sins.

Despite the straightforward clarity of Isaiah 53:7–8, the idea that Yahweh's servant, the promised Messiah, would be slaughtered like a sacrificial lamb never found its way into the canon of rabbinical tradition. After the crucifixion and resurrection of Jesus, the full significance of Isaiah's prophecy was obvious to every Christian who seriously considered the passage. Isaiah 53 instantly rose to prominence as a focal point in the study, testimony, and teaching of the church (Luke 22:37; Acts 8:32–35; 1 Pet. 2:24–25). A common theme in the apostles' preaching was "that it was *necessary* for the Christ to suffer" (Acts 17:3; cf. 3:18; 26:23; Luke 24:26).

Meanwhile, the keepers of rabbinical tradition held firmly to their belief that the Messiah could only be a triumphant champion. Rather than deal with Isaiah 53, they ignored it or tried to explain away its apparent references to Christ. In the teaching and liturgy of the synagogues, that part of Isaiah fell into disuse and faded into the distant background. (As explained in chapter 2, even to this day the passage is always omitted from the scheduled public readings in synagogues worldwide.)

One of the serious charges Jesus brought against the Jewish leaders during his earthly ministry was that they had allowed their religious traditions to overshadow and annul the simple truth of Scripture. That is a common fallacy in all religions that are dominated by elaborate ritual. Sacrament and ceremony inevitably eclipse sound doctrine. Jesus's utter contempt for the practice of citing human tradition to dispel the plain teaching of God's Word is evident in the sharply sarcastic way he rebuked the scribes and Pharisees:

> You have a fine way of rejecting the commandment of God in order to establish your tradition! For Moses said, "Honor your father and your mother"; and, "Whoever reviles father or mother must surely die." But you say, "If a man tells his father or his mother, 'Whatever you would have gained from me is Corban'" (that is, given to God)—then you no longer permit him to do anything for his father or mother, thus making void the word of God by your tradition that you have handed down. *And many such things you do.* (Mark 7:9–13)

It is clear from the force of Jesus's rebuke that the practice of modifying (and even countermanding) the Word of God with far-fetched interpretations or man-made amendments was well established as part of the rabbinical tradition by Jesus's time. Having engineered the crucifixion of Christ, the Jewish Council (including the chief priests and leading Jewish scholars of that time) were simply unwilling to see Christ's death and resurrection as a fulfillment of any Old Testament prophecy—even a passage as clear as Isaiah 53.

When Peter stood in Solomon's portico on the temple mount and announced that Jesus had fulfilled "what God foretold by the mouth of all the prophets, that his Christ would suffer" (Acts 3:18), leading members of the Sanhedrin, the ruling Jewish council, had them arrested and ordered them to speak no more about Jesus (Acts 4:1–18). The Jewish leaders could not—and did not—deny the truth of the apostolic message. They were simply unwilling to believe it:

> When they saw the boldness of Peter and John, and perceived that they were uneducated, common men, they were astonished. And they recognized that they had been with Jesus. But seeing the man who was healed standing beside them, they had nothing to say in opposition. But when they had commanded them to leave the council, they conferred with one another, saying, "What shall we do with these men? For that a notable sign has been performed

through them is evident to all the inhabitants of Jerusalem, and we cannot deny it." (vv. 13–16)

That was the response of the elite leaders. That was the start of the official rejection of Jesus Christ that was soon ensconced as established Jewish tradition—and still dominates today.

It was not, however, the universal response of all ethnic Hebrews. Untold thousands of Jewish people *have* embraced Jesus as their Messiah—starting in the first century at Pentecost (the Jewish Feast of Weeks, a harvest festival established in Ex. 34:22), when "there were added [to the church] that day about three thousand souls" (Acts 2:41). For at least five years after the resurrection of Christ (before the martyrdom of Stephen, Acts 8:4), the disciples were still ministering in and around Jerusalem, and virtually all who came to faith in Christ at that time were Jewish. "The word of God continued to increase, and the number of the disciples multiplied greatly in Jerusalem, *and a great many of the priests* became obedient to the faith" (Acts 6:7).

The links between the Old Testament sacrificial system and the death of "Christ, our Passover lamb" (1 Cor. 5:7) were too numerous and too striking to deny. Any clear-minded, open-hearted penitent who understood the lessons of Israel's priesthood and bloody sacrificial system could easily see the fulfillment of Isaiah 53 in the death and resurrection of Christ. And many did.

Throughout Israel's history, until the destruction of the temple by the Romans in AD 70, countless millions of animals had been sacrificed. Sacrifices were offered not only at Passover, but also morning and evening in the temple (Ex. 29:38–42) and as personal sin offerings by individuals (Lev. 5:5–7). Even before the sacrificial regulations were spelled out in the book of Leviticus, there was the example of Abel's acceptable sacrifice (Gen. 4:4–5) and Abraham's offering of a ram in place of his son Isaac (Gen. 22:13). The Jewish people had been taught that sin causes death, that "the soul who sins shall die" (Ezek. 18:4, 20). And every animal sacrificed throughout Israel's history vividly demonstrated the reality that the inevitable penalty for sin is death. The truth was writ large across all the rituals prescribed in the Old Testament: "Indeed, under the law almost everything is purified with blood, and without the shedding of blood there is no forgiveness of sins" (Heb. 9:22).

As we have previously pointed out, the endless repetition of sacrifices made the point that animal sacrifices could not really atone for human guilt. "It is impossible for the blood of bulls and goats to take away sins" (Heb. 10:4). Furthermore, if sins are to be atoned for by a substitute, shouldn't the substitute have some conscious sense of the price that is being paid and why? After all, we sin deliberately, willfully. A dying animal is doing nothing knowingly or willfully.

But, as commentator Alec Motyer points out, in the death of Christ,

> the fatal flaw in existing substitutionary procedures was exposed and met in one stroke. For the point where animal substitution failed was also the point where sin is most serious. Sin as failure . . . need be no more than a pity; sin as moral defect . . . is distressing but leaves it arguable that what cannot be helped cannot be blameworthy; but *sin as wilfullness . . . is the thing God cannot overlook.* It is the very heart of our sinfulness that we sin because we want to. We do not want "this man to reign over us" (Lk. 19:14). Because of this, no animal can do more than picture substitution: only a person can substitute for a person; only a consenting will can substitute for a rebellious will. The servant, indeed, fulfills the stated requirements for a substitute: he identified with sinners in their condemnation ([Isa. 53:]4–5); he was without stain of our sin (9); he was acceptable to the holy God (6, 10). He also adds what no other ever did or could: the will to accept and submit to the substitute's role.[2]

Those "same sacrifices that [were] continually offered every year [could never] make perfect those who draw near. Otherwise, would they not have ceased to be offered, since the worshipers, having once been cleansed, would no longer have any consciousness of sins?" (Heb. 10:1–2).

Don't imagine, however, that Christ's death provided a whole new way of salvation. Before the cross, repentant sinners were saved by grace, trusting that God would mercifully provide for them a sacrifice

---

2. J. Alec Motyer, *The Prophecy of Isaiah* (Downers Grove, IL: InterVarsity Press, 1993), 433; emphasis added.

that would satisfy him. Abraham's answer to Isaac epitomizes the spirit of saving faith shared by all the Old Testament saints: "God will provide for himself the lamb" (Gen. 22:8). They were saved, not by the blood of animals, but by divine grace, through faith, in anticipation of the perfect sacrifice Messiah would offer. The animal sacrifices merely symbolized that reality and served as an expression of obedient faith. Those sacrifices were never efficacious for redemption. God's forgiveness in the Old Testament was an expression of his divine forbearance. The shedding of Christ's blood as a propitiation is what finally atoned for all the sins God graciously passed over in Old Testament times (Rom. 3:25).

The sacrificed animals vividly pictured the fact that the penalty of sin is death. They also showed that God was willing to provide an innocent substitute who would die in place of penitent sinners. Messiah, the Lord Jesus, was always the one ordained in the eternal counsel of Yahweh to be that ultimate sacrifice (1 Pet. 1:19–20). He alone is "the Lamb of God, who takes away the sin of the world!" (John 1:29).

John the Baptist was the last and greatest of the Old Testament prophets, the forerunner of the Messiah, and the one who had the privilege of introducing the true Messiah to Israel. Isaiah wrote of John the Baptist:

A voice cries:
"In the wilderness prepare the way of the LORD;
    make straight in the desert a highway for our God.
Every valley shall be lifted up,
    and every mountain and hill be made low;
the uneven ground shall become level,
    and the rough places a plain.
And the glory of the LORD shall be revealed,
    and all flesh shall see it together,
        for the mouth of the LORD has spoken." (Isa. 40:3–5; cf. Mal.
        3:1; 4:5–6; Matt. 3:3; 11:13–14; John 1:23)

When John pointed out Jesus as "the Lamb of God, who takes away the sin of the world!" (John 1:29, 36), he surely had Isaiah 53 in mind. Peter was likewise alluding to Isaiah's prophecy when he wrote, "You were ransomed . . . with the precious blood of Christ, like that of a lamb without blemish or spot" (1 Pet. 1:18–19). Israel *will* have him as their living, exalted King, but first he had to die "like a lamb that is led to the slaughter" (Isa. 53:7).

The servant's preternatural silence as he suffers is the sign Isaiah's prophecy highlights.

Silent before His Accusers

We have seen (both in the introduction and at the beginning of chapter 1) that Isaiah includes four Servant Songs, all with messianic themes (42:1–9; 49:1–13; 50:4–11; and 52:13–53:12). All of them highlight the meekness and mercy of the servant of Yahweh. Another repeated theme in the songs is the hateful rejection the servant receives (49:7; 50:6). The voice of the servant speaks in the second and third of the songs, but the first and fourth songs both speak of his quietude ("He will not cry aloud or lift up his voice, or make it heard in the street," 42:2. And "like a sheep that before its shearers is silent, so he opened not his mouth," 53:7). Fittingly, then, he does not speak in the first or fourth songs. In Isaiah 42, the hushed tone signifies his gentleness and composure. In the Isaiah 53 passage, his silence reflects his submission to God, his willingness to obey Yahweh no matter the cost—even unto death.

The word translated "oppressed" in verse 7 refers to the suffering and abuse the servant endured in connection with his arrest and trials. It is used in an emphatic sense and could be translated, "He himself was oppressed."

Beginning with his arrest in Gethsemane in the middle of the night, Jesus suffered physical, psychological, and emotional abuse. He endured the outrageous injustice of mock trials, in which he was falsely accused by false witnesses giving false testimony. No proof that he had committed any crime was ever presented, and his guiltlessness was formally declared both by Herod (Luke 23:14–15) and by Pilate (Luke 23:4, 14, 22). His innocence was affirmed as well by Pilate's wife (Matt. 27:19), the repentant thief (Luke 23:41), the centurion, and the execution squad (Matt. 27:54). Yet Pilate nonetheless gave in to the demands of the people and their leaders and unjustly sentenced him to be crucified. So severe was the physical abuse inflicted on him that "his appearance was so marred, beyond human semblance, and his form beyond that of the children of mankind" (Isa. 52:14). By the time the Jewish leaders and the Romans finished abusing him, his injuries were severe enough to make "men hide their faces" (53:3).

The servant was also "afflicted." The passive form of the Hebrew verb in Isaiah 53:7 means that he allowed himself to be afflicted. It could be translated "He humbled himself." The same word is used of Pharaoh's refusal to humble himself in Exodus 10:3. It means "to be made low, or put down." Perhaps Paul had Isaiah 53:7 in mind when he wrote of Christ, "And being found in human form, *he humbled himself* by becoming obedient to the point of death, even death on a cross" (Phil. 2:8).

Jesus was submissive to the Father's plan in his death. After all, human judgment had no independent authority over him. As he told Pilate, "You would have no authority over me at all unless it had been given you from above" (John 19:11). Neither the Sanhedrin, nor Herod, nor Pilate possessed enough power to pass judgment on Christ; they merely carried out what God's "plan had predestined to take place" (Acts 4:28). That did not, however, relieve those human rulers of their responsibility for misusing their human authority. In Acts 2:23, where Peter states that Jesus was "delivered up according to the definite plan and foreknowledge of God," he goes on to state that he was "nailed to a cross by the hands of godless men" (NASB). God's sovereign control over human events can never be used as an excuse for the evil that men do.

As an expression of his humility, the servant "opened not his mouth." His humble silence was not the normal response of any person enduring oppression and torment. The typical response for someone suffering unjustly would be to cry aloud and broadcast the complaint—or at least to groan, as the children of Israel did when they were in bondage in Egypt (Ex. 2:23). Job (Job 7:1–21; 23:2–4) and Paul (Acts 23:3) vocally protested when they were afflicted with abuse they had done nothing to deserve. People typically do not suffer in silence—and the more intense and unjust the suffering, the less likely anyone is to bear it in silent passivity.

But the servant "opened not his mouth; like a lamb that is led to the slaughter."

Jesus was arrested in the middle of the night as if he were a criminal (Luke 22:52), betrayed by Judas, savagely abused by both the Jewish leaders and the Romans, and finally led to execution, all without any resistance or complaint. Throughout the entire ordeal, the New Testament repeatedly mentions his stone silence. When he was questioned by the high priest, he remained silent (Matt. 26:63). On trial before the Sanhedrin, he remained silent (Mark 14:61). When the Jewish religious leaders accused him before Pilate, he remained silent (Matt. 27:12). When Herod questioned him, he did not answer (Luke 23:9). And when Pilate himself questioned him, he still did not reply (John 19:9). It is true that he spoke a few necessary words in each of those situations. But he never said a word in defense of his innocence or in protest of his unjust treatment. "Like a sheep that before its shearers is silent, so he opened not his mouth."

His silence signaled his willingness to die. It's worth stressing again that Jesus's ministry was not a noble plan gone wrong. He himself said, "I lay down my life that I may take it up again. No one takes it from me, but I lay it down of my own accord. I have authority to lay it down, and I have authority to take it up again" (John 10:17–18). The whole reason he came into this world was to die voluntarily as the Lamb of God to take away the sin of the world. As he contemplated the cross, Jesus said, "Now is my soul troubled. And what shall I say? 'Father, save me from this hour'? But *for this purpose I have come to this hour*" (John 12:27).

Christ's silence was also the silence of judgment. To those who stubbornly hardened their hearts and persistently refused to listen to him—people who, "though he had done so many signs before them, . . . still did not believe in him" (John 12:37)—he gave one final exhortation: "The light is among you for a little while longer. Walk while you have the light, lest darkness overtake you. The one who walks in the darkness does not know where he is going. While you have the light, believe in the light, that you may become sons of light" (vv. 35–36).

After that came the silence of judgment as Jesus "departed and hid himself from them" (v. 36).

Here, as the servant of the Lord silently, without protest, accepted both the unrighteous judgment of men and the righteous judgment of God on behalf of sinners, Old Testament soteriology reaches its apex. "Mercy and truth are met together; righteousness and peace have kissed each other" (Ps. 85:10 KJV).

That is the message of the gospel, a message of sin and judgment, but also of substitutionary atonement, forgiveness, and above all, God's love. It includes the fact that the true Messiah (the silent servant of Isaiah 53) is the only acceptable sacrifice for sin, slaughtered by God for us as our Passover lamb (1 Cor. 5:7, 21).

Silent in His Death

The words "oppression" and "judgment" in Isaiah 53:8 are legal terms. "Oppression," as noted above in connection with verse 7, refers to the injustice and suffering the servant endured during his arrest and trials. The two terms are connected; the unjust judgments constitute the oppression. The "judgment" in view here comprises every phase of the various trials Jesus was subjected to. The phrase "taken away" refers to the carrying out of his sentence when he was taken away to be executed. There was no attempt to give Jesus a fair trial. Multiple verdicts declared him innocent, and then he was handed over to the executioners at the behest of an angry mob. His death was in reality an act of state-sanctioned murder.[3]

It was Pilate who ultimately ordered the slave of the Lord to be crucified (a form of execution usually reserved for slaves). Thus he "was cut off out of the land of the living." That is a common Hebrew expression that refers to being killed (cf. Jer. 11:19; Dan. 9:26). Here in Isaiah 53:8 it refers to the servant's violent, premature death as a result of bearing God's righteous judgment on the sin of fallen mankind. The Messiah would be executed; judicially murdered; led to his death like a lamb led to slaughter (cf. Jer. 11:19). *Despite* all that Jesus was—God incarnate, who did miraculous works that no one else ever did (John 15:24), and who spoke like no one else ever did (John 7:46; cf. Matt. 7:28–29)—he was executed. *Because* of who he is, this was the most horrendous injustice in human history.

---

3. For more details on the injustice of Christ's trials, see John MacArthur, *The Murder of Jesus* (Nashville: Word, 2000).

The telling statement "And as for his generation, who considered that he was cut off out of the land of the living?" was all too true. Who gave serious thought to the injustice being committed against Jesus? Who protested his brutal treatment and execution? Where were the upright men among the religious leaders of the nation? Where were the high priest and the rest of the leading priests? Where were the scribes, Pharisees, Sadducees, and all the others who proclaimed their devotion to God's law? For that matter, where were Jesus's own disciples? They had all deserted him (Matt. 26:56), just as Zechariah 13:7 had predicted. Only John returned to join a handful of women at the cross—as a silent witness. Why weren't the strict procedural rules required in capital cases followed instead of turning Christ's trial into a kangaroo court?

A famous nineteenth-century study of the Jewish jurisprudence described what a just trial would have looked like in first-century Israel:

> On the day of the trial, the executive officers of justice caused the accused person to make his appearance. At the feet of the Elders were placed men who, under the name of *auditors*, or *candidates*, followed regularly the sittings of the Council. The papers in the case were read; and the witnesses were called in succession. The president addressed this exhortation to each of them: "It is not conjectures, or whatever public rumour has brought to thee, that we ask of thee; consider that a great responsibility rests upon thee: that we are not occupied by an affair, like a case of pecuniary interest, in which the injury may be repaired. If thou causest the condemnation of a person unjustly accused, his blood, and the blood of all the posterity of him, of whom thou wilt have deprived the earth, will fall upon thee; God will demand of thee an account, as he demanded of Cain an account of the blood of Abel. Speak."
>
> A woman could not be a witness, because she would not have the courage to give the first blow to the condemned person; nor could a child, that is irresponsible, nor a slave, nor a man of bad character, nor one whose infirmities prevent the full enjoyment of his physical and moral faculties. *The simple confession of an individual against himself,* or the declaration of a prophet, however renowned, would not decide a condemnation. The Doctors say—

"We hold it as fundamental, that *no one shall prejudice himself*. If a man accuses himself before a tribunal, we must not believe him, unless the fact is attested by two other witnesses; and it is proper to remark, that the punishment of death inflicted upon Achan, in the time of Joshua was an exception, occasioned by the nature of the circumstances; for our law does not condemn upon the simple confession of the accused, nor upon the declaration of one prophet alone."

The witnesses were to attest to the identity of the party, and to depose to the month, day, hour, and circumstances of the crime. After an examination of the proofs, those judges who believed the party innocent stated their reasons; those who believed him guilty spoke afterwards, and *with the greatest moderation*. If one of the *auditors*, or *candidates*, was entrusted by the accused with his defence, or if he wished in his own name to present any elucidations in favour of innocence, he was admitted to the seat, from which he addressed the judges and the people. But this liberty was not granted to him, if his opinion was in favour of condemning. Lastly; when the accused person himself wished to speak, they gave the most profound attention. When the discussion was finished, one of the judges recapitulated the case; they removed all the spectators; two scribes took down the votes of the judges; one of them noted those which were in favour of the accused, and the other, those which condemned him. Eleven votes, out of twenty-three, were sufficient to acquit; but it required thirteen to convict. If any of the judges stated that they were not sufficiently informed, there were added two more Elders, and then two others in succession, till they formed a council of sixty-two, which was the number of the Grand Council. If a majority of votes acquitted, the accused was discharged *instantly*; if he was to be punished, the judges postponed pronouncing sentence till the third day; during the intermediate day they could not be occupied with anything but the cause, and they abstained from eating freely, and from wine, liquors, and everything which might render their minds less capable of reflection.

On the morning of the third day they returned to the judgment seat. Each judge, who had not changed his opinion, said, *I continue of the same opinion and condemn*; any one, who at first condemned, might at this sitting acquit; but he who had once acquitted was not allowed to condemn. If a majority condemned, two *magistrates* immediately accompanied the condemned person to the place of punishment. The Elders did not descend from their seats; they placed at the entrance of the judgment hall an officer of justice with a small flag in his hand; a second officer, on horseback, followed the prisoner, and constantly kept looking back to the place of departure. During this interval, if any person came to announce to the Elders any new evidence favourable to the prisoner, the first officer waved his flag, and the second one, as soon as he perceived it, brought back the prisoner. If the prisoner declared to the *magistrates*, that he recollected some reasons which had escaped him, they brought him before the *judges* no less than five times. If no incident occurred, the procession advanced slowly, preceded by a herald who, in a loud voice, addressed the people thus: "This man (stating his name and surname) is led to punishment for such a crime; the witnesses who have sworn against him are such and such persons; if any one has evidence to give in his favour, let him come forth quickly." . . .

At some distance from the place of punishment, they urged the prisoner to confess his crime, and they made him drink a stupefying beverage, in order to render the approach of death less terrible.[4]

Why was the rule of law deliberately contravened by those who engineered Jesus's trial and crucifixion? Why the urgency to put him to death even as the nation prepared to celebrate the Passover? Doesn't that prove sinister intent on their part?

Early in Christian history those very questions were asked. In response, a false account of Jesus's execution from the Jewish leaders' perspective was recorded in the Talmud:

There is a tradition: On the eve of the Sabbath and the Passover they hung Jesus. And the herald went forth before him for forty days crying, "Jesus goeth to be executed, because he has practised sorcery and seduced Israel and estranged them from God. Let any one who can bring forward any justifying plea for him come and

---

4. M. Dupin, "The Trial of Jesus Before Caiaphas and Pilate," cited in Simon Greenleaf, *An Examination of the Testimony of the Four Evangelists by the Rules of Evidence Administered in Courts of Justice* (London: A. Maxwell & Son, 1847), 887–90; emphases original.

give information concerning it," but no justifying plea was found for him, and so he was hung on the eve of Sabbath and the Passover. Ulla said, "But doest thou think that he belongs to those for whom a justifying plea is to be sought? He was a very seducer, and the All-merciful has said [Deut. 13:8], 'Thou shalt not spare him, nor conceal him.'"[5]

In other words, Rabbi Ulla was arguing that Jesus's crimes were so egregious that there was no need to solicit testimony in his defense. Nevertheless, the Talmud says the rabbi's argument was rejected (and Jesus was given forty days to seek testimony that might exonerate him) *"because he stood near to the kingdom"*—that is, because he belonged to the royal line of David.[6]

The Gospel accounts of the last week of Jesus's earthly life are detailed and consistent. They predate the talmudic legends by more than a century. So the rabbis' tale of a fair trial lasting forty days is simply not credible. But it is interesting for several reasons.

It is significant, first of all, that this and other revisionist legends claimed Jesus's crimes were "sorcery" and other moral transgressions.[7] They did not question his lineage; they tacitly affirmed it. David Baron was a British Jew who converted to Christianity in the nineteenth century and wrote several significant works (including an excellent commentary on Isaiah 53). He pointed out that even the Jewish authorities' attempts to justify their treatment of Jesus prove that they knew the truth about him. Baron said, "The fact that Christ was of the Royal Davidic house was written deep on the consciousness of the Jewish nation, and shines out even from beneath the blasphemous legends which the Rabbis invented about Him in self-justification."[8]

Also, the talmudic account of Jesus's trial reflects a deep animosity toward Christ that began with the Sanhedrin during Jesus's earthly ministry (Mark 3:6; John 11:53) and still finds expression today. Some devout followers of traditional Judaism have such antipathy toward

---

5. David Baron, *The Servant of Jehovah: The Sufferings of the Messiah and the Glory That Should Follow* (New York: Marshall, Morgan & Scott, 1922), 105–6.
6. David Baron, *The Ancient Scriptures and the Modern Jew* (London: Hodder & Stoughton, 1901), 18.
7. See chap. 4, note 17.
8. Ibid.

Jesus that they will not speak of him by name but substitute derogatory Yiddish expressions. An article from a Jewish website mocking Moody Bible Institute's Jewish Studies program explains the practice:

> In Yiddish as in no other language, the basic assumptions of Christianity were undercut. By the time Moody [Bible Institute] began teaching it, Jesus had long been a figure of both fear and derision in the Yiddish speaking world. The savior was regularly referred to by dismissive nicknames like *Yoizel*, *Getzel*, and most creatively *Yoshke Pandre*. The layers of meaning in this last name are amazing: Using the diminutive Yiddish suffix "-ke," *Yoshke* might be translated as "Little Joe," tweaking Jesus's non-biological relationship to the credulous husband of Mary. *Pandre*, meanwhile, is Yiddish for "panther," a reference to the allegations [made by the heretic Celsus and repeated in the Talmud] that the father of Jesus was neither God, nor Joseph the carpenter, but a plundering Roman soldier called Pantera (Latin for "panther"). Thus the name slyly makes Jesus's birth illegitimate and those associated with it either rapists or fools.[9]

The article goes on to describe other Yiddish expressions for Jesus that are too profane to repeat. The thread of bitter scorn for Jesus is traceable from the Sanhedrin of Jesus's day, through the Talmud, down to the present time.

Obviously, not all Jewish people hold Jesus in such high contempt. He is despised by some; merely rejected by others. (And to be fair, Jewish hatred of Jesus has often been made worse by deliberate, systematic mistreatment at the hands of people who claimed to be acting in Jesus's name. Perhaps no single group of people has suffered more or longer than the Jews at the hands of various tyrants and religious zealots who are driven by ethnic or racial hatred.)

Still, it is a fact that every major branch of Judaism rejects the claims of Christ and repudiates the claim that he is Messiah. Devout Jews regard "messianic Jews" (ethnic Jews who believe in Jesus) as apostate, and therefore no longer truly Jewish. Orthodox Jews will

---

9. Peter Manseau, "Missionary Yiddish," January 22, 2009, http://jewcy.com/jewish-religion -and-beliefs/missionary_Yiddish.

often "sit shiva," observing a weeklong ritual of mourning tantamount to a funeral for the dead, if one of their community trusts in Jesus.

While the confession "we esteemed him not" in Isaiah 53:3 is an appropriate confession for anyone turning from unbelief to faith, it has a particular significance for the Jewish nation because (as we noted in chapter 4) they were the nation chosen to bring Messiah into the world; the Scriptures were given though them; and they possessed spiritual advantages and a relationship with Yahweh that no other nation was ever privileged to enjoy (Rom. 3:1–2; 9:4–5).

And yet, as Scripture says, when the promised Messiah came, "his own people did not receive him" (John 1:11). Indeed, their chief priests were the architects of the conspiracy that took Jesus's life.

The Jewish leaders' harsh, unjust, malevolent treatment of him did not alter the fact that the servant was voluntarily giving his life *for them*. Isaiah wrote, "[He was] stricken for the transgression of my people." Isaiah uses the expression "my people" as a technical term for the Jewish nation about two dozen times. "The ox knows its owner, and the donkey its master's crib, but Israel does not know, my people do not understand" (Isa. 1:3; see also 3:12; 5:13; 32:13; 40:1).

By the way, this verse clearly distinguishes "my servant" from "my people," showing why Israel *cannot* be the servant of Isaiah 53. "Who considered that he [my servant] was . . . stricken for the transgression of my people?" The point here is that though the people regarded the servant as "stricken, smitten *by God*, and afflicted" (v. 4), they did not realize the stroke of judgment was not for his own transgressions (he had none), but for the sins of the nation (and not for the nation only, but for all the sins of all his people, from every tongue, tribe, and nation).

John's Gospel recounts how (in the meeting where the conspiracy against Jesus was hatched) Caiaphas, the high priest, argued that putting Jesus to death would be the lesser of two evils: "It is better for you that one man should die for the people, not that the whole nation should perish" (John 11:50). The apostle goes on to explain, "He did not say this of his own accord, but being high priest that year he prophesied that Jesus would die *for the nation, and not for the nation only*, but also to gather into one the children of God who are scattered abroad [i.e., the Gentiles who would come to faith in Jesus]" (vv. 51–52).

Israel collectively misjudged Jesus. They believed he was struck dead by God for sins and blasphemies, as his accusers claimed. In reality, he *was* stricken by God—but for the transgressions of his people, to bring salvation to both Jews and Gentiles (Acts 20:21; Rom. 1:16; 3:29–30; 9:24; 1 Cor. 1:24; 12:13; Eph. 2:12–14).

Silent in the Grave

Isaiah 53:9 introduces an astonishing set of details: "And they made [or assigned] his grave [to be] with the wicked." Since he was crucified with criminals, it was expected that Jesus's body would be disposed of in the same manner as theirs. The Romans generally left the dead bodies of crucified criminals hanging on their crosses like symbolic roadkill, to be devoured by birds and wild animals. In the ancient world, to expose someone's dead body and refuse to bury it was the ultimate act of dishonoring that person, as the Philistines did to the bodies of Saul and his sons (1 Sam. 31:10–12)—and as the followers of Antichrist will do to the bodies of the two witnesses in the tribulation (Rev. 11:7–9; see also Jer. 25:33).

To leave a corpse exposed like that was strictly forbidden by God (Deut. 21:22–23). But the Romans purposely left the remains of their crucified victims out in the open. Crucifixions were usually done within sight of high-traffic thoroughfares. Thus the corpses of the condemned served as a graphic illustration of the fate that awaited those who dared to challenge the might of Rome. Eventually, officials would dispose of whatever bones and skulls were left at a common grave site. In Jerusalem, that location was the Valley of Hinnom, a ravine on the outskirts of Jerusalem just south of the city.

Hinnom had a dark and evil past. It was a place where babies were sacrificed to Molech, the detestable false god of the Ammonites (1 Kings 11:7), by burning them to death (2 Kings 17:17; 21:6; Jer. 32:35)—an appalling practice strictly prohibited by God (Lev. 18:21; 20:2–5; Jer. 7:31–32; 32:35). The Aramaic name for the valley was transliterated into Greek and used in the New Testament as a name for hell. The English transliteration is *Gehenna*. In Old Testament times the place came to be known as "Topheth." The meaning of that name is uncertain. Most resources say it means "the place of burning" (from the Aramaic word for "fireplace"). That is an apt description. Other linguists say it is derived from the Hebrew word for "drum," and it is a reference to the drums that were constantly beaten to drown out the screams of the babies who were being burned alive. Jeremiah said the place should be called "the Valley of Slaughter" (Jer. 19:6).

In Jesus's time, the Hinnom valley was Jerusalem's garbage dump, where a fire burned continuously in the midst of the rubbish (cf. Isa. 66:24; Matt. 3:12; Mark 9:48). After the bones of a crucified criminal were picked clean by scavenger birds, the final remains would be thrown into that fire.

That would not happen to God's servant. The voice of Messiah speaks in Psalm 16:10: "You will not abandon my soul to Sheol, or let your holy one see corruption" (cf. Acts 2:27–31; 13:35–37). In an amazing turn of events, Isaiah says the servant instead would be "with a rich man in his death."

That rich man was Joseph of Arimathea (Matt. 27:57), who had become "a disciple of Jesus, but secretly for fear of the Jews" (John 19:38). He not only provided his own unused tomb (Luke 23:53) for Jesus to be buried in, but also boldly asked Pilate for the body (Matt. 27:58). He then entombed Jesus's body, with the help of Nicodemus, another prominent person who was discretely a disciple of Jesus (John 19:39–42). So instead of his decomposed body being unceremoniously thrown into Jerusalem's garbage dump, Christ's body was buried in the new, unused tomb of a wealthy man—exactly as Isaiah had predicted seven centuries earlier. God arranged for his Son's honorable burial to demonstrate to the world that his servant, Israel's Messiah, was innocent.

The final phrase in verse 9 reveals the significance of the servant's burial: this was God's way of vindicating Christ's blamelessness. He would not allow any further humiliation of his Son. The closing words of this section, "he had done no violence [sin of action], and there was no deceit in his mouth [sin in the heart]," was a testimony by the Father to Jesus's complete, sinless perfection.

It was also the first small step of his exaltation.

7

The Suffering and Exalted Servant

So, there is no doubt that the Prophet is here comparing two opposite things: namely, (1) that Jesus Christ should be for a long time, as it were, hidden, indeed, as it were, plunged into the depths of hell, and even, when He should come, He should have no great pomp in order to be prized by men; but entirely the contrary, that He should be rejected, that He should be held in such contempt that no one would ever think that the salvation of the people should be accomplished by His means; but (2) He shall not therefore be less exalted.

John Calvin[1]

It was the very day of his resurrection when Jesus encountered those two disciples traveling from Jerusalem to the nearby village of Emmaus. Mark 16:12–13 barely mentions the event in passing. Luke tells us what happened.

The walk to Emmaus was seven miles (Luke 24:13). At a very brisk pace, that would be at least a two-hour journey. Because people tended to travel in small groups and converse while walking, they traveled at a slightly slower pace. So the walk to Emmaus would take about two and a half to three hours. These two disciples "were talking with each other about all these things that had happened" (v. 14). Specifically,

---

1. Leroy Nixon, trans., *The Gospel According to Isaiah* (Grand Rapids, MI: Eerdmans, 1953), 14.

they were reviewing and trying to make sense of the troubling events of the past three days—from Jesus's arrest on Thursday night to the empty tomb that very morning.

A lone pedestrian caught up with them. "While they were talking and discussing together, Jesus himself drew near and went with them" (v. 15).[2] Jesus asked, "What is this conversation that you are holding with each other as you walk?" (v. 17). They replied by giving a brief account

> concerning Jesus of Nazareth, a man who was a prophet mighty in deed and word before God and all the people, and how our chief priests and rulers delivered him up to be condemned to death, and crucified him. But we had hoped that he was the one to redeem Israel. Yes, and besides all this, it is now the third day since these things happened. (vv. 19–21)

They went on to say they had heard from "some women" about the empty tomb, and "a vision of angels, who said that he was alive." Some companions of theirs had even gone to the tomb and found it empty, but "him they did not see" (vv. 22–24).

These two did not realize that they were saying this to the risen Lord himself!

That's when Jesus responded by rebuking them for being "foolish ones, and slow of heart to believe all that the prophets have spoken! Was it not necessary that the Christ should suffer these things and enter into his glory?" (vv. 25–26).

The career of Messiah, our Lord told them, falls into two categories: *suffering* and *glory*. Had they understood that simple principle from the writings of the prophets, their faith would not have been so shaken.

After they finally realized whom they had been talking to, "They

---

2. Luke says these two disciples (one named Cleopas; the other anonymous) were "kept from recognizing him" (v. 16). That obviously means God sovereignly restrained their ability to discern who he was (cf. v. 31)—not necessarily by a miracle that literally clouded their vision, but more likely by providentially using their grief and confusion to keep them from realizing that the risen, glorified body of Jesus would look dramatically different from the battered corpse that was taken off the cross and placed in a tomb just days earlier. They were not the only ones who failed to recognize the risen Jesus immediately. Mary Magdalene mistook him for a gardener at the tomb (John 20:25). The Eleven likewise failed to recognize him at first when he met them on the shore in Galilee (John 21:4). It was the same body, but what was "sown in dishonor [had been] raised in glory. [What was] sown in weakness [was] raised in power" (1 Cor. 15:43).

said to each other, 'Did not our hearts burn within us while he talked to us on the road, while he opened to us the Scriptures?'" (v. 32).

That same evening, Jesus appeared to the eleven remaining apostles and some of his other followers, who were hiding at a secret location in Jerusalem, fearful of the Jewish authorities (John 20:19). After reassuring the panic-stricken disciples that it was really him and not a ghost, Jesus said to them:

> "These are my words that I spoke to you while I was still with you, that everything written about me in the Law of Moses and the Prophets and the Psalms must be fulfilled." Then he opened their minds to understand the Scriptures, and said to them, "Thus it is written, that the Christ should suffer and on the third day rise from the dead." (Luke 24:44–46)

In other words, Jesus reiterated what he had told the two disciples earlier that day: the Old Testament taught that Messiah had to suffer. Only then would he be glorified and exalted. His exaltation began when he rose from the dead and then ascended to the Father's right hand.

Those who do not grasp that his suffering was the prerequisite to glory have not understood the first thing about the gospel. This is a theme that resonates through the Christian message (Matt. 26:64; Acts 2:33; 7:55; Rom. 8:34; Eph. 1:20; Col. 3:1; Heb. 1:3; 1 Pet. 3:22).

But as we have seen from the beginning, belief that Messiah would suffer simply did not figure into the popular messianic hope. Jewish doctors of theology focused on his glory and glossed over the necessity of his suffering. They fully expected their Messiah to establish his kingdom and deliver Israel from her enemies—and they earnestly hoped that day would come sooner rather than later. But they failed to understand the Old Testament's teaching that Messiah would suffer and die before he conquered and ruled.

The expectation that Messiah would quickly bring the glory of his kingdom to earth was so strong and so persistent that even at his ascension the leading disciples were still asking him, "Lord, will you at this time restore the kingdom to Israel?" (Acts 1:6). Whatever hope they may have had that the kingdom would begin immediately must have been dashed when he replied, "It is not for you to know times or seasons that the Father has fixed by his own authority" (v. 7). And within minutes, "as they were looking on, he was lifted up, and a cloud took him out of their sight" (v. 9).

They eventually understood and accepted that suffering, not just glory, was a necessary part of Messiah's ministry. Peter would later write, "Concerning this salvation, the prophets who prophesied about the grace that was to be yours searched and inquired carefully, inquiring what person or time the Spirit of Christ in them was indicating when he predicted the *sufferings* of Christ and the *subsequent glories*" (1 Pet. 1:10–11).

It is impossible to understand the person and work of the Lord Jesus Christ apart from those two categories. Together, they encompass the entire range of Old Testament prophecies about Messiah. Both themes run consistently through the prophets' messages. Indeed, there are numerous texts scattered across the whole Old Testament ("beginning with Moses and all the Prophets") that Jesus might have explained on that two-and-a-half-hour walk to Emmaus.

As we have previously suggested, Old Testament passages that prefigured or foretold Jesus's sufferings would include the symbolism in Abraham's willingness to sacrifice Isaac; the Passover lamb; the bronze serpent lifted up in the wilderness (John 3:14); the blood-shedding that was so prominent in the sacrificial system; the piercing and mockery portrayed in Psalm 22; the suffering described in Psalms 69, 118, and other messianic psalms; and the betrayal and piercing alluded to in Zechariah 11:12–13; 12:10.

But nowhere in the Old Testament do the twin themes of suffering and glory come together so clearly and with so much detail as in Isaiah 52:13–53:12. By now you surely understand why this detailed messianic prophecy is exceptionally noteworthy, revealing so many precise, historically verified details of Messiah's life, death, resurrection, and exaltation seven centuries before his birth.

Verses 10 to 12 comprise the fifth and final stanza of this fourth and last of Isaiah's Servant Songs. Earlier stanzas have portrayed the servant of the Lord as the astonishing servant, the rejected servant, the substituted servant, and the silent servant. But "this final stanza is like a reservoir into which flow all the main lines of thought."[3] It begins with a triumphant promise and ends with a triumphant proclamation.

To understand the final stanza, we need to look again at the opening section of this passage, Isaiah 52:13–15. Verse 13 presents an enigma to the Jewish reader concerning the servant of the Lord, the Messiah: "He shall be high and lifted up." The phrase "high and lifted up" speaks of his deity. Those same words are used in Isaiah 6:1 and 57:15 to describe God. His divine majesty and glory will startle the nations, and that's what will reduce their rulers to a stunned silence when he returns in glory (52:15).

But on the other hand, the servant is also a man. According to verse 14: "His appearance was so marred, beyond human semblance, and his form beyond that of the children of mankind." As God, he is highly exalted; as man he was marred and disfigured.

Here is the mystery that seemed impossible for Old Testament readers to fathom: how could this glorious, startling, divine deliverer be at the same time the most marred and disfigured of men? The answer lies in understanding that the Messiah would be humbled and endure suffering at his first coming. "Being found in human form," Paul wrote, "he humbled himself by becoming obedient to the point of death, even death on a cross" (Phil. 2:8). Afterward, he would be exalted by the Father. Because of Christ's willing obedience, "God has highly exalted him and bestowed on him the name that is above every name, so that at the name of Jesus every knee should bow, in heaven and on earth and under the earth, and every tongue confess that Jesus Christ is Lord, to the glory of God the Father" (vv. 9–11).

That the servant would be both humiliated and exalted is God's plan. Yahweh is the speaker before and after Israel's confession— in verses 13–15 of chapter 52, which describe the servant's suffering, and again in the second half of verse 11 and verse 12 of chapter 53, which describe his exaltation. What happened to Jesus Christ was not an unexpected tragedy, but the exact fulfillment of God's plan. The suffering servant of the Lord was no hapless victim; he is (even in the extremity of his crucifixion) the victorious Son of God. He was chosen by the Father and empowered by the Spirit both to suffer and to be

---

3. J. Alec Motyer, *The Prophecy of Isaiah* (Downers Grove, IL: InterVarsity Press, 1993), 436.

glorified—all to bring his people forgiveness for their sins and eternal life in heaven. He is the only acceptable sacrifice to take away the sins of the world (John 1:29).

So God himself provides the answer to Israel's enigma regarding his servant. In Isaiah 53:12 he says that although the servant was humiliated and "numbered with the transgressors" when he "bore the sin of many," he will nevertheless be highly exalted when God causes him to "divide . . . a portion with the many, and . . . divide the spoil with the strong." This is the most glorious and important truth ever revealed to human-ity—the good news of salvation for sinners by the death of the servant of the Lord. And it was all foretold to the Jewish nation in Isaiah 53.

"To Him Shall Come and Be Ashamed All Who Were Incensed Against Him" (Isa. 45:24)

Isaiah 53 is, as we have said from the start, the confession that will be made when the people of Israel finally recognize and receive him as the true Messiah. Up to this point in Isaiah 53 the provisions and benefits of the servant's death have been viewed from the perspective of repentant Israel. That perspective continues for the first half of the final stanza (verse 10 and the first part of verse 11).

But in the latter part of the fifth stanza (the second half of verse 11, and verse 12) there is a shift in voice and perspective. Starting midway through verse 11, this is no longer the confession of repentant Israel. This is God giving his verdict on the servant's suffering and death. The possessive pronoun in the expression "my servant" signals the change of voice. God is now the speaker, and he affirms the truthfulness of Israel's confession.

So in Isaiah 52:13–15 and 53:11–12 we are hearing the voice of God, with words of commendation for the faithfulness of his servant. The passage between those two declarations is the part that foretells the future repentance of Israel.

That day will come, as surely as God is faithful. The whole promise of the new covenant (Jer. 31:31–36) is punctuated with this promise: "Thus says the LORD: 'If the heavens above can be measured, and the foundations of the earth below can be explored, then I will cast off all the offspring of Israel for all that they have done'" (v. 37). In other words, it is no more possible for God to abandon his chosen nation than it would be to measure infinity. The apostle Paul explicitly raises and answers the question: "I ask, then, has God rejected his people? By no means! For I myself am an Israelite, a descendant of Abraham, a member of the tribe of Benjamin" (Rom. 11:1). Ezekiel 36:22–38 is an extended promise to Israel that God is not yet through dealing with them as a nation. "You shall dwell in the land that I gave to your fathers, and you shall be my people, and I will be your God" (v. 28).

Paul dealt with all of this in detail in Romans 9–11. In the end, he affirms that all the old-covenant promises to Israel will be fulfilled. Just as the threats and curses for their apostasy were fulfilled literally, so shall be the promises about their restoration to the Promised Land:

> A partial hardening has come upon Israel, until the fullness of the Gentiles has come in. And in this way *all Israel will be saved*, as it is written,
>
> "The Deliverer will come from Zion,
>   he will banish ungodliness from Jacob";
> "and this will be my covenant with them
>   when I take away their sins." (Rom. 11:25–27)

This is no recent innovation in Christian doctrine regarding the end times. Jesus himself said, "Jerusalem will be trampled underfoot by the Gentiles, *until the times of the Gentiles are fulfilled*" (Luke 21:24). Theologians throughout church history—including many in the Reformed tradition—have long taught that national Israel, "the natural branches, [will] be grafted back into their own olive tree" (Rom. 11:24). That is to say, they will, ultimately, turn from their unbelief, embrace Jesus as Messiah, and inherit all the blessings of the Abrahamic and Davidic covenants.

That view was taught by many of the church fathers, including Justin Martyr, Origen, John Chrysostom, Jerome, and Cyril of Alexandria. Tertullian wrote, "At His last coming [Christ] will favour with His acceptance and blessing the circumcision also, even the race of Abraham, which by and by is to acknowledge Him."[4]

---

4. Tertullian, *The Five Books Against Marcion*, 5.9, in *The Ante-Nicene Fathers*, ed. A. Roberts and J. Donaldson, 10 vols. (Grand Rapids. MI: Eerdmans, 1951), 3:448.

The greatest of all the theologians in the early centuries of the church, Augustine, also affirmed his belief in Israel's future salvation, a view that he said was common in his day: "It is a familiar theme in the conversation and heart of the faithful, that in the last days before the judgment the Jews shall believe in the true Christ, that is, our Christ, by means of this great and admirable prophet Elias who shall expound the law to them."[5]

Thomas Aquinas, the most influential (and probably the best) of the medieval Roman Catholic theologians, also believed in the national salvation of Israel. He believed that in the end times, "the remnants of Israel will be converted."[6] He wrote, "As by the fall of the Jews, the Gentiles who had been enemies were reconciled, so after the conversion of the Jews near the end of the world, there will be a general resurrection by which men will rise from the dead to immortal life."[7] He wrote, "the blindness of the Jews will endure until all the pagans chosen for salvation have accepted the faith. And this is in accord with what Paul says . . . about the salvation of the Jews, namely, that after the conversion of the pagans, all Israel will be saved."[8]

The most skilled theologian among the magisterial Reformers, John Calvin, wrote in his comments on Isaiah 59:20 that

> Paul quotes this passage, (Rom. xi. 26,) in order to shew that there is still some remaining hope among the Jews; although from their unconquerable obstinacy it might be inferred that they were altogether cast off and doomed to eternal death. But because God is continually mindful of his covenant, and "his gifts and calling are without repentance," (Rom. xi. 29,) Paul justly concludes that it is impossible that there shall not at length be some remnant that come to Christ, and obtain that salvation which he has procured. Thus the Jews must at length be collected along with the Gentiles, that out of both "there may be one fold" under Christ. (John x. 16.).[9]

---

5. Augustine, *The City of God*, 20.29, in *The Nicene and Post-Nicene Fathers*, ed. Philip Schaff, 14 vols. (New York: Scribners, 1887), 2:448.

6. Thomas Aquinas, *Summa Theologica* (New York: Cosimo, 2007), 2:1072.

7. Thomas Aquinas, *On the Epistle of Romans*.

8. John Y. B. Hood, *Aquinas and the Jews* (Philadelphia: University of Philadelphia Press, 1995), 77. The excerpt is translated from Aquinas's Latin commentary on Romans.

9. John Calvin, *Commentary on the Book of the Prophet Isaiah*, trans. William Pringle, 4 vols. (Edinburgh: Calvin Translation Society, 1853), 4:269.

The Geneva Bible was the Bible of the original English Reformers. It was the most influential English Bible before the King James Version. It contained notes, written by many of the leading Protestant theologians of the day. The notes on Romans 11:24 and 25 read in part:

> He [Paul] speaks of the whole nation, not of any one part. . . . The blindness of the Jews is neither so universal that the Lord has no elect in that nation, neither will it be continual: for there will be a time in which they also (as the prophets have foretold) will effectually embrace that which they now so stubbornly for the most part reject and refuse.

Many of the English and American Puritans, including John Owen, Thomas Manton, John Flavel, William Perkins, Thomas Boston, Increase Mather, and Cotton Mather, also believed there will be a national conversion of Israel.

Jonathan Edwards, considered by many to be the greatest theologian America has ever produced, stated bluntly, "Nothing is more certainly foretold than this national conversion of the Jews is in the eleventh chapter of Romans. And there are also many passages of the Old Testament which cannot be interpreted in any other sense."[10]

The eighteenth-century English Baptist theologian John Gill believed in "the conversion of the Jews, and the settlement of them in their own land."[11] He wrote,

> The conversion of the Jews . . . will follow upon the destruction of antichrist. . . . There are many prophecies that speak of their conversion; as that they shall be born at once; not in a civil sense, set up and established as a nation; but in a spiritual sense, born again of water and of the spirit; they shall be brought into a thorough conviction of sin, and a true sense of it, and shall mourn for it; particularly the sin of their obstinate rejection of the true Messiah, and their continued unbelief in him; when they shall be led and go forth with weeping and with supplication, and shall seek the Lord their God, and David their king, the Messiah, and receive him and

---

10. Jonathan Edwards, *A History of the Work of Redemption* (Worcester, MA: Thomas & Whipple, 1808), 487.

11. John Gill, *A Complete Body of Doctrinal and Practical Divinity*, 3 vols. (London: Ridgway, 1796), 2:155.

submit unto him; and join themselves to Christian churches, and be subject to the ordinances of Christ: and this will be universal; all Israel shall be saved, the whole nation shall be born at once, suddenly; for which for many hundreds of years they have been kept a distinct people, and have not been reckoned and mixed among the nations, though scattered in the midst of them; which is a most marvellous thing in providence, and plainly shows that God has some great things to do for them and by them.[12]

Charles Hodge, one of the leading Presbyterian theologians of the nineteenth century, wrote, "The second great event, which, according to the common faith of the Church, is to precede the second advent of Christ, is the national conversion of the Jews."[13]

In a sermon entitled "The Harvest and the Vintage" Charles Spurgeon said regarding the future conversion of national Israel:

It is certain that the Jews, as a people, will yet own Jesus of Nazareth, the Son of David as their King, and that they will return to their own land, and they shall build the old wastes, they shall raise up the former desolations, and they shall repair the old cities, the desolations of many generations.[14]

J. C. Ryle, a contemporary of Spurgeon, also expressed his conviction that Israel will one day be restored:

It always seemed to me that as we take literally the texts foretelling that the walls of Babylon shall be cast down, so we ought to take literally the texts foretelling that the walls of Zion shall be built up, that as according to prophecy the Jews were literally scattered, so according to prophecy the Jews will be literally gathered.[15]

Contemporary theologians such as Geerhardus Vos, George Eldon Ladd, John Murray, William Hendriksen, R. C. Sproul, Millard Erickson, and Wayne Grudem have also taught that there will be a future conversion of the nation of Israel.

---

12. Ibid., 2:155.

13. Charles Hodge, *Systematic Theology* (New York: Scribner's, 1884), 3:805.

14. Charles Spurgeon, *The Metropolitan Tabernacle Pulpit*, 63 vols. (London: Passmore & Alabaster, 1904), 50:553.

15. J. C. Ryle, "Watch!," in *Coming Events and Present Duties* (London: William Hunt, 1879), 19.

When that day comes, the Jewish people will look at the one whom they pierced and reverse their opinion concerning him. They had thought that he was stricken by God and afflicted because he was a blaspheming sinner. Then, however, they will understand that what happened to him was to pay for their transgressions, which were laid on him (2 Cor. 5:21) to bring spiritual well-being and healing to sinners.

The Suffering Servant

One of the most amazing features of Isaiah 53 is the fact that the future generation of Jewish believers who will make this confession express a full understanding of the significance of the cross of Christ. Their knowledge of the gospel—rooted in this ancient prophecy—will finally be correct and complete. They will confess that "although [Christ] had done no violence, and there was no deceit in his mouth" (v. 9), "yet it was the will of the LORD to crush him" and "put him to grief" when he "makes [himself] an offering for guilt" (v. 10). Every vital detail of the doctrine of Christ's vicarious, substitutionary atonement for sinners is expressed in that statement. It's no exaggeration to say that this is the core truth of the Christian faith.

To be sure, men did their worst to the servant. They abused him to the point that he hardly looked human (52:14). They despised, rejected, oppressed, afflicted, and attempted to dishonor him even in his burial (53:3, 7, 8, 9). He was "crucified and killed by the hands of lawless men" (Acts 2:23).

Yet as we have stressed more than once already, the text shockingly says, "It was the will of the LORD to crush him; *he* has put him to grief" (Isa. 53:10). Yahweh ordained that something horrific, inexplicable, and incomprehensible would happen to his servant. The servant's death was God's doing, according to God's plan. As the first half of Acts 2:23 acknowledges, Jesus was "delivered up according to the definite plan and foreknowledge of God." Without diminishing the evil of the act, Scripture plainly teaches that this was precisely what God's hand and purpose "predestined to take place" (Acts 4:27–28). It was ultimately *the Lord God* who pierced him for our transgressions, chastised him to bring us peace, wounded him to heal us, and laid our iniquities on him.

But even more shocking is that God, who takes no pleasure in the death of the wicked (Ezek. 18:23, 32; 33:11), took pleasure in the death of his servant, the righteous one. The Hebrew word translated "will" in verse 10 by the English Standard Version literally means, "to delight in," or "to take pleasure in." The New American Standard Bible translates the phrase more literally: "The LORD *was pleased* to crush Him."

The phrase "he has put him to grief" is a strong phrase, describing the intensity of Christ's suffering. It indicates an experience excruciating enough to completely debilitate him. God did not merely crush the servant in the sense of killing him; he did so in the most appalling manner imaginable.

As we have pointed out several times now, Jesus did not die the death of a well-meaning martyr. Martyrs throughout the history of the church have died singing hymns of praise to God, confidently testifying to their faith in the Lord. They died with hope and joy in their hearts because they died under the sweet comforts of grace.

But Jesus received no help or succor in his death. He suffered under the relentless, unrelieved terrors of divine wrath and fury against sin. God arrived in the blackness at Calvary to bring judgment, not on the ungodly, but on his Son. God brought the outer darkness of hell to Calvary that day as he unleashed the full extent of his wrath against the sins of all who would ever believe in Jesus Christ.

Infinite wrath moved by infinite righteousness brought infinite punishment on the eternal Son.

Surely "this is a hard saying; who can listen to it?" (cf. John 6:60). Even many Christians reject the truth of penal substitution, likening it to "divine child abuse." One writer cynically wrote, "If God wants to forgive us, why doesn't he just do it? How does punishing an innocent person make things better? That just sounds like one more injustice in the cosmic equation. It sounds like divine child abuse. You know?"[16] In reality, the fact that God the Father made his own Son's soul an offering for sin is the greatest possible expression of his love for humanity. "In this is love, not that we have loved God but that he loved us and sent his Son to be the propitiation for our sins" (1 John 4:10).

---

16. Brian McLaren, *The Story We Find Ourselves In: Further Adventures of a New Kind of Christian* (San Francisco: Jossey-Bass, 2003), 143. McLaren, Tony Campolo, Steve Chalke, and others have all in recent years made this same scoffing remark about "divine child abuse."

Jesus was able to absorb the infinite judgment of eternal hell for all who will ever believe in just three hours (and then rise from the dead) because he himself is infinite God, with infinite power. Scripture is clear on this: he bore in his own body our sins (1 Pet. 2:24). Although he knew no sin, he was made sin for us (2 Cor. 5:21). He was pierced for our transgressions and crushed for our iniquities (Isa. 53:5). He was made a curse for us (Gal. 3:13). This was the cup that he pleaded with the Father in Gethsemane to remove from him, if possible.

The Lord's cry at the ninth hour, "'Eloi, Eloi, lema sabachthani?' . . . means, 'My God, my God, why have you forsaken me?'" (Mark 15:34). That plea reveals that the Father did not immediately comfort his Son when the darkness lifted. This is the only time in the New Testament where Jesus refers to God as anything other than "Father." The doubled phrase "My God, my God" is an expression of affection mingled with disappointment (cf. Luke 10:41; 13:34; 22:31). The Father was present in the fury of judgment but absent in terms of comfort.

His absence was necessary, however. While hell includes the full fury of God's personal presence to punish, that presence will not bring any comfort, sympathy, or relief. If Jesus was to endure the full suffering of hell, that suffering had to include both the punishment of God and the absence of his comfort.

How could God possibly have been "pleased" by bringing such agony and torment on his Son?

It was the *outcome* that pleased him, not the *pain*. His pleasure in crushing Jesus and putting him to grief was not in the torment inflicted on his Son, but in the Son's fulfilling his Father's purpose—not his agony, but his accomplishment; not his suffering, but the salvation that suffering accomplished. God was pleased because the servant willingly sacrificed himself as a guilt offering; he gave his life to save sinners.

The Old Testament guilt offering (sometimes referred to as the trespass offering) was one of the five main sacrifices in the Levitical system. Those sacrifices, described in the first seven chapters of Leviticus, also included the burnt offering, the grain offering, the peace offering, and the sin offering. The first three, the burnt, grain, and peace offerings, were voluntary for individual Israelites, but the sin and guilt offerings were mandatory. Sin offerings and guilt offerings were offered every day in the morning and evening sacrifices, as well as on the Sabbath (Num. 28:1–10). Four of the offerings (all except the grain offering) involved animal sacrifices. These pictured the deadly result of sin—the sobering reality that "the soul who sins shall die" (Ezek. 18:4, 20). Yet again, they also offered hope, because God allowed a substitute to die in the sinner's place, foreshadowing Christ's death as the ultimate sacrifice for sin (2 Cor. 5:21; Eph. 5:2; Heb. 7:27; 9:26; 10:12).

The fifth and final sacrifice, the guilt offering, added an important dimension that is not found in the others. It is the principle of restitution, satisfaction, or propitiation. Restitution was required when someone deprived another (whether God or another human) of his or her rightful due. The guilt offering was thus the most complete of the five major offerings.

In the future the Jews as a nation will see all of this in the offering of Christ, whose sacrifice provided complete satisfaction for the demands of God's justice, made full restitution, and served as a thorough propitiation. The sinner's debt is paid in full by God's "canceling the record of debt that stood against us with its legal demands. This he set aside, nailing it to the cross" (Col. 2:14). Repentant sinners, having died to sin through their union with Christ in his death (Rom. 6:2–4), are freed from sin's guilt (Rom. 6:11, 18, 22; 8:2). His death is the propitiation for the sins of all who believe (1 John 2:1–2).

The Honored Servant

In the concluding portion of their confession, in the second part of Isaiah 53:10 and the first part of verse 11, the believing remnant turn from the suffering the servant endured when God crushed him, to celebrate the honor that was bestowed on him afterward. Their confession mentions four specific aspects of how God will honor his servant.

First, "he shall see his offspring." Unlike humans, who see their children, possibly their grandchildren, and sometimes their great-grandchildren, Messiah will see all the generations of his spiritual offspring—those whom he is not ashamed to call brethren (Heb. 2:11). They are given to him by the Father (John 6:37), and Christ brings them to glory (v. 10).

He will be able to do that because "he shall prolong his days." That phrase is a Hebraism for a long, enduring life (cf. Deut. 4:40; Prov. 28:16; Eccles. 8:13). In Revelation 1:18 Jesus declared, "I died, and behold I am alive forevermore." The writer of Hebrews noted that "he is able to save to the uttermost those who draw near to God through him, since he always lives to make intercession for them" (Heb. 7:25; cf. v. 16).

The servant will also be honored because through his willing acceptance of God's crushing judgment, he accomplished the work of redemption. That caused "the will of the LORD [to] prosper in his hand." The work of redemption Christ achieved was to the praise of God's glory (Eph. 1:12), and because of it "God has highly exalted him and bestowed on him the name that is above every name, so that at the name of Jesus every knee should bow, in heaven and on earth and under the earth, and every tongue confess that Jesus Christ is Lord, to the glory of God the Father" (Phil. 2:9–11).

Finally, the servant will be honored by the satisfaction of seeing the plan of redemption through to its conclusion. Despite the "anguish of his soul he shall see and be satisfied" (Isa. 53:11). He will have the joy of seeing his spiritual offspring, the redeemed, gathered into God's kingdom. It will be his honor to see them surround his throne, worshiping and serving him, to the praise of his glory throughout all eternity. In particular, he will delight in seeing the salvation of Israel:

> For Zion's sake I will not keep silent,
>   and for Jerusalem's sake I will not be quiet,
> until her righteousness goes forth as brightness,
>   and her salvation as a burning torch.
> The nations shall see your righteousness,
>   and all the kings your glory,
> and you shall be called by a new name
>   that the mouth of the LORD will give.
> You shall be a crown of beauty in the hand of the LORD,
>   and a royal diadem in the hand of your God.
> You shall no more be termed Forsaken,
>   and your land shall no more be termed Desolate,
> but you shall be called My Delight Is in Her,
>   and your land Married;

for the LORD delights in you,
    and your land shall be married.
For as a young man marries a young woman,
    so shall your sons marry you,
and as the bridegroom rejoices over the bride,
    so shall your God rejoice over you. (Isa. 62:1–5)

Most important, Jesus would be satisfied that his work of substitutionary atonement was completed, as indicated by his triumphant, final cry from the cross, "It is finished" (John 19:30). As he said to the Father on the night before his death, "I glorified you on earth, having accomplished the work that you gave me to do" (John 17:4; cf. 4:34; 5:36).

8

The Sin-Bearing Servant

"The Lord hath laid on him the iniquity of us all." It was the sovereign decree of heaven which constituted Christ the great substitute for his people. No man taketh this office upon himself. Even the Son of God stoopeth not to this burden uncalled. He was chosen as the covenant-head in election; he was ordained in the divine decree to stand for his people. God the Father cannot refuse the sacrifice which he has himself appointed. "My son," said good old Abraham, "God shall provide himself a lamb for a burnt-offering." He has done so in the Saviour; and what God provides, God must and will accept.

Charles Spurgeon[1]

Isaiah 53 answers the most vitally important question that any fallen human being could ever ask: *How can a sinner be fully reconciled to God?* That is a question everyone eventually needs to face squarely. The question generally arises when someone is struggling under the weight of his or her own guilt, suffering the anguish of sin's consequences, or feeling the profound grief that always results when sin's wages are being paid. Job and his counselors raised the question more than once during his ordeal. Job asked, "How can a man be in the right before God?" (Job 9:2). "Who can bring a clean thing out of an unclean?" (14:4).

---

1. Charles Spurgeon, *The Metropolitan Tabernacle Pulpit*, 63 vols. (London: Passmore & Alabaster, 1864), 10:176.

Later in the story, one of Job's counselors, Bildad, echoed the human quandary: "How then can man be in the right before God? How can he who is born of woman be pure? Behold, even the moon is not bright, and the stars are not pure in [God's] eyes; how much less man, who is a maggot, and the son of man, who is a worm!" (25:4–6).

No one is above the dilemma. No one is righteous enough to escape God's judgment. Solomon wrote, "Surely there is not a righteous man on earth who does good and never sins" (Eccles. 7:20). The apostle Paul wrote, "None is righteous, no, not one" (Rom. 3:10); and, "There is no distinction: for all have sinned and fall short of the glory of God" (vv. 22–23). Notice carefully that when Scripture mentions our fallenness and the universality of sin, the point is never to excuse (or even to mitigate) the guilt we bear as sinners. No one should ever think, *I'm not so bad. After all, everyone sins.* But when Scripture speaks of the fact that all have sinned, it is always to stress the truth that without a Savior, the whole human race would be utterly doomed.

The true, clear, and satisfying answer to Job's dilemma is found in Isaiah 53. Here is how God "justifies the ungodly" (Rom. 4:5). Here is how a man can be right with God, and God can remain just while justifying sinners (cf. Rom. 3:26). *"By his knowledge shall the righteous one, my servant, make many to be accounted righteous, and he shall bear their iniquities"* (Isa. 53:11).

We'll work our way through that potent verse in this chapter, and you will see that the entire New Testament gospel is packed into that terse statement. Every controverted doctrine that is essential for understanding the biblical doctrine of atonement is there: propitiation through the death of an innocent victim; salvation by grace through faith alone; justification through the imputation of righteousness; and atonement by penal substitution.

Thus Isaiah 53 not only summarizes the gospel; it also gives a clear and thorough interpretation of it. Anyone who has studied systematic theology will immediately see the striking fact that Isaiah's soteriology is identical to that of Paul's and the apostles'.

No wonder. Isaiah 53 is the gospel according to God. It is neither an accident nor a surprise that this is the same message proclaimed by

Jesus and the apostles in the New Testament. There is only one true gospel (cf. Gal. 1:8–9).

God's Perspective on the Servant's Work

One of the intriguing features of this passage is that all the gospel principles Isaiah highlights most clearly and emphatically are doctrines that frequently come under attack from pseudo-Christian cults, errant and apostate denominations, false teachers of every stripe, and massive religious institutions whose attachment to their own tradition is stronger than their commitment to Scripture. Isaiah here unequivocally affirms the doctrines of justification by faith, imputed righteousness, substitutionary atonement, and Messiah's death as a sacrifice offered to propitiate Yahweh.

Those doctrines were the very same principles that were recovered by the Protestant Reformers after nearly being smothered to death under centuries of accumulated error and stifling church tradition. The Reformers dusted them off, recognized their true importance, and proclaimed them as essential gospel truths. They are the same truths that set the hearts of English and American Puritans aflame. They are the same doctrines proclaimed by the Puritans' spiritual heirs—men like George Whitefield, Jonathan Edwards, Charles Spurgeon, and others. When taught clearly and fearlessly by preachers who truly believe in the authority of Scripture and proclaim it "as what it really is, the word of God" (1 Thess. 2:13), those truths have always been used by God to draw people to Christ and transform whole communities—and sometimes reform an entire culture.

In recent years, some of the most disturbing attacks on those doctrines have come from supposedly Protestant writers who approach biblical scholarship as if the goal were to invent new perspectives on time-honored doctrines, find novel interpretations of core biblical passages, or even devise a whole new kind of Christianity.

None of their ideas are really novel. Every essential point of gospel truth has been continuously under attack on one front or another since apostolic times. Most of the New Testament epistles address doctrinal errors that were a threat to the faith and spiritual health of believers in the early church. The classic example, of course, is the book of Galatians, which Paul wrote to correct (and condemn) an error that was rife in the Galatian churches. False teachers were attacking the principle of *sola fide*—telling Gentile Christians that faith alone was not a sufficient instrument of justification. The false teachers of Galatia said Gentile converts first needed to be circumcised. Others even today peddle a similar error by saying the ritual of baptism is the new birth Jesus spoke of in John 3. People cannot be saved unless they are baptized, they claim. Thus baptism—a work that must be performed—is subtly added to faith as a requirement for entry into the Christian life. Another currently popular view is the notion that justification is a process that will not be complete until God declares the believer righteous at the final judgment. They invariably suggest that verdict will hinge (at least in part) on good works performed by the one being judged.

All such views destroy the truth that believers are *now* saved (not sometime in the future) "by grace . . . through faith. And this is not your own doing; it is the gift of God, *not a result of works,* so that no one may boast" (Eph. 2:8–9). Jesus said, "Whoever hears my word and believes him who sent me has eternal life. He does not come into judgment, but has passed from death to life" (John 5:24). The verb tenses are significant. The person who believes "*has* eternal life" as a present possession. And it is already a past-tense reality that such a person "*has passed* from death to life."

Scripture is full of statements that confirm all the controverted gospel truths. "Whoever believes in [Jesus] is not condemned, but whoever does not believe is condemned already" (John 3:18). "We . . . have believed in Christ Jesus, in order to be justified by faith in Christ and not by works of the law, because by works of the law no one will be justified" (Gal. 2:16). "To the one who does not work but believes in him who justifies the ungodly, his faith is counted as righteousness" (Rom. 4:5). "He saved us, not because of works done by us in righteousness, but according to his own mercy" (Titus 3:5). "If it is by grace, it is no longer on the basis of works; otherwise grace would no longer be grace" (Rom. 11:6).[2]

---

2. Good works are the inevitable *fruit* of our faith, not an additive that makes faith effectual. When we believe, we are justified, and we are spiritually reborn—raised from a state of spiritual death. This new birth (*regeneration*) is what makes good works inevitable. It changes the heart and character of the believer, giving him new desires and a new willingness to obey. So no genuine

The doctrines of penal substitution, blood atonement, and propitiation are also affirmed by the rest of Scripture.[3] A number of significant texts further make clear that it was God himself who ordained that Christ should die for sin—and then punished him on the cross (Luke 2:44–46; Acts 2:23–24; 4:26–28; Rom. 8:32; 1 John 4:10). "What God foretold by the mouth of all the prophets, that his Christ would suffer, *he thus fulfilled*" (Acts 3:18).

But before any of the New Testament was even written, Isaiah 53 affirmed all those truths in God's own words—and in the plainest possible language. One verse after Isaiah writes, "It was the will of the LORD to crush him; he has put him to grief" (Isa. 53:10), the Lord himself speaks: "By his knowledge shall the righteous one, my servant, make many to be accounted righteous, and he shall bear their iniquities" (v. 11).

That statement runs contrary to every religion ever invented by the human mind. Rather than instructing people how they can better themselves to earn divine favor, reach nirvana, gain enlightenment, or whatever, the gospel according to God announces that Yahweh's servant, Israel's Messiah—the Lord of the church—does everything necessary to justify sinners. Specifically, God counts them as righteous because his servant has borne their sin. "Out of the anguish of his soul" those sins are atoned for.

Notice, by the way, how contrary this is to the many popular man-centered approaches to evangelism so prevalent in today's church. This gospel is not a plea for sinners to be satisfied with God; it is the announcement that God is satisfied with what his servant did on behalf of sinners.

In the last two verses of Isaiah's amazing prophecy, God is the main speaker. We know that, because the pronouns change from plural to singular: "*my* servant," "*I* will divide"—and the context makes clear that God is now the one speaking. The suffering servant is Yahweh's servant. This can be none other than the voice of God.

---

believer will ever be utterly devoid of good works. Furthermore, no true believer will ever abandon the faith (1 John 2:19). Nevertheless, we are "created in Christ Jesus *for* good works" (Eph. 2:10), not "[as] a result of" them (v. 9). And our *justification* is grounded in what Christ has done for his people—not what they do for him.

3. See, for example, Steve Jeffrey, Michael Ovey, and Andrew Sach, *Pierced for Our Transgressions* (Wheaton, IL: Crossway, 2007). See also John MacArthur, *The Gospel according to Paul* (Nashville: Thomas Nelson, 2017).

It is closure from the same almighty voice that spoke first in Isaiah 52:13–15. There he spoke of the servant's career and said it would include both glory (vv. 13 and 15) and suffering (v. 14). Starting in Isaiah 53:1, we hear the testimony of repentant Israelites at Messiah's return, confessing their sin in having rejected him. Finally, in Isaiah 53:11, both the voice and the perspective shift again. God is speaking in real time (as far as the people in Isaiah's generation were concerned). In verse 11 and the first half of verse 12, he therefore deals with the cross as a future event. His words affirm the testimony of the repentant Israelites. Specifically, he verifies that they are correct in understanding the atonement as a vicarious, propitiatory sacrifice. "He bore the sin of many" (v. 12).

Commentator J. Alec Motyer points out that the doctrine of substitutionary atonement is both clear and thorough in Israel's confession:

> Isaiah 53:11 is one of the fullest statements of atonement theology ever penned. (i) The Servant knows the needs to be met and what must be done. (ii) As "that righteous one, my servant" he is both fully acceptable to the God our sins have offended and has been appointed by him to his task. (iii) As righteous, he is free from every contagion of our sin. (iv) He identified himself personally with our sin and need. (v) He accomplishes the task fully. Negatively, in the bearing of iniquity; positively, in the provision of righteousness.[4]

Yahweh also affirms the servant's humanity when he says that he "poured out his soul to death and was numbered with the transgressors." He therefore acknowledges him as a true mediator because he "makes intercession for the transgressors" (v. 12). The New Testament points out that only someone who is both God and man could fill such a role—and there is only one person in the history of humanity who meets that qualification. (We'll return to this point shortly.)

God refers to his servant as "the righteous one." That description likewise fits only one human being in all history—the Lord Jesus Christ. As we noted at the beginning of this chapter, the Bible says repeatedly and in no uncertain terms that no one can be righteous:

There is no one who does not sin. (1 Kings 8:46)

---

4. J. Alec Motyer, *The Prophecy of Isaiah* (Downers Grove, IL: InterVarsity, 1993), 442.

Who can say, "I have made my heart pure;
I am clean from my sin"? (Prov. 20:9)

The LORD looks down from heaven on the children of man,
to see if there are any who understand,
who seek after God.

They have all turned aside; together they have become corrupt;
there is none who does good,
not even one. (Ps. 14:2–3)

If we say we have no sin, we deceive ourselves, and the truth is not
in us. (1 John 1:8)

The only sinless person who ever lived was the Lord Jesus Christ. To his challenge, "Which one of you convicts me of sin?" (John 8:46), his enemies made no reply. He "knew no sin" (2 Cor. 5:21); he was "without sin" (Heb. 4:15); he "committed no sin" (1 Pet. 2:22); he was "holy, innocent, unstained" (Heb. 7:26); and "in him there is no sin" (1 John 3:5). Only he, the servant of the Lord, the Messiah, can be described as "the righteous one"—a term used repeatedly in the New Testament to refer to Jesus. "You denied the Holy and Righteous One," Peter boldly declared to the Jewish people (Acts 3:14). On trial for his life, Stephen fearlessly challenged his accusers, "Which of the prophets did your fathers not persecute? And they killed those who announced beforehand the coming of the Righteous One, whom you have now betrayed and murdered" (Acts 7:52). After Paul's dramatic encounter with the glorified Christ on the road to Damascus, Ananias told him, "The God of our fathers appointed you to know his will, to see the Righteous One and to hear a voice from his mouth" (Acts 22:14).

God declares that the Righteous One will "make many to be accounted righteous." The "many" whom he will justify are the people of God, those who believe and for whose sins he died and made atonement (Rom. 5:15, 19; 1 Cor. 10:33; Heb. 9:28). His righteousness will be imputed to them, and on that ground alone (because of what Christ has done for them, not for any merit of their own) they are reckoned as righteous before God.

The many will be justified "by his knowledge." Some think that phrase could refer to the servant's own knowledge. Indeed, Isaiah says, "the Spirit of knowledge" rests on him (Isa. 11:2). Jesus said, "All things have been handed over to me by my Father, and no one knows the Son except the Father, and no one knows the Father except the Son and anyone to whom the Son chooses to reveal him" (Matt. 11:27).

But the point here is not about some special knowledge that the Righteous One possesses. He doesn't justify sinners because he has superior insights. It wasn't his intellectual prowess that justified the many. It was his death. Moreover, his knowledge is not the instrument of justification; the sinner's faith is. And that's what the expression "his knowledge" refers to in this text. The Hebrew phrase means, "By *the knowledge of him* shall the righteous one, my servant, make many to be accounted righteous." It is the same knowledge Jesus spoke of when he said in his High Priestly Prayer, "And this is eternal life, that they know you, the only true God, and Jesus Christ whom you have sent" (John 17:3). It is also the same knowledge Paul mentioned in Philippians 3:10: " . . . that I may know *him* [Jesus Christ] and the power of his resurrection."

The text is a succinct statement of how sinners are justified. They do not gain a right standing with God because they are *made* righteous. (If that were the case, we would indeed have to wait until the final judgment to discover whether we are justified.) The text could not be more clear: believers gain a right standing with God because they are "*accounted* righteous." "God credits [them with] righteousness apart from works" (Rom. 4:6 NASB)—like Abraham, who "believed the Lord, and he counted it to him as righteousness" (Gen. 15:6).

In short, a righteousness not their own is imputed to them—credited to their account. That's what Paul was speaking of in Philippians 3:9, when he said he wanted to be "found in [Christ], not having a righteousness of [his] own that comes from the law, but that which comes through faith in Christ, the righteousness from God that depends on faith." It's what he had in mind when he said of his fellow Israelites, "I bear them witness that they have a zeal for God, but not according to knowledge. For, being ignorant of the righteousness of God, and *seeking to establish their own, they did not submit to God's righteousness*" (Rom. 10:2–3). Later in that same chapter, Paul reinforces the truth that salvation comes only through the knowledge of Christ. After declaring that "everyone who calls on the name of the Lord will be saved" (v. 13), he asks a series of pointed questions:

> How then will they call on him in whom they have not believed? And how are they to believe in him of whom they have never heard? And how are they to hear without someone preaching? And how are they to preach unless they are sent? As it is written, "How beautiful are the feet of those who preach the good news!" (vv. 14–15)

Sinners must have *knowledge* of Christ in order to believe in him.

By the way, that passage from Romans 10 is God's testimony about the urgency of proclaiming the message of Jesus Christ to the ends of the earth. Those who come to God in penitent faith will be justified only if they *know* and *trust* the servant who gave his life in order to "bear their iniquities."

In the second half of Isaiah 53:12, the verbs revert to past tense again. God is still the one speaking, but now he speaks of the death of his servant as a past event. (God can do that because he transcends time and eternity.) Still describing the willing sacrifice made by "the righteous one, my servant," Yahweh says, "he poured out his soul to death." The Hebrew verb there means "to lay bare." It has a strong connotation of defenselessness. Literally, it means "he exposed his soul to death," in the sense that he handed it over; he willingly gave up his life. It's an echo of the same truth confessed by repentant Israel in verse 7: He died "like a lamb that is led to the slaughter."

The stress is on the willingness of the servant's sacrifice. "For this reason the Father loves me," Jesus said, "because I lay down my life that I may take it up again. No one takes it from me, but I lay it down of my own accord. I have authority to lay it down, and I have authority to take it up again" (John 10:17–18). "He poured out his soul to death." He was acting with a definite purpose; not being manipulated by those who subjected him to such suffering.

The servant also "was numbered with the transgressors." That is not a direct reference to his being crucified between two thieves (though that arrangement does serve as a living picture of the extreme humiliation this verse is talking about). It is first about his willingness to be identified with transgressors in his incarnation. Though sinless himself—indeed, though decked with the glory of God, sharing the same authority as God the Father, dwelling in the high and holy place of heaven—he "did not count equality with God a thing to be grasped, but emptied himself, by taking the form of a servant, being born in the likeness of men. And being found in human form, he humbled himself by becoming obedient to the point of death, even death on a cross" (Phil. 2:6–8).

He came to earth as an infant, grew up in poverty, lived among sinners, mingled with sinners, and ultimately died in place of sinners. From a visual standpoint Jesus did not stand out from everybody else; unlike countless portraits of him over the centuries, he had no halo. Nothing about his physical appearance marked him as a supernatural being. In fact, as we have seen from the start, the disconnect between his ordinary appearance and the miraculous power he possessed was a stumbling block for many who rejected him (Isa. 53:2). Therefore they decided that the power this ordinary-looking man had must have come from Satan.

Although he came to earth "in the *likeness* of sinful flesh" and therefore was numbered with the transgressors, Jesus was able to do what no human being can do: he bore the sin of many and thereby "condemned sin in the flesh" (Rom. 8:3).

The final word from the Father about the servant is that he "makes intercession for the transgressors." An intercessor or mediator is one who acts as a link between two parties. Jesus Christ is the bridge between God and sinners. "There is one mediator between God and men, the man Christ Jesus" (1 Tim. 2:5). He is the one who pleads our case before God, presenting the merits of his sacrifice as payment in full for our sins.

The apostle John may be purposely alluding to Isaiah 53:12 when he says, "We have an advocate with the Father, Jesus Christ the righteous" (1 John 2:1). As a matter of fact, Christ's priestly mediation for believers began even before his death. In his High Priestly Prayer recorded in John 17 we get a glimpse of him in his role as the Great High Priest interceding for his people. Offering himself as an atonement was the pinnacle of his high-priestly work, but he continues even now in the role of our Great High Priest. He "always lives to make intercession for [believers]" (Heb. 7:25).

The verbs translated, "poured out," "was numbered," and "bore" are in the perfect tense, signifying a completed action. But the verb translated "makes intercession" is imperfect, describing continuous, ongoing action. Jesus is our ceaseless defender, intercessor, and mediator (Rom. 8:34; Heb. 7:25; 1 John 2:1).

God himself affirms the vicarious sacrifice of Christ as the only offering that can satisfy his justice and (at the same time) justify sinners. Only those who know Christ will be declared righteous by God. Knowledge of the Savior is therefore essential—no one backs into heaven without saving knowledge of him. Thus, the mandate for Christians is not to inflate their self-esteem, manipulate God so they can become healthy and wealthy, or to use marketing gimmicks to grow large churches, but rather to spread the saving knowledge of Jesus Christ to the world by proclaiming the gospel. Our Lord's command is to "go therefore and make disciples of all nations, baptizing them in the name of the Father and of the Son and of the Holy Spirit, teaching them to observe all that I have commanded you" (Matt. 28:19–20).

With Yahweh's own words in Isaiah 53:12, "Therefore I will divide him a portion with the many, and he shall divide the spoil with the strong," this magnificent passage ends where it began in verse 13 of chapter 52, with the exaltation of Jesus Christ. He will return in order to defeat the world's rebellion against God, judge the ungodly, and establish his glorious thousand-year kingdom on the earth (Rev. 19:11–20:6). He will receive the title deed to the earth (Revelation 5). The kingdoms of the world will become "the kingdom of our Lord and of his Christ, and he shall reign forever and ever" (Rev. 11:15). And "at the name of Jesus every knee [will] bow, in heaven and on earth and under the earth" (Phil. 2:10).

The "many" and the "strong" are the multitudes whom Christ has justified and for whom he poured out his blood (Matt. 26:28). Their strength is not a fleshly might of their own, but the power of the indwelling Holy Spirit. They, too, will be exalted as joint heirs with him (Rom. 8:17). All the redeemed of all ages will be part of an everlasting fellowship with him that will enrich their lives. Everything he possesses of the eternal glories in the new heaven and the new earth will be our possession as well. We will reign with him on earth in the millennial kingdom and forever in the new heaven and new earth.

Bear in mind that God himself categorically affirms that the confession of faith found in Isaiah 53 is a true and sound understanding of the work of Christ on the cross. This must be the confession of all who come to faith in Christ. They must acknowledge him as the only acceptable sacrifice for sin, embrace him as the substitute who died in their place, and confess that he rose from the dead. That still is the only way of salvation (John 14:6; Acts 4:12).

Seven Important Questions That Summarize Isaiah 53

We might summarize Isaiah 53 by asking a series of questions.

First: *What is the theme of this chapter?* Its theme is suffering—horrific, gruesome, traumatic, agonizing suffering. The servant was "a man of sorrows and acquainted with grief" (v. 3). He bore griefs, carried sorrows, and was "stricken, smitten by God, and afflicted" (v. 4). He was pierced, crushed, chastised, and wounded (v. 5). He was oppressed, and afflicted like a lamb led to slaughter (v. 7). He experienced oppression and judgment, was cut off out of the land of the living, and stricken for the transgression of his people (v. 8). He was crushed and put to grief (v. 10), and verse 11 refers to the anguish of his suffering.

The servant's suffering leads to a second question: *Was his suffering deserved?* No, the suffering was not deserved by the one who suffered, since "he had done no violence, and there was no deceit in his mouth" (v. 9). And since what comes out of the mouth reflects what is in the heart (Matt. 12:34), there was no evil or deceit in his mouth because there was none in his heart. In fact, he is identified in verse 11 as "the righteous one."

Third: *Did God attempt to protect the servant from suffering?* No, he did not. In fact, "it was the will of the LORD to crush him . . . [and] put him to grief" (v. 10).

Fourth: *Is that failure on God's part to protect the silent, sinless servant consistent with God's righteous nature?* Yes, because the servant's suffering was substitutionary, endured not for his own sins, but for the sins of others. "But he was pierced for our transgressions; he was crushed for our iniquities; upon him was the chastisement that brought us peace, and with his wounds we are healed" (v. 5); "the LORD has laid on him the iniquity of us all" (v. 6); "he was cut off out of the land of the living, stricken for the transgression of my people" (v. 8); "he shall bear their iniquities" (v. 11); "he bore the sin of many" (v. 12).

Fifth: *Why would the servant willingly submit to that?* Why should any man who is righteous suffer so horribly, be unprotected by God, and suffer vicariously for sins he didn't commit? Because he gladly and lovingly obeyed the will of his Father. He made himself an offering for the sins of others (v. 10); he freely "poured out his soul to death" (v. 12).

What an amazing person to suffer so greatly, to suffer undeservedly, to suffer without the protection of a righteous God, though he was righteous, to suffer vicariously, to suffer willingly.

Sixth: *What is the outcome of his suffering?* First, he will by his suffering justify the many. He will give them his righteousness. "Out of the anguish of his soul he shall see and be satisfied; by his knowledge shall the righteous one, my servant, make many to be accounted righteous, and he shall bear their iniquities" (v. 11).

Second, he will be exalted:

Behold, my servant shall act wisely;
    he shall be high and lifted up, and shall be exalted. . . .
So shall he sprinkle many nations.
    Kings shall shut their mouths because of him,
for that which has not been told them they see,
    and that which they have not heard they understand.
        (Isa. 52:13, 15)

Seventh: *Who is this servant who willingly endured such suffering?* It can be none other than the Lord Jesus Christ. How can anyone fail to see that?

My earnest hope is that if you have read this far, you see the truth—and that whether you are a Jew or a Gentile, your own humble confession will echo the message of Isaiah 53. There is no more burden-lifting truth than this in all of Scripture: "Surely he has borne our griefs and carried our sorrows. . . . He was pierced for our transgressions; he was crushed for our iniquities; upon him was the chastisement that brought us peace, and with his wounds we are healed" (Isa. 53:4–5).

Part 2

THE LIFE AND TIMES OF ISAIAH THE PROPHET

9

Here I Am! Send Me

Isaiah was undoubtedly the greatest of the Hebrew prophets, the foremost man in the nation in his time, and possibly, after David, the most conspicuous personage in the history of Israel; and, perhaps, more than any other prophet, he has powerfully influenced Jews and Christians for over twenty-seven hundred years. In a critical and eventful period of his nation's history he served the offices of prophet, statesman, reformer, teacher, writer, orator and poet.

W. Graham Scroggie[1]

In this part of our study, we're going to consider the life and ministry of Isaiah and the historical context of his writings. It will be helpful to see how Isaiah 53 fits in the range of prophetic messages penned by the inspired prophet. What we discover is that the luster of this prophetic gem is greatly intensified by its setting within the broad panorama of Isaiah's life and prophecies.

We began the introduction to this book by noting that Isaiah's very name speaks of salvation. It could be translated "Yahweh saves," or "Yahweh is salvation." The name is a suitable summary of Isaiah's prophetic message, which (as we have seen) strikes that note resoundingly in chapter 53.

Isaiah is in many ways a mysterious figure. He appears only as a

---

1. W. Graham Scroggie, *The Unfolding Drama of Redemption*, 3 vols. (London: Pickering & Inglis, 1953), 1:322–23.

minor character in the Old Testament's Historical Books. He is mentioned only thirteen times in 2 Kings and three times in 2 Chronicles—always in connection with his prophecies. We know from Isaiah 8:3 that he was married, though we are never told his wife's name. He calls her simply "the prophetess." Together they had at least two sons whose names are given, Shear-jashub (Isa. 7:3) and Maher-shalal-hash-baz (8:3). Those few biographical details must be gleaned from Isaiah's own prophecies. Apart from the name of his father, the Old Testament's Historical Books contain no personal information about him.

The prophet introduces himself in Isaiah 1:1 as "the son of Amoz." He is identified that way a total of thirteen times in references scattered across 2 Kings, 2 Chronicles, and Isaiah. Perhaps the prophet's father was such a prominent person when the biblical record was being written that no more background information was deemed necessary. On the other hand, Amoz is mentioned nowhere in the Bible except as the father of Isaiah, so Isaiah's family background is essentially unknown to readers in later generations. There is no record even to tell us what tribe he was from. One ancient Jewish tradition says Isaiah was a cousin of King Uzziah, but there is no biblical evidence for that.

There are, however, a few clues that suggest Isaiah was from an important or influential family. He had enough social stature to be able to pay an unannounced personal visit to the king (Isa. 7:3), and he had a close enough relationship with Uriah the high priest and Zechariah the prophet that he could call them as character witnesses to confirm his prophetic qualifications (8:2).

We're not told how or when Isaiah died—an unusual omission for such a prominent biblical figure. The Mishnah, a written record of ancient Jewish oral traditions, says Isaiah was killed by Manasseh, one of the last kings of Judah. We'll take a closer look at the reign of King Manasseh in chapter 10, but for now it's sufficient to note that the Mishnah's account is in perfect accord with what the Bible says about the character of Manasseh, who "shed very much innocent blood, till he had filled Jerusalem from one end to another" (2 Kings 21:16). Numerous Jewish and Christian sources dating as far back as the second century (AD) state that Isaiah was sawn asunder with a wood saw.[2] Hebrews 11:37 makes a possible allusion to Isaiah's martyrdom, citing the faith of Old Testament saints who "were sawn in two."

Isaiah is sometimes referred to as the "Paul" of the Old Testament—and the comparison is fitting. Like Paul, Isaiah clearly had a well-developed intellect and a thorough knowledge of the Word of God. The focus at the center of the prophet's message is the promised Messiah and the gracious means by which he provides salvation for his people. That was also the apostle's principal theme: "Jesus Christ and him crucified" (1 Cor. 2:2; see also 1:23). You have surely noticed from our study so far that Isaiah 53 is dominated by the same redemptive doctrines that are the distinctive features of Pauline theology: Christ crucified and risen, substitutionary atonement, justification by faith, and the sovereignty of God.

The Historical Setting

Isaiah evidently lived a long life, judging from the fact that his prophetic career spanned the reigns of at least four monarchs, "Uzziah, Jotham, Ahaz, and Hezekiah" (Isa. 1:1). His opening verse thus enables us to identify precisely where Isaiah fits in the Old Testament chronology. The window he gives us actually begins in 739 BC (the year Uzziah's reign ended) and extends beyond Hezekiah's time. Hezekiah died around 686 BC. We know Isaiah outlived him, because 2 Chronicles 32:32 says Isaiah wrote a full account of Hezekiah's life. (That work is not included in the canon of Scripture, and there are no surviving copies of it. The only inspired text Isaiah wrote is the Old Testament book that bears his name.)

Isaiah compiled his prophecies and wrote them down for posterity, probably completing the work within a decade after Hezekiah's death. That time frame is deduced from the fact that the latest event Isaiah records as *history* (not prophecy) is the assassination of Sennacherib (Isa. 37:36–38). The Assyrian king was killed by two of his own sons in 681 BC—about five years after the death of Hezekiah.

---

2. For example, *Justin Martyr's Dialogue with Trypho the Jew*, trans. Henry Brown (London: George Bell, 1846), 256. St. Jerome's Latin commentary on Isa. 57:1 (c. AD 410) calls this "*certissima traditio*," a highly certain tradition.

That means the prophet's ministry lasted some sixty years (or longer). As we have pointed out previously, this timeline also means Isaiah 53 was written at least seven hundred years before the event it describes.

We saw in chapter 2 that Isaiah arranged his prophecies thematically in two major sections, with the dividing point coming between chapters 39 and 40. The first thirty-nine chapters begin and end with prophetic warnings about the *judgment and captivity* that were coming to the kingdom of Judah. Chapters 40–66 then promise *grace and salvation.*

The second part of Isaiah is best understood as a single promise of deliverance woven together from several discrete prophecies that Isaiah received over the course of his ministry. Twenty-four verses in Isaiah 40–66 include the words "thus says the LORD." Those are individual prophecies that were given to Isaiah, and he was then directed by the Holy Spirit (cf. 2 Pet. 1:21) to braid them together in one glorious vision. It is a majestic revelation of the salvation that would be brought to the people of God by the coming Messiah.

Those final twenty-seven chapters describe not only the deliverance of Israel from their captivity and the redemption of sinners from the guilt and bondage of sin but also the ultimate unshackling of all the nations and peoples of the earth from the dominion of Satan. In short, Isaiah's account of God's promised salvation is one long crescendo that ultimately describes how the curse of Genesis 3:17–19 will be completely overthrown in the coming millennial kingdom under the rule of Messiah. As we observed in chapter 2 of this book, Isaiah gradually builds that crescendo in three movements of nine chapters each. Chapters 40–48 are mainly about Judah's *release from the Babylonian captivity.* The theme in chapters 49–57 is *redemption from sin.* And chapters 58–66 culminate with a prophecy about the *reign of righteousness on the earth*, when the Messiah takes his rightful throne in Jerusalem and Yahweh says, "I will extend peace to her like a river" (66:12).

People in Isaiah's time had good reason to be eager for the promised peace of the messianic kingdom. Over the course of Isaiah's career, Jerusalem was frequently under siege by hostile armies. Times of peace were fragile. And "peace" was usually bargained for by making unholy alliances with pagan rulers or by paying tribute to evil empires. (Even the best Jewish kings of that era tended to be too pragmatic and prone to compromise when it came to handling international affairs.) The inevitable result for the entire Jewish nation was a recurring spiral of spiritual decline and a loss of the blessedness that comes with keeping the faith.

How did God's people get into such a destructive cycle?

The Divided Kingdom

If you are at all familiar with the broad sweep of Old Testament history, you know that after the death of Solomon, around 930 BC, Israel split into two kingdoms. It was a major turning point that marked the abrupt end of Israel's golden era. The northern kingdom, retaining the name *Israel*, was a federation of ten tribes ruled by a series of ungodly kings who had no legitimate claim to the Davidic throne. The split began when the ten tribes rejected Rehoboam, Solomon's rightful heir. In effect, they were repudiating God's chosen royal bloodline and thereby showing contempt for Scripture's messianic promises. In their rebellion, they anointed a rival king of their own choosing, Jeroboam. They abandoned Jerusalem, the temple, and the Levitical priesthood. They adopted Samaria as their capital city. And they maintained this succession of usurper kings for more than two hundred years. Naturally, all their kings were apostates, and the spiritual history of the northern tribes is an unbroken story of backsliding and decline. Although the Lord sent them prophets (starting with Elijah and his successor Elisha), the kingdom of Israel never truly repented. Finally, in 722 BC, the capital city, Samaria, was overthrown by the Assyrians, and most of the people in the northern kingdom were swept into exile from which they never fully returned as a nation under God (2 Kings 17:24).

The southern kingdom, *Judah*, consisted of only two tribes—Judah and Benjamin. They alone remained loyal to the Davidic throne when the kingdom split away after Solomon's death (1 Kings 12:21).[3] Judah

---

3. According to 1 Kings 12:20, "There was none that followed the house of David but the tribe of Judah only." But the very next verse says that "all the house of Judah *and the tribe of Benjamin*, 180,000 chosen warriors" went to war against Jeroboam. Some Benjaminites on the tribe's northern borders may have sided with Jeroboam, because Benjamin's territory was split. Bethel, for example, lay within Benjamin's borders (Josh. 18:21–22), and Scripture says Jeroboam placed a golden calf there (1 Kings 2:29). Nevertheless, the greater part of Benjamin remained loyal to

was the largest of all the tribes, and Benjamin was the smallest. But the city of Jerusalem lay within Benjamin's territory, and the tribe of Judah occupied a vast region stretching from Benjamin's southern border to Kadesh Barnea. (Kadesh was that place in the Sinai wilderness from which the Israelites of Moses's time were originally supposed to enter the Promised Land. But they rebelled and were condemned to forty years of wandering in the desert.)

By combining their lands and populations, Judah and Benjamin constituted a kingdom that was roughly two-thirds the size of the other ten tribes. Moreover, when most in the northern kingdom were taken captive by the Assyrians, members of every tribe and "great numbers" from Ephraim, Manasseh, and Simeon (three of the northern tribes) fled their own land and moved into the territory of Judah (2 Chron. 15:9). So Judah constituted a formidable political entity, with all the tribes represented.

Nevertheless, many of Judah's kings were no better than their illegitimate northern rivals. The Davidic dynasty did produce a few godly reformers. But overall, Judah's spiritual history is a spotted chronicle— a long tale of decline and disobedience, interrupted occasionally with some bright eras of revival and blessing. Periods of reform typically lasted no longer than a generation or two.

Isaiah ministered in the kingdom of Judah. Keep in mind that the prophet's ministry spanned many decades and at least four royal administrations. The four kings whom Isaiah names in his opening verse run the gamut between good and evil. But Isaiah starts the record of his prophecies by addressing all Judah as a "sinful nation, a people laden with iniquity, offspring of evildoers, children who deal corruptly" (Isa. 1:4). The first thirty-nine chapters are then filled with warnings aimed at kings and people, urging them not to follow the trail blazed by their northern cousins. In the end, Judah did not heed any of those warnings.

Uzziah and Jotham

The first king Isaiah had any connection with was Uzziah (alternatively known as Azariah—cf. 2 Kings 14:21 and 2 Chron. 26:1). Uzziah

---

Rehoboam (2 Chron. 11:1–12). The southern kingdom later recovered Bethel and, presumably, all remaining territory that was originally part of Benjamin's allotment (2 Kings 23:15).

was a fundamentally good king with godly instincts. Under his leadership, Judah thrived materially, because Uzziah generally "did what was right in the eyes of the LORD" (2 Chron. 26:4). Toward the end of his reign, however, Uzziah became too caught up in his own political and economic successes. "When he was strong, he grew proud, to his destruction. For he was unfaithful to the LORD his God and entered the temple of the LORD to burn incense on the altar of incense" (v. 16).

Only priests were permitted to offer incense at the temple. For this arrogant intrusion into the priestly office, Uzziah was stricken with leprosy on the spot. He remained leprous "to the day of his death, and being a leper lived in a separate house, for he was excluded from the house of the LORD" (v. 21).

We can safely infer that Isaiah was born and grew up under Uzziah's regime because the king ruled for fifty-two years (2 Kings 15:2), and Isaiah did not receive his formal call to the prophetic office until the king died. On that occasion, Isaiah saw a vision of "the Lord sitting upon a throne, high and lifted up; and the train of his robe filled the temple" (Isa. 6:1). Isaiah had apparently received other visions prior to Uzziah's death (cf. 1:1), but the experience he describes in chapter 6 was the first climactic turning point in the prophet's life and career. Isaiah tells the story as a flashback, so even though it comes six chapters into the book of Isaiah, it is his account of how his public ministry began—setting the date for us with a fair amount of precision: "In the year that King Uzziah died" (Isa. 6:1). That, once again, was 739 BC.

The next king in Isaiah's list is Jotham, about whom we needn't say much. Scripture says of Jotham, "He did what was right in the eyes of the LORD according to all that his father Uzziah had done, except he did not enter the temple of the LORD" (2 Chron. 27:2a)—meaning, of course, that Jotham didn't meddle with priestly duties as his father had done. He learned, it seems, from his father's error.

But then the text adds ominously, "The people still followed corrupt practices" (v. 2b). Apparently Jotham, despite his personal uprightness and decency, was not an effective leader, and he failed to move the nation in a more godly direction. He did little to eliminate false worship or curb the nation's downward spiritual drift (2 Kings 15:35). When a society acquires a taste for compromise and adopts a certain level of contempt for the things of God, it is no easy task to reform the culture. That difficulty will come into play again shortly, when we consider the reign of Jotham's grandson, Hezekiah.

Jotham's reign lasted sixteen years, and when he died, his son and successor led the kingdom of Judah into an era of unprecedented apostasy and rebellion.

Ahaz

Third in the list of four kings named in Isaiah 1:1 was Ahaz, a worthless man driven only by evil passions, rank superstition, and an unholy fascination with pagan religion. Ahaz was utterly unfit to give spiritual leadership to the Jewish nation. Although he was the reigning king on Judah's throne when Israel was overthrown by the Assyrians, Ahaz learned nothing from the divine judgment that befell the northern kingdom. In fact, he seemed to be trying hard to mimic or even exceed the wickedness of Israel's kings. According to 2 Chronicles 28:2–3, "He walked in the ways of the kings of Israel. He even made metal images for the Baals, and he made offerings in the Valley of the Son of Hinnom and burned his sons as an offering, according to the abominations of the nations whom the LORD drove out before the people of Israel."

In other words, Ahaz sacrificed his own infant offspring as a burnt offering to Molech (cf. 2 Kings 16:3) in that evil ravine on Jerusalem's outskirts called "Hinnom"—*Gehenna* in Aramaic. (We discussed this place at the end of chapter 6. It was a site so long associated with wickedness and fire that it became a metaphor for hell.)

Ahaz clearly hated God, engaging in every abominable practice that had originally provoked the Lord to condemn the barbarous religions of the Canaanites when he drove them from the land in the time of Joshua.

The king despised the Lord so much that he even tried to refuse a promise of divine deliverance when he knew he needed it most. Indeed, "in the time of his distress he became yet *more* faithless to the LORD—this same King Ahaz" (2 Chron. 28:22). When the kings of Damascus and Syria were threatening an attack on Jerusalem, Isaiah came to Ahaz with an encouraging message from God, assuring him that he did not need to fear the military might of these hostile nations. The Lord offered to give Ahaz any sign the king would ask for. The idea was that the fulfillment of the sign would confirm the truth of Isaiah's reassuring prophecy. In other words, Ahaz was literally given a promise of deliverance and a blank check from God to ask for anything he wanted! "Ask a sign of the LORD your God; let it be deep as Sheol or high as heaven" (Isa. 7:11).

But Ahaz was so hostile to God and so disinclined to pray that he rebuffed the Lord's gracious proposal. "I will not ask," he told the prophet (v. 12). He even tried vainly to conceal his utter contempt for God under a cloak of artificial piety by adding, "and I will not put the LORD to the test." He flatly refused to ask for any sign at all—even something as simple as a straw in the wind or an omen on the order of Gideon's fleece.

So God himself chose a profound, heavenly sign. Isaiah delivered the message in this now-familiar prophecy: "Therefore the Lord himself will give you a sign. Behold, the virgin shall conceive and bear a son, and shall call his name Immanuel" (Isa. 7:14). The sign God gave looked far beyond the life of Ahaz and pointed to the coming of Messiah as the greatest possible proof of God's care and protection for his people.

Having thus stupidly refused the Lord's care and safekeeping, Ahaz sought military protection from Assyria—a larger, more powerful, and (if possible) more pagan nation than Damascus and Syria combined. It was a sinful alliance, strictly forbidden by the Mosaic law (Ex. 23:31–33). Then compounding that sin, Ahaz purchased the help of Assyria's king by stealing valuable furnishings from the temple. He "took the silver and gold that was found in the house of the LORD and in the treasures of the king's house and sent a present to the king of Assyria" (2 Kings 16:8).

In order to solidify his alliance with Assyria even further, Ahaz undertook a campaign of religious syncretism, blending the forms and rituals of Assyrian idolatry with Jewish ceremony. On the temple grounds, Ahaz installed an altar of his own (patterned on a pagan model he saw in Damascus). He removed the Lord's bronze altar and rearranged the temple in accord with his own preferences (vv. 10–20). His obvious aim was to marry Assyrian paganism with Jewish traditions. This of course corrupted every activity at the temple in a way that eliminated any pretense of true worship. It was a shameless violation of the first commandment, the very foundation of Jewish law: "You shall have no other gods before me" (Ex. 20:3).

In effect, the temple itself became a center of pagan worship. By the end of Ahaz's reign, paganism had overwhelmed and virtually eradicated every vestige of legitimate corporate worship in Judah. "Ahaz gathered together the vessels of the house of God and cut in pieces the vessels of the house of God, and he shut up the doors of the house of the LORD, and he made himself altars in every corner of Jerusalem" (2 Chron. 28:24).

Those were dark days in Israel—spiritually, economically, and politically. The people themselves were severely backslidden and practically indifferent to Ahaz's dalliance with pagan abominations. Yet they so thoroughly despised him for his tyrannical wickedness that when he died, "they buried him in the city, in Jerusalem, for they did not bring him into the tombs of the kings of Israel. And Hezekiah his son reigned in his place" (2 Chron. 28:27).

Hezekiah

Immediately things changed for the better. "Hezekiah began to reign when he was twenty-five years old, and he reigned twenty-nine years in Jerusalem. . . . And he did what was right in the eyes of the LORD, according to all that David his father had done" (2 Chron. 29:1–2).

Hezekiah is the last of the four kings named in Isaiah's opening verse. He was one of the most faithful kings who ever sat on David's throne, and his story is remarkable. He was a consistently good and godly ruler who came at a point in history when it may have seemed the Davidic dynasty was irretrievably corrupt. His godly influence was a welcome respite after his own father's relentlessly wicked and worldly bias.

Reform and revival thus came unexpectedly, seemingly out of nowhere. How could a reformer like Hezekiah emerge from the household of a man as wicked as Ahaz? Scripture tells us nothing about Hezekiah's upbringing. We don't know who instructed him in the ways of the Lord. But it was obvious from the very start that he was genuinely devoted to the God of Abraham, Isaac, and Jacob. Furthermore, he was a zealous, energetic reformer. Hezekiah set to work right away on a campaign to restore the faith his father had sought so recklessly to eradicate:

> In the first year of his reign, in the first month, he opened the doors of the house of the LORD and repaired them. He brought in the priests and the Levites and assembled them in the square on the east and said to them, "Hear me, Levites! Now consecrate yourselves, and consecrate the house of the LORD, the God of your fathers, and carry out the filth from the Holy Place. For our fathers have been unfaithful and have done what was evil in the sight of the LORD our God. They have forsaken him and have turned away their faces from the habitation of the LORD and turned their backs. They also shut the doors of the vestibule and put out the lamps and have not burned incense or offered burnt offerings in the Holy Place to the God of Israel." (2 Chron. 29:3–7)

Hezekiah forbade pagan worship in the high places. He even "broke in pieces the bronze serpent that Moses had made, for until those days the people of Israel had made offerings to it" (2 Kings 18:4). The bronze serpent, of course, was an important piece of ancient Israel's spiritual heritage. It was also one of the principal Old Testament symbols of Christ (Num. 21:4–9; John 3:14–15). But the people had sinned by making it an idol. They even named it "Nehushtan," as if it were a god. Therefore Scripture commends Hezekiah for destroying it. His personal faith and devotion to the Lord are beyond question.

Yet despite Hezekiah's reforms, the people of Judah generally remained half-hearted, earthly minded, and spiritually complacent—easily led one way or the other. When the Assyrians were poised to invade Jerusalem, Hezekiah's key advisors urged him to make an alliance with Egypt in order to turn back the threat. That would have been a repeat of the sin that launched Ahaz's worst acts of apostasy. The fact that Hezekiah's closest counselors were in favor of such a compromise is a fair gauge of the spiritual condition of the rest of the populace. Most of the nation remained easily susceptible to spiritual deception despite Hezekiah's godly leadership. Again we see that it is easier to steer people into apostasy than to lead them out of it.

This history explains why Isaiah's prophecies in those first thirty-nine chapters are punctuated by rebukes and admonitions regarding the faithlessness of God's people. The Lord himself reprimanded the people of Judah repeatedly for their tendency to put their trust in fleshly power and the weapons of carnal warfare:

> "Ah, stubborn children," declares the LORD,
>> "who carry out a plan, but not mine,
> and who make an alliance, but not of my Spirit,
>> that they may add sin to sin;
> who set out to go down to Egypt,
>> without asking for my direction,
> to take refuge in the protection of Pharaoh
>> and to seek shelter in the shadow of Egypt!
> Therefore shall the protection of Pharaoh turn to your shame,
>> and the shelter in the shadow of Egypt to your humiliation." . . .
>
> And now, go, write it before them on a tablet
>> and inscribe it in a book,
> that it may be for the time to come
>> as a witness forever.
> For they are a rebellious people,
>> lying children,
> children unwilling to hear
>> the instruction of the LORD;
> who say to the seers, "Do not see,"
>> and to the prophets, "Do not prophesy to us what is right;
> speak to us smooth things,
>> prophesy illusions,
> leave the way, turn aside from the path,
>> let us hear no more about the Holy One of Israel."
>>> (Isa. 30:1–3, 8–11)

There's more:

> Woe to those who go down to Egypt for help
>> and rely on horses,
> who trust in chariots because they are many
>> and in horsemen because they are very strong,

but do not look to the Holy One of Israel
    or consult the LORD! (31:1)

To his credit, Hezekiah harkened to the word of the Lord. Unlike his evil father, and against his own political advisors' counsel, he did not put his trust in military might buttressed by foreign alliances. He looked to the Lord as his strength and salvation.

The testimony of Hezekiah's faith was so well known that the Assyrians used it to taunt faithless people in Jerusalem. With the Assyrian army in battle array outside the city, Sennacherib instructed his chief officer, the Rabshakeh, to call out in Hebrew to the Jewish people, "Hear the words of the great king, the king of Assyria! Thus says the king: 'Do not let Hezekiah deceive you, for *he will not be able to deliver you. Do not let Hezekiah make you trust in the LORD by saying, "The LORD will surely deliver us.* This city will not be given into the hand of the king of Assyria"'" (Isa. 36:13–15). The Rabshakeh followed that message with vile, insulting threats aimed at striking fear and revulsion into the hearts of the Jews. (His jeering diatribes contain some of the most crass, vulgar sayings recorded anywhere in Scripture.)

When Hezekiah saw the Assyrian army camped on his doorstep and heard the menacing words of the Rabshakeh, he covered himself with sackcloth (a symbol of mourning, humility, and contrition) and sent messengers to seek further counsel from Isaiah.

Isaiah responded to the king with a letter saying, "Thus says the LORD: Do not be afraid because of the words that you have heard, with which the young men of the king of Assyria have reviled me. Behold, I will put a spirit in him, so that he shall hear a rumor and return to his own land, and I will make him fall by the sword in his own land" (Isa. 37:6–7).

The prophet records what happened next:

Hezekiah received the letter from the hand of the messengers, and read it; and Hezekiah went up to the house of the LORD, and spread it before the LORD. And Hezekiah prayed to the LORD: "O LORD of hosts, God of Israel, enthroned above the cherubim, you are the God, you alone, of all the kingdoms of the earth; you have made heaven and earth. Incline your ear, O LORD, and hear; open your eyes, O Lᴏʀᴅ, and see; and hear all the words of Sennacherib, which he has sent to mock the living God. Truly, O Lᴏʀᴅ, the kings of Assyria have laid waste all the nations and their lands, and have cast their gods into the fire. For they were no gods, but the work of men's hands, wood and stone. Therefore they were destroyed. So now, O Lᴏʀᴅ our God, save us from his hand, that all the kingdoms of the earth may know that you alone are the Lᴏʀᴅ." (vv. 14–20)

There you see the godliness and faith of Hezekiah. He makes a stark and refreshing contrast to his father, the evil Ahaz, who foolishly spurned the Lord's kind reassurance and tried instead to seal victory for himself by making sinful compromises with the Lord's enemies.

As he had promised, the Lord delivered Hezekiah. He also answered Sennacherib's fleshly arrogance with several heavy strokes from the rod of divine judgment, beginning that very night:

The angel of the Lᴏʀᴅ went out and struck down 185,000 in the camp of the Assyrians. And when people arose early in the morning, behold, these were all dead bodies. Then Sennacherib king of Assyria departed and returned home and lived at Nineveh. And as he was worshiping in the house of Nisroch his god, Adrammelech and Sharezer, his sons, struck him down with the sword. And after they escaped into the land of Ararat, Esarhaddon his son reigned in his place. (vv. 36–38)

The Word of the Lord Is Good

Then the story takes an unexpected turn. Hezekiah's triumph is followed by a severe trial rather than a happily-ever-after ending. He was immediately brought face-to-face with his mortality. "In those days Hezekiah became sick and was at the point of death" (38:1).

As was his pattern, the king appealed for the Lord's help and mercy, so the Lord sent this message through Isaiah: "I have heard your prayer; I have seen your tears. Behold, I will add fifteen years to your life" (v. 5).

Hezekiah responded by writing a psalm of thanksgiving and testimony. One line in particular, written in the form of a prayer to God, demonstrates the humility of the king's heart, the depth of his devotion, and the keenness of his spiritual perception: "Behold, it was for my welfare that I had great bitterness; but in love you have delivered my life from the pit of destruction, for you have cast all my sins behind your back" (v. 17). Hezekiah clearly understood that he personally needed salvation and cleansing from sin, and God alone could provide that. He even confessed that the trials God put him through were for Hezekiah's own benefit. No one can doubt the authenticity of his faith and salvation.

"Nothing Shall Be Left"

Nevertheless, the king's reforms and the influence of his godly leadership ultimately did not stave off the apostasy of Judah. Despite Isaiah's warnings to the people of Judah, the southern kingdom finally followed the same path of apostasy that had led to the judgment of their brethren in the northern kingdom, Israel. (We will examine how that came to pass in the chapter that follows.)

Isaiah knew what was coming, even during the reforms of Hezekiah. The last four verses of the first thirty-nine chapters of Isaiah summarize the dire prophecy of judgment to come:

> Then Isaiah said to Hezekiah, "Hear the word of the LORD of hosts: Behold, the days are coming, when all that is in your house, and that which your fathers have stored up till this day, shall be carried to Babylon. Nothing shall be left, says the LORD. And some of your own sons, who will come from you, whom you will father, shall be taken away, and they shall be eunuchs in the palace of the king of Babylon." (Isa. 39:5–7)

At first glance, Hezekiah's response to that prophecy may sound selfishly indifferent: "'The word of the LORD that you have spoken is good.' For he thought, 'There will be peace and security in my days'" (39:8). It suggests, however, that Hezekiah knew God's judgment was long overdue, and that Judah had no rightful claim to the blessings of peace and security. God's promise to extend such grace beyond Hezekiah's lifetime was evidently more than Hezekiah expected. The knowledge that calamity would not befall the nation in his lifetime understandably came to him as a great relief.

That is the bitter ending to the first half of Isaiah, and it is the last time Hezekiah's name appears in the book.

It's worth noting, by the way, that Isaiah's first major division ends with four chapters of historical material. They serve as a kind of buffer between Isaiah's two major prophetic sections. Isaiah seems to have included this passage in order to give the proper context to his prophecies against Assyria. The historical interlude begins with Sennacherib's siege against Jerusalem and stops just before recording the death of Hezekiah. In fact, those chapters (Isaiah 36–39) duplicate 2 Kings 18:13–20:19 virtually word for word, but Isaiah omits two verses that are found at the end of 2 Kings 20 (vv. 20–21), describing the end of Hezekiah's life: "The rest of the deeds of Hezekiah and all his might and how he made the pool and the conduit and brought water into the city,[4] are they not written in the Book of the Chronicles of the Kings of Judah? And Hezekiah slept with his fathers, and Manasseh his son reigned in his place."

If the tradition is true (and it certainly is plausible) that Isaiah was subsequently put to death by Manasseh, the prophet's death perfectly symbolizes the nation's ultimate rejection of his prophetic pleas.

But God nevertheless graciously withheld his judgment on Judah for another hundred years after the death of Hezekiah. Judah would be blessed with several more opportunities to reform before Jerusalem was finally overthrown.

---

4. This was a famous tunnel, still in existence today, that carried water one-third of a mile through solid rock from Jerusalem's only natural spring to the pool of Siloam. Cf. 2 Chron. 32:30.

10

Judah's Demise

Judah was carried away out of their land [2 Kings 25:21], about 860 years after they were put in possession of it by Joshua. Now the scripture was fulfilled, *The Lord shall bring thee, and the king which thou shalt set over thee, into a nation which thou hast not known*, Deut. [28:36]. Sin kept their fathers forty years out of Canaan, and now turned *them* out. The Lord is known by those judgments which he executes, and makes good that word which he has spoken, Amos [3:2]. *You only have I known of all the families of the earth, therefore I will punish you for all your iniquities.*

Matthew Henry[1]

Judgment *did* finally come to Judah, and the wealth and people of the Jewish nation were carried away to Babylon in precisely the way Isaiah 39:6–7 predicted. Nebuchadnezzar was the human instrument whom God used to bring judgment to Judah.

By the end of the seventh century BC (within sixty-five years after Hezekiah's death) the Neo-Assyrian Empire had begun to unravel. A relentless succession of insurrections, civil wars, and incursions from neighboring powers gradually weakened the massive empire. In 612 BC, a large coalition of enemy armies attacked Nineveh, the Assyrian capital. The city was completely laid waste (in fulfillment of

---

1. Matthew Henry, *Commentary on the Whole Bible*, 6 vols. (Old Tappan, NJ: Revell, n.d.), 2: 835; emphasis original.

Nah. 3:5–7), but the Assyrian king escaped. About seven years later, the allied armies of the Medes and Chaldeans, led by Nebuchadnezzar, crushed the combined forces of Egypt and Assyria at the Battle of Carchemish. The nucleus of world power moved to Babylon under Nebuchadnezzar.

This new empire, the Neo-Babylonian (or Chaldean) Empire, would dominate the world for only eighty-seven years, but it was a highly prosperous and influential kingdom while it lasted. Babylon had been the center of world power once before, more than nine hundred years before Nebuchadnezzar. He set out to re-create (and surpass) the city's ancient glory. He rebuilt Babylon into a spectacular metropolis with wide avenues and lush gardens. He restored ancient temples, constructed magnificent civic edifices (including several palaces for himself), and surrounded the city with imposing fortifications—thick walls connected by manned towers with enormous gates placed at key intervals, all made of colorful glazed brick.[2] The labor force he used for all this construction work consisted mainly of people he had taken captive from the rest of Mesopotamia and the eastern Mediterranean region.

Meanwhile, Nebuchadnezzar waged far-reaching military campaigns in an effort to expand his realm.

In 597 BC, angered by a Jewish revolt, Nebuchadnezzar sent his armies to take control of Jerusalem. Over the next two or three decades most of the inhabitants of Judah were forcibly relocated to Babylon. Nothing was left of the famous glory that distinguished the Hebrew nation during Solomon's reign. The Promised Land lay desolate until the Jews were permitted to return—and when they came back, it was without a king. In fact, after the Babylonian conquest, the continuity of the Davidic line appeared to be irreparably broken. No descendant of David's has sat on a throne in Jerusalem from that day until now.

But Scripture *cannot* be broken (John 10:35). God's purposes cannot be thwarted. All his promises are yea and amen (2 Cor. 1:20). "It is impossible for God to lie" (Heb. 6:18). Of course that means God

---

2. The famous Ishtar gate was part of Nebuchadnezzar's wall. It was discovered and excavated in the early twentieth century, then carried to Berlin where it was reassembled brick by brick and can be seen today in Berlin's Pergamon Museum. It is made of blue, glazed brick, lavishly embellished with colorful bulls, dragons, and decorative trim. It includes an inscription written by Nebuchadnezzar himself, who says he designed the city's gates and "magnificently adorned them with luxurious splendour for all mankind to behold in awe."

enforces his threats of judgment just as faithfully as he fulfills his promises of blessing. Yet no interruption in the line of Davidic kings could ever prevent Messiah from coming as promised. Nor will the passage of time prevent him from returning someday to reestablish his throne. Jeremiah 3:17 describes a time yet future when "Jerusalem shall be called the throne of the LORD, and all nations shall gather to it, to the presence of the LORD in Jerusalem, and they shall no more stubbornly follow their own evil heart."

Judah after Isaiah

God's dealings with his half-hearted and disobedient people remind us that "the steadfast love of the LORD is from everlasting to everlasting" (Ps. 103:17). "His anger is but for a moment, and his favor is for a lifetime" (30:5). And the timeline of Isaiah proves that God's patience far exceeds the severity of his judgment.

Remember, Hezekiah died in 686 BC. Nebuchadnezzar took power over Jerusalem about ninety years later, in 597. In the interim, God was remarkably gracious to Judah. The people did not heed Isaiah's words of warning; they had failed to follow the godly leadership of Jotham; they had indulged in gross wickedness under Ahaz; and then they refused to embrace Hezekiah's reforms with a whole heart. God nevertheless stayed his hand of judgment for almost nine more decades *after* Hezekiah died.

By contrast, the period from the start of God's judgment to the end of Judah's captivity was barely seventy years (Jer. 25:11–12).[3]

Judah's apostasy teaches us a vital cautionary lesson. It gives us a clear warning about the danger of *backsliding*. That's the biblical term used to describe the Hebrew nation's frequent turning away from the Lord into unbelief and disobedience. It's a fitting expression. The Lord

---

3. Nebuchadnezzar's conquest of Jerusalem occurred in 597 BC, and Judah's captivity ended with the Decree of Cyrus, in approximately 536. So the years of strict captivity numbered fewer than sixty-five. Seventy was the number of years the ground would lay fallow. Apparently, the counter began with Jeremiah's prophecy, delivered in the final decade of the seventh century BC, when the political situation in and around Judah was too volatile for the land to be cultivated as it normally would have been. This judgment was foretold in Moses's time (Lev. 26:32–35) and was meant to last "until the land had enjoyed its Sabbaths. All the days that it lay desolate it kept Sabbath, to fulfill seventy years" (2 Chron. 36:21). Because Israel had not observed the required Sabbath-year rest since the time of Saul (some 490 years before the captivity), the Lord caused the land to lay desolate one year for every year of Jubilee the nation had neglected.

himself uses it in Isaiah 57:17: "I hid my face and was angry, but he went on backsliding in the way of his own heart." In Jeremiah 8:5 the Lord asks rhetorically, "Why then has this people turned away in perpetual backsliding? They hold fast to deceit; they refuse to return." The Hebrew words in those texts are derived from a root that speaks of falling back, losing ground, turning away, or returning again and again to the same place. It evokes the picture of someone who cannot seem to get the necessary traction to advance spiritually—and makes no serious effort anyway. In Hosea 4:16, the Lord compares Israel to "a backsliding heifer" (KJV). The Hebrew word for "backsliding" in that verse carries the connotation of a stubborn animal that lazily slips backward on a slippery hill and then deliberately refuses to press upward again. Most modern translations of Hosea 4:16 make clear that what the Lord is talking about is a headstrong refusal to move ahead: "Like a stubborn heifer, Israel is stubborn."

Charles Spurgeon, perhaps the nineteenth century's finest preacher, spent the last few years of his life warning Christians about the dangers of backsliding. He cited several examples from church history to prove that when God's people begin to depart from sound, settled, biblical truth, they are leaving the security of God's blessing and protection, stepping instead onto a precarious downhill pathway that always ends in disaster. He likened it to a steep downgrade with a slippery surface where it is impossible to maintain a secure footing. Stumble, and momentum will take over. The pull of gravity is relentless and the path filled with hazards, so it is ultimately impossible to descend without falling. For those whose feet have already started to slip, there is virtually no way to regain control, much less recapture lost ground.

That is a fair description of Judah's experience in the era of the divided kingdom, especially after the death of Hezekiah.

Manasseh: Worse Than the Canaanites

Here's an abbreviated summary of what happened after the passing of the four kings named in Isaiah 1:1. Second Chronicles 32:33 says, "Hezekiah slept with his fathers, and they buried him in the upper part of the tombs of the sons of David, and all Judah and the inhabitants of Jerusalem did him honor at his death. And Manasseh his son reigned in his place." Manasseh turned out to be twice as much a child of hell as his grandfather. Remember, according to Jewish tradition, Manasseh is the king who had Isaiah killed. Scripture says this of him:

> He did what was evil in the sight of the LORD, according to the abominations of the nations whom the LORD drove out before the people of Israel. For he rebuilt the high places that his father Hezekiah had broken down, and he erected altars to the Baals, and made Asheroth, and worshiped all the host of heaven and served them. And he built altars in the house of the LORD, of which the LORD had said, "In Jerusalem shall my name be forever." And he built altars for all the host of heaven in the two courts of the house of the LORD. And he burned his sons as an offering in the Valley of the Son of Hinnom, and used fortune-telling and omens and sorcery, and dealt with mediums and with necromancers. He did much evil in the sight of the LORD, provoking him to anger. And the carved image of the idol that he had made he set in the house of God. . . . *Manasseh led Judah and the inhabitants of Jerusalem astray, to do more evil than the nations whom the LORD destroyed before the people of Israel.* The LORD spoke to Manasseh and to his people, but they paid no attention. (2 Chron. 33:2–10)

Notice that the evil practices Manasseh personally indulged in ranged from the routine idolatry of fortune-telling to the sacrificial slaughter of some of his own children! This is a direct descendant of David (and an ancestor of Christ). But Scripture expressly categorizes him as more evil than the Canaanites who had utterly contaminated the Promised Land with idolatry before the time of Joshua! That is a telling indictment.

During Hezekiah's reign, Jerusalem was literally the only major city in the world that was free from the horrors of pagan bloodlust. Under Assyrian domination, the rest of the "civilized" world was devoted to superstitious beliefs that were not really civilized at all. Unspeakable religious atrocities—up to and including human sacrifice—were commonplace in Nineveh, Babylon, and virtually all other major urban strongholds in Mesopotamia. Bloody rituals were, we might say, stylish. In the words of one writer, Manasseh affirmed and promoted this grotesque trend—"not in the temper of an amateur, as had his grand-father Ahaz, but in the temper of a fanatic."[4]

Manasseh eagerly overthrew the culture of Levitical worship that his father had so carefully tried to revive and preserve. He systemati-cally replaced Jewish beliefs and practices with "things from the east" (Isa. 2:6). In other words, he imported Assyrian-style religious perver-sions ranging from abominable pagan images to ritualized cruelty. More than any king before him, he filled the land with idols (v. 8). He turned all of Jerusalem, including the temple, into an egregious cen-ter of open idolatry—profaning God's house in ways even his wicked grandfather never dreamed of.

He seemed to be trying to revive Baal worship, including devotion to the sinister Ammonite god, Molech—a demonic deity who (it was believed) could be appeased only with infant sacrifices.

The place where Manasseh built his shrine to Molech was "the Val-ley of the Son of Hinnom" (2 Chron. 33:6; Jer. 7:31; 32:35). As you know by now, that very spot had been used for the same wicked pur-pose before. It is the place where Ahaz, Manasseh's wicked grandfather, had sacrificed children (2 Chron. 28:3; see our previous remarks about the Valley of Hinnom near the end of chapter 6, and in chapter 9).

Manasseh revived the evil practice of child sacrifice with such ambi-tious zeal that in effect he made "an institution of what Ahaz had tried as a desperate expedient."[5] Isaiah 57:5 indicates that under Manasseh's influence many people in Judah embraced the practice of child sacrifice.

Amazing Grace—and Amon

Archaeologists have found Assyrian inscriptions dating from Manasseh's reign that list him as a vassal of the Assyrian kings Esar-haddon and Ashurbanipal (Sennacherib's son and grandson, respec-tively). Manasseh's reign was mostly free from any outside military threat, chiefly because he paid tribute to these Assyrian kings.

The fact that Manasseh's reign was peaceful does not in any way diminish the evil that he did. He was to a very large degree personally

---

4. John Franklin Genung, "Manasseh: A king of Judah," in *The International Standard Bible Encyclopaedia*, ed. James Orr, 5 vols. (Chicago: Howard-Severance, 1915), 3:1978.
5. Ibid.

responsible for provoking the severity of the judgment that finally befell Judah. Scripture is emphatic about this:

> Manasseh led [the people of Judah] astray to do more evil than the nations had done whom the LORD destroyed before the people of Israel. And the LORD said by his servants the prophets, "Because Manasseh king of Judah has committed these abominations and has done things more evil than all that the Amorites did, who were before him, and has made Judah also to sin with his idols, therefore thus says the LORD, the God of Israel: Behold, I am bringing upon Jerusalem and Judah such disaster that the ears of everyone who hears of it will tingle." (2 Kings 21:9–12)

Although Manasseh was one of Judah's very worst kings, near the end of his reign, the Lord showed him extraordinary grace, bringing him, it seems, to the point of true repentance.

God's grace came with the appearance of disaster. Manasseh must have done something that seemed suspicious or disloyal to the reigning Assyrian monarch, so he was arrested, brutally bound, and carried to Babylon to be put on trial. Scripture says this was the sovereign design of God: "Therefore *the LORD* brought upon [Judah] the commanders of the army of the king of Assyria, who captured Manasseh with hooks and bound him with chains of bronze and brought him to Babylon" (2 Chron. 33:11).

In Babylon, Manasseh called on the name of the Lord. "He entreated the favor of the LORD his God and humbled himself greatly before the God of his fathers. He prayed to him, and God was moved by his entreaty and heard his plea and brought him again to Jerusalem into his kingdom. *Then Manasseh knew that the LORD was God*" (vv. 12–13).

Returning to Jerusalem, Manasseh instituted new, far-reaching reforms. "He took away the foreign gods and the idol from the house of the LORD, and all the altars that he had built on the mountain of the house of the LORD and in Jerusalem, and he threw them outside of the city. He also restored the altar of the LORD and offered on it sacrifices of peace offerings and of thanksgiving, and he commanded Judah to serve the LORD, the God of Israel" (vv. 15–16).

But those corrections, while apparently indicative of a real change in Manasseh's heart, were not as thorough as his father's reforms had been, and the compromise Manasseh had previously sponsored had a long-lasting gravitational and cross-generational pull on the people of Judah. Verse 17 of 2 Chronicles 33 adds this: "Nevertheless, the people still sacrificed at the high places, but only to the LORD their God." In other words, it was a partial reformation. People now worshiped the true God (at least in name), but not in a way that showed real obedience to his Word. Manasseh's late reforms may have temporarily slowed the nation's descent on the downgrade, but Judah could not be turned away from the calamity that lay waiting at the end of the slippery slide.

Manasseh's reign lasted fifty-five years (longer than any other king in Judah during the divided kingdom). He was succeeded by his son Amon, who quickly led the kingdom back to the path of apostasy and closer than ever to the precipice of divine judgment. Amon "walked in all the way in which his father walked and served the idols that his father served and worshiped them. He abandoned the LORD, the God of his fathers, and did not walk in the way of the LORD" (2 Kings 21:21–22). After just two years of his miserable leadership, Amon was assassinated by his own servants, and he was succeeded by Josiah.

Josiah, the Best of Judah's Kings

Josiah was a reformer like his great-grandfather Hezekiah. He was merely eight years old when he took the throne, which suggests he was born close to the time when his grandfather, Manasseh, repented of his evil. Scripture gives no details about the first eighteen years of Josiah's reign, telling us only that "he did what was right in the eyes of the LORD and walked in all the way of David his father, and he did not turn aside to the right or to the left" (2 Kings 22:2).

Then, eighteen years after ascending the throne, Josiah undertook a project to repair and refurbish the temple. While those reparations were underway, the high priest discovered a scroll containing the Book of the Law. The scroll was read to Josiah, and his immediate response was sorrowful repentance. "When the king heard the words of the Book of the Law, he tore his clothes" (2 Kings 22:11).

Because of Josiah's humility and faith, the Lord promised him that the threatened judgment would not fall during his lifetime. The first 24 verses of 2 Kings 23 describe the many reforms Josiah instituted. Then Scripture says this of him: "Before him there was no king like him, who turned to the LORD with all his heart and with all his soul and with all his might, according to all the Law of Moses, nor did any like him arise after him" (v. 25). Josiah's thirty-one-year-long reign was one final token of divine mercy and opportunity for his rebellious people.

Sadly, however, Josiah was not able to lead his countrymen off the downgrade and out of apostasy. He died from a battle wound when he was shot by an Egyptian archer in a skirmish against Pharaoh Necho at Megiddo. His death marked the end of all reforms under the kings of Judah.

Jehoahaz and Jehoiakim

Josiah was followed by Jehoahaz, of whom Scripture says, "Jehoahaz was twenty-three years old when he began to reign, and he reigned three months in Jerusalem. . . . He did what was evil in the sight of the LORD, according to all that his fathers had done" (vv. 31–32). Jehoahaz is also called Shallum (Jer. 22:11). He had an older half-brother who ought to have succeeded their father to the throne (1 Chron. 3:15), but 2 Chronicles 36:1 says, "The people of the land took Jehoahaz the son of Josiah and made him king in his father's place in Jerusalem." His reign was cut short when he was taken captive by Pharaoh and brought to Egypt, where he died.

The Egyptian king replaced Jehoahaz on Judah's throne with his older half-brother, Jehoiakim, allowing Jehoiakim to remain in Jerusalem. Jehoiakim served at Pharaoh's pleasure and had no regard whatsoever for the Lord. Scripture says he "did what was evil in the sight of the LORD, according to all that his fathers had done" (2 Kings 23:37). Jewish tradition records that he was the worst kind of tyrant—proudly sinister, morally perverse, openly scornful of everything holy. He became notorious for the wanton, godless way he indulged in blatant carnal self-gratification. The record of his misconduct reveals how far and how quickly the spiritual state of Judah devolved after the death of Josiah. According to ancient rabbinical sources, Jehoiakim

lived in incestuous relations with his mother, daughter-in-law, and
stepmother, and was in the habit of murdering men, whose wives
he then violated and whose property he seized. His garments were
of "*sha'atnez*" [mixed fabric, expressly forbidden by Deut. 22:11],
and in order to hide the fact that he was a Jew, he had made himself
an epispasm [an artificial reversal of his circumcision] by means of
an operation, and had tattooed his body. . . . He even boasted of
his godlessness, saying, "My predecessors, Manasseh and Amon,
did not know how they could make God most angry. But I speak
openly; all that God gives us is light, and this we no longer need,
since we have a kind of gold that shines just like the light; furthermore, God has given this gold to mankind [Ps. 115:16] and is not
able to take it back again." . . .

When Jehoiakim was informed that Jeremiah was writing his
Lamentations, he sent for the roll, and calmly read the first four
verses, remarking sarcastically, "I still am king." When he came to
the fifth verse and saw the words, "For the Lord hath afflicted her
for the multitude of her transgressions" (Lam. i. 5), he took the
roll, scratched out the names of God occurring therein, and threw
it into the fire.[6]

Jeremiah's prophetic career overlapped Jehoiakim's reign. The
prophet published many harsh prophecies against the king's evil pro-
miscuity. Jeremiah 36 is Jeremiah's own account of how Jehoiakim
burned a scroll containing *all* the words God had ever spoken to the
prophet (v. 2). But "the word of the Lord remains forever" (1 Pet.
1:25). So Jeremiah simply had his scribe, Baruch, take up a new scroll,
and "at the dictation of Jeremiah [he rewrote] all the words of the
scroll that Jehoiakim king of Judah had burned in the fire. *And many
similar words were added to them*" (v. 32).

Jeremiah 22:18–19 is a prophecy concerning Jehoiakim's death:

Therefore thus says the Lord concerning Jehoiakim the son of
Josiah, king of Judah:

"They shall not lament for him, saying,
    'Ah, my brother!' or 'Ah, sister!'

6. Isadore Singer, ed., *The Jewish Encyclopedia*, 12 vols. (New York: Funk & Wagnalls, 1904), 7:85.

> They shall not lament for him, saying,
>   'Ah, lord!' or 'Ah, his majesty!'
> With the burial of a donkey he shall be buried,
>   dragged and dumped beyond the gates of Jerusalem."

Jehoiakim reigned eleven years during a sea change in world politics. Soon after he had taken the throne in Jerusalem, Nebuchadnezzar rose to power in Babylon. He made Jehoiakim his vassal for three years (2 Kings 24:1), but Jehoiakim, who had dutifully served the Egyptian pharaoh, rebelled against Nebuchadnezzar. Jehoiakim's rebellion (a fitting expression of his defiant character) thus became the trigger that unleashed the wrath of Nebuchadnezzar against Judah. Nebuchadnezzar's armies proved to be the instrument by which God finally judged the apostate Jewish nation:

> The LORD sent against [Jehoiakim] bands of the Chaldeans and bands of the Syrians and bands of the Moabites and bands of the Ammonites, and sent them against Judah to destroy it, according to the word of the LORD that he spoke by his servants the prophets. Surely this came upon Judah at the command of the LORD, to remove them out of his sight, for the sins of Manasseh, according to all that he had done, and also for the innocent blood that he had shed. For he filled Jerusalem with innocent blood, and the LORD would not pardon. (2 Kings 24:2–4)

Nebuchadnezzar had Jehoiakim bound in chains, intent on carrying him to Babylon (2 Chron. 36:6). But the siege went on for many months, and Jehoiakim evidently died before Nebuchadnezzar was able to bring him to Babylon. Josephus says Nebuchadnezzar commanded the king's body "to be thrown before the walls, without any burial,"[7] just as Jeremiah 22:19 had prophesied.

The End of the Divided Kingdom and the Beginning of the Babylonian Captivity

Jehoiakim's successor was Jehoiachin (also known as Jeconiah and Coniah). It was 597 BC, the year Jerusalem fell. The city's walls were

---

7. *Antiquities of the Jews,* 10.6.3., in *The Works of Flavius Josephus,* trans. William Whiston, 2 vols. (London: Henry G. Bohn, 1845), 1:419.

already being breached by Nebuchadnezzar's armies. So almost as soon as Jehoiachin ascended the throne, he surrendered to Nebuchadnezzar and was brought to Babylon—along with practically every government official in Judah (2 Kings 24:12–16). Jehoiachin was kept there in captivity for the remainder of his life. This was the first major deportation of what would become the Babylonian captivity. Isaiah had forewarned the nation about this, starting nearly a century before it came to pass. Indeed, a detailed warning of this exact judgment was included in Moses's law (Lev. 26:14–39), centuries before Isaiah.

Nebuchadnezzar formally deposed Jehoiachin as king almost immediately, though he let him live. In fact, he outlived Nebuchadnezzar, and according to 2 Kings 25:27–30, Nebuchadnezzar's successor elevated Jehoiachin to a place of honor. "So Jehoiachin put off his prison garments. And every day of his life he dined regularly at the king's table, and for his allowance, a regular allowance was given him by the king, according to his daily needs, as long as he lived" (vv. 29–30). That is the last verse of 2 Kings, and it seemed like the permanent end of the Davidic dynasty.

Jehoiachin (Jeconiah) was in fact the last person in David's direct line to sit on the throne of Judah. Like so many of his predecessors, he "did what was evil in the sight of the LORD, according to all that his father had done" (2 Kings 24:9). Jeremiah 22:30 records a divine curse on his entire line of descent: "Thus says the LORD: 'Write this man down as childless, a man who shall not succeed in his days, for none of his offspring shall succeed in sitting on the throne of David and ruling again in Judah.'"

The point was not that Jehoiachin would literally be childless. He wasn't (1 Chron. 3:17–20). But as far as the Davidic dynasty was concerned, he may as well have been, because no one in his bloodline would ever inherit the throne of David.

On the face of it, that prophecy would seem to have brought an end to the royal line of Israel, in breach of the Davidic covenant. But Matthew 1:11–16 traces the royal line from Jehoiachin ("Jechoniah") through Joseph. Christ was the adopted son of Joseph and a true descendant of David through Mary's line (Luke 3:23–31). Jesus therefore inherited the right to the throne from Joseph's line, and the curse against Jehoiachin's actual bloodline did not apply to him. Thus God fulfilled both the promise and the curse, which from the time of Jeremiah to the birth of Christ may have seemed irreconcilable.

The last titular king of Judah was Zedekiah, Jehoiachin's uncle. (We met him earlier, back in chapter 4 of this book.) He was appointed by Nebuchadnezzar, who changed the puppet king's name from Mattaniah (2 Kings 24:17). Scripture says of him, "He did what was evil in the sight of the LORD, according to all that Jehoiakim had done" (v. 19).

The choice to put Zedekiah on the throne seems to have been a calculated move by Nebuchadnezzar to enfeeble the Jewish people. Nebuchadnezzar had begun the deportations to Babylon by bringing Judah's most noble, capable, and fit inhabitants first. "He carried away all Jerusalem and all the officials and all the mighty men of valor, 10,000 captives, and all the craftsmen and the smiths. None remained, except the poorest people of the land. . . . The chief men of the land he took into captivity from Jerusalem to Babylon. And the king of Babylon brought captive to Babylon all the men of valor, 7,000, and the craftsmen and the metal workers, 1,000, all of them strong and fit for war" (vv. 14–16).

It seems Nebuchadnezzar chose Zedekiah by singling out the most passive person with modest leadership abilities and blood ties to the kingly line.

But Zedekiah tried to rebel, and Nebuchadnezzar's angry response to his rebellion resulted in the final major deportation of Jews from the Promised Land. Babylonian forces then leveled the city of Jerusalem—including the temple. Nebuchadnezzar deposed Zedekiah, poked his eyes out, and carried everyone else (except a few of the very poorest) into captivity in Babylon (2 Kings 25:1–21). Whatever remained that had any value was either taken or destroyed. The land was left desolate.

Every prophecy Isaiah had ever uttered about the judgment and captivity of Judah was thus fulfilled to the letter. Those who had scoffed at Isaiah's words of judgment now knew for certain that he was a true prophet. The captivity therefore had the beneficial effect of drawing many Jews in captivity back to the faith of their fathers. Psalm 137 is a famous lament and prayer for deliverance penned by some unknown writer while the nation was being held in captivity:

By the waters of Babylon,
there we sat down and wept,
    when we remembered Zion.
On the willows there
    we hung up our lyres.
For there our captors
    required of us songs,
and our tormentors, mirth, saying,
    "Sing us one of the songs of Zion!"

How shall we sing the LORD's song
    in a foreign land?
If I forget you, O Jerusalem,
    let my right hand forget its skill! (vv. 1–5)

Once Isaiah's dire warnings about the Babylonian captivity were fulfilled, the promises of salvation he penned seized the full attention of the faithful remnant, as they longed for deliverance. They knew just as surely as judgment had come, there would come a time when "the ransomed of the LORD shall return and come to Zion with singing; everlasting joy shall be upon their heads; they shall obtain gladness and joy, and sorrow and sighing shall flee away" (Isa. 51:11).

That explains why, beginning with Isaiah 40, through chapter 66, Isaiah's prophecy is dominated by a series of promises and prophecies about deliverance. By now you understand why chapter 53 anchors and explains all the other promises. The atonement accomplished through the suffering of Yahweh's servant is the necessary ground and prerequisite for every other expression of God's grace and deliverance.

Acknowledgments

My profound thanks to Phil Johnson and Dave Enos, who helped draft this material from transcripts of my sermons; Keith Erickson, who did a masterful job proofreading the final draft; and to Lydia Brownback and the rest of the team at Crossway for their careful, skillful work in putting the final polish on the project.

Appendix

"The Man of Sorrows"

A Sermon by Charles Spurgeon[1]

A man of sorrows, and acquainted with grief.
Isaiah 53:3

Possibly a murmur will pass round the congregation, "This is a dreary subject and a mournful theme." But, O beloved, it is not so, for great as were the woes of our Redeemer, they are all over now, and are to be looked back upon with sacred triumph.

However severe the struggle, the victory has been won; the laboring vessel was severely tossed by the waves, but she has now entered into the desired haven. Our Savior is no longer in Gethsemane agonizing, or upon the cross expiring. The crown of thorns has been replaced by many crowns of sovereignty. The nails and the spear have given way to the scepter. Nor is this all, for though the suffering is ended, the blessed results never end.

We may remember the travail, for the Man Child is born into the

1. This sermon was preached by Charles Haddon Spurgeon in March 1873. From *The Metropolitan Tabernacle Pulpit*, 63 vols. (London: Passmore & Alabaster, 1873), 19:121–32. British spellings have been Americanized, paragraph breaks and Scripture references have been inserted, punctuation has been simplified, some archaic expressions have been modernized, and Spurgeon's closing plea to his congregation has been abridged. Capitalization of deity pronouns and of some other terms reflects that used by Crossway, the publisher of this book. Scripture quotations are either from the KJV or slightly paraphrased by Spurgeon.

world. The sowing in tears is followed by a reaping in joy. The bruising of the heel of the woman's seed is well recompensed by the breaking of the Serpent's head. It is pleasant to hear of battles fought when a decisive victory has ended war and established peace. So with the double reflection that all the work of suffering is finished by the Redeemer, and that, henceforth, he beholds the success of all his labors, we shall rejoice even while we enter into fellowship with his sufferings.

Let it never be forgotten that the subject of the sorrows of the Savior has proved to be more efficacious for comfort to mourners than any other theme in the compass of revelation, or out of it. Even the glories of Christ afford no such consolation to afflicted spirits as the sufferings of Christ. Christ is in all attitudes the consolation of Israel, but he is most so as a man of sorrows. Troubled spirits turn not so much to Bethlehem as to Calvary. They prefer Gethsemane to Nazareth. The afflicted do not so much look for comfort to Christ as he will come a second time in splendor of state, as to Christ as he came the first time, a weary man and full of woes.

The passion-flower yields us the best perfume. The tree of the cross bleeds the most healing balm. In this case, like cures like, for there is no remedy for sorrow beneath the sun like the sorrows of Immanuel. As Aaron's rod swallowed up all the other rods, so the griefs of Jesus make our griefs disappear. Thus you see that in the black soil of our subject, light is sown for the righteous—light which springs up for those who sit in darkness and in the region of the shadow of death.

Let us go, then, without reluctance to the house of mourning, and commune with "the Chief Mourner," who above all others could say, "I am the man that hath seen affliction" (Lam. 3:1).

We will not stray from our text this morning, but keep to it so closely as even to dwell upon each one of its words. The words shall give us our divisions—"A man;" "a man of sorrows;" "acquainted with grief."

A Man

There is no novelty to anyone here present in the doctrine of the real and actual manhood of the Lord Jesus Christ. But, although there be nothing novel in it, there is everything *important* in it. Therefore, let us hear it again.

This is one of those gospel church bells which must be rung every Sunday. This is one of those provisions of the Lord's household, which, like bread and salt, should be put upon the table at every spiritual meal. This is the manna which must fall every day round about the camp. We can never meditate too much upon Christ's blessed person as God and as man.

Let us reflect that he who is here called a man was certainly "very God of very God," "a man," and "a man of sorrows," and yet at the same time, "God over all, blessed for ever" (Rom. 9:5). He who was "despised and rejected of men" was beloved and adored by angels, and he from whom men hid their faces in contempt, was worshiped by cherubim and seraphim. This is the great mystery of godliness. God was "manifest in the flesh" (1 Tim. 3:16). He who was God, and was in the beginning with God, was made flesh, and dwelt among us. The Highest stooped to become the lowest; the Greatest took his place among the least. Strange, and needing all our faith to grasp it, yet is it true that he who sat upon the well of Sychar, and said "Give me to drink," was none other than he who digged the channels of the ocean, and poured into them the floods.

Son of Mary, thou art also Son of Jehovah! Man of the substance of thy mother, thou art also essential Deity; we worship thee this day in spirit and in truth!

Remembering that Jesus Christ is God, it now behooves us to recollect that his manhood was nonetheless real and substantial. It differed from our own humanity in the absence of sin, but it differed in no other respect.

It is idle to speculate upon a heavenly manhood, as some have done, who have, by their very attempt at accuracy, been borne down by whirlpools of error. It is enough for us to know that the Lord was born of a woman, wrapped in swaddling bands, laid in a manger, and needed to be nursed by his mother as any other little child. He grew in stature like any other human being, and as a man we know that he ate and drank, that he hungered and thirsted, rejoiced and sorrowed. His body could be touched and handled, wounded and made to bleed. He was no phantasm, but a man of flesh and blood, even as ourselves; a man needing sleep, requiring food, and subject to pain; and a man who, in the end, yielded up his life to death.

There may have been some distinction between his body and ours, for inasmuch as it was never defiled by sin, it was not capable of corruption. Otherwise in body and in soul, the Lord Jesus was perfect man after the order of our manhood, "made in the likeness of sinful flesh," and we must think of him under that aspect. Our temptation is to regard the Lord's humanity as something quite different from our own. We are apt to spiritualize it away, and not to think of him as really bone of our bone and flesh of our flesh. All this is akin to grievous error. We may fancy that we are honoring Christ by such conceptions, but Christ is never honored by that which is not true.

He was a man, a real man, a man of our race, the Son of Man; indeed a representative man, the second Adam. "As the children are partakers of flesh and blood, he also himself took part of the same" (Heb. 2:14). "He made himself of no reputation, and took upon him the form of a servant, and was made in the likeness of men" (Phil. 2:7).

Now this condescending participation in our nature brings the Lord Jesus very near to us in relationship. Inasmuch as he was man, though also God, he was, according to Hebrew law, our *goel*—our kinsman, next of kin. Now it was according to the law that if an inheritance had been lost, it was the right of the next of kin to redeem it. Our Lord Jesus exercised his legal right, and seeing us sold into bondage and our inheritance taken from us, came forward to redeem both us and all our lost estate.

A blessed thing it was for us that we had such a kinsman. When Ruth went to glean in the fields of Boaz, it was the most gracious circumstance in her life that Boaz turned out to be her next of kin. And we who have gleaned in the fields of mercy praise the Lord that his only begotten Son is the next of kin to us, our brother, born for adversity.

It would not have been consistent with divine justice for any other substitution to have been accepted for us, except that of a man. Man sinned, and man must make reparation for the injury done to the divine honor. The breach of the law was caused by man, and by man must it be repaired. Man had transgressed; man must be punished. It was not in the power of an angel to have said, "I will suffer for man"—for angelic sufferings would have made no amends for human sins. But the man, the matchless man, being the representative man, and of right by kinship allowed to redeem, stepped in, suffered what was due, made amends to injured justice, and thereby set us free! Glory be unto his blessed name!

And now, beloved, since the Lord thus saw in Christ's manhood a suitableness to become our Redeemer, I trust that many here who have been under bondage to Satan will see in that same human nature an attraction leading them to approach him. Sinner, you have not to come to an absolute God; you are not bidden to draw nigh to the consuming fire. You might well tremble to approach him whom you have so grievously offended. But there is a man ordained to mediate between you and God, and if you would come to God, you must come through him—the man Christ Jesus. God out of Christ is terrible out of his holy places. He will by no means spare the guilty—but look at yonder Son of man!

> His hand no thunder bears,
> No terror clothes his brow;
> No bolts to drive your guilty souls
> To fiercer flames below.

He is a man with hands full of blessing, eyes wet with tears of pity, lips overflowing with love, and a heart melting with tenderness. Do you not see the gash in his side? Through that wound there is a highway to his heart, and he who needs his compassion may soon excite it. O sinners! The way to the Savior's heart is open, and penitent seekers shall never be denied. Why should the most despairing be afraid to approach the Savior? He has deigned to assume the character of the Lamb of God. I never knew even a little child that was afraid of a lamb. The most timorous will approach a lamb, and Jesus used this argument when he said to every laboring and heavy-laden one: "Take my yoke upon you, and learn of me, for I am meek and lowly in heart" (Matt. 11:29).

I know you feel yourselves sad and trembling, but need you tremble in his presence? If you are weak, your weakness will touch his sympathy, and your mournful inability will be an argument with his abounding mercy. If I were sick and might have my choice where I would lie, with a view to healing, I would say, place me where the best and kindest physician upon earth can see me. Put me where a man with great skill, and equal tenderness, will have me always beneath his eye. I shall not long groan there in vain—if he can heal me, he will.

Sinner, place yourself by an act of faith this morning beneath the cross of Jesus. Look up to him and say, "Blessed Physician, whose wounds for me can heal me, whose death for me can make me live, look down upon me! You are a man. You know what man suffers. You are man. Will you let a man sink down to hell who cries for help? You art a man, and you can save. And will you let a poor unworthy one who longs for mercy be driven into hopeless misery, while he cries to you to let your merits save him?"

Oh, guilty ones, have faith that you can reach the heart of Jesus. Sinner, fly to Jesus without fear. He waits to save. It is his office to receive sinners and reconcile them to God. Be thankful that you do not have to go to God first, as you are. But you are invited to come to Jesus Christ, and through him to the Father. May the Holy Spirit lead you to devout meditation upon the humility of our Lord; and so may you find the door of life, the portal of peace, the gate of heaven!

Then let me add, before I leave this point, that every child of God ought also to be comforted by the fact that our Redeemer is one of our own race, seeing that he was made like unto his brethren, that he might be a merciful and faithful High Priest; and he was tempted in all points, like as we are, that he might be able to succour them that are tempted (Heb. 2:17; 4:15).

The sympathy of Jesus is the next most precious thing to his sacrifice. I stood by the bedside of a Christian brother the other day, and he remarked, "I feel thankful to God that our Lord took our sicknesses. Of course," said he, "the grand thing was, that he took our sins, but next to that, I, as a sufferer, feel grateful that he also took our sicknesses."

Personally, I also bear witness that it has been to me, in seasons of great pain, superlatively comfortable to know that in every pang which racks his people the Lord Jesus has a fellow-feeling. We are not alone, for one like unto the Son of man walks the furnace with us (cf. Dan. 3:25). The clouds that float over our sky have darkened the heavens for him also—

He knows what strong temptations mean,

For he has felt the same.

How completely it takes the bitterness out of grief to know that it once was suffered by him.

The Macedonian soldiers, it is said, made long forced marches which seemed to be beyond the power of mortal endurance, but the reason for their untiring energy lay in Alexander's presence. He was accustomed to walk with them, and bear the like fatigue. If the king himself had been carried like a Persian monarch in a palanquin, in the midst of easy, luxurious state, the soldiers would soon have grown tired; but, when they looked upon the king of men himself, hungering when they hungered, thirsting when they thirsted, often putting aside the cup of water offered to him, and passing it to a fellow-soldier who looked more faint than himself, they could not dream of repining. Why, every Macedonian felt that he could endure any fatigue if Alexander could.

This day, assuredly, we can bear poverty, slander, contempt, or bodily pain, or death itself, because Jesus Christ our Lord has borne it. By his humiliation it shall become pleasure to be abased for his sake, by the spittle that distilled on his cheeks it shall become a fair thing to be made a mockery for him. By the buffeting and the blindfolding it shall become an honor to be disgraced. And by the cross it shall become life itself to surrender life for the sake of such a cause and so precious a Master!

May the man of sorrows now appear to us, and enable us to bear our sorrows cheerfully. If there be consolation anywhere, surely it is to be found in the delightful presence of the Crucified: "A man shall be a hiding-place from the wind, and a covert from the tempest" (Isa. 32:2).

We must pass on to dwell awhile upon the next words:

A Man of Sorrows

The expression is intended to be very emphatic, it is not "a sorrowful man," but "a man of sorrows"—as if he were made up of sorrows, and they were constituent elements of his being. Some are men of pleasure, others men of wealth, but he was "a man of sorrows." He and sorrow might have changed names. He who saw him, saw sorrow, and he who would see sorrow must look on him. "Behold, and see," he says, "if there was ever sorrow like unto my sorrow which was done unto me" (Lam. 1:12).

Our Lord is called the man of sorrows, for this was his peculiar token and special mark. We might well call him "a man of holiness," for there was no fault in him; or a man of labors, for he did his Father's business earnestly; or "a man of eloquence," for never man spoke like this man. We might right fittingly call him in the language of our hymn, "The man of love," for never was there greater love than glowed in his heart. Still conspicuous as all these and many other excellencies were, yet had we gazed upon Christ and been asked afterward what was the most striking peculiarity in him, we should have said *his sorrows*.

The various parts of his character were so singularly harmonious that no one quality predominated, so as to become a leading feature. In his moral portrait, the eye is perfect, but so also is the mouth. The cheeks are as beds of spices, but the lips also are as lilies, dropping sweet-smelling myrrh. In Peter, you see enthusiasm exaggerated at times into presumption; and in John, love for his Lord would call fire from heaven on his foes. Deficiencies and exaggerations exist everywhere but in Jesus. He is the perfect man, a whole man, the holy one of Israel.

But there was a peculiarity, and it lay in the fact that "his visage was so marred more than any man, and his form more than the sons of men" through the excessive griefs which continually passed over his spirit. Tears were his insignia, and the cross his escutcheon. He was the warrior in black armor, and not as now the rider upon the white horse. He was the Lord of grief, the Prince of pain, the Emperor of anguish, a "man of sorrows, and acquainted with grief."

> Oh! king of grief! (a title strange, yet true,
> To thee of all kings only due),
> Oh! king of wounds! how shall I grieve for thee,
> Who in all grief preventest me.

Is not the title of "man of sorrows" given to our Lord by way of eminence? He was not only sorrowful, but preeminent among the sorrowful. All men have a burden to bear, but his was heaviest of all. Who is there of our race that is quite free from sorrows? Search ye the whole earth through, and everywhere the thorn and thistle will be found, and these have wounded every one of woman born. High in the lofty places of the earth there is sorrow, for the royal widow weeps for her lord. Down in the cottage where we fancy that nothing but content can reign, a thousand bitter tears are shed over dire penury and cruel oppression. In the sunniest climes the serpent creeps among the flowers. In the most fertile regions poisons flourish as well as wholesome herbs. Everywhere "men must work and women must weep." There is sorrow on the sea, and sadness on the land. But in this common lot, the "firstborn among many brethren" has more than a double portion. His cup is more bitter, his baptism more deep, than the rest of the family.

Common sufferers must give place, for none can match with him in woe. Ordinary mourners may be content to rend their garments, but he himself is rent in his affliction; they sip at sorrow's bowl, but he drains it dry. He who was the most obedient Son smarted most under the rod when he was stricken of God and afflicted; no other of the smitten ones have sweat great drops of blood, or in the same bitterness of anguish, cried, "My God, my God, why hast thou forsaken me" (Mark 15:34).

The reasons for this superior sorrow may be found in the fact that with his sorrow there was no admixture of sin. Sin deserves sorrow, but it also blunts the edge of grief by rendering the soul untender and unsympathetic. We do not start at sin as Jesus did, we do not tremble at the sinner's doom as Jesus would. His was a perfect nature, which, because it knew no sin, was not in its element amid sorrow, but was like a land bird driven out to sea by the gale. To the robber the jail is his home, and the prison fare is the meat to which he is accustomed, but to an innocent man a prison is misery, and everything about it is strange and foreign. Our Lord's pure nature was peculiarly sensitive of any contact with sin.

We, alas, by the fall, have lost much of that feeling. In proportion as we are sanctified, sin becomes the source of wretchedness to us. Jesus being perfect, every sin pained him much more than it would any of us. I have no doubt there are many persons in the world who could live merrily in the haunts of vice—could hear blasphemy without horror, view lust without disgust, and look on robbery or murder without abhorrence. But to many of us, an hour's familiarity with such abominations would be the severest punishment. A sentence in which the name of Jesus is blasphemed is torture to us of the most exquisite kind. The very mention of the shameful deeds of vice seizes us with horror. To live with the wicked would be a sufficient hell to the righteous. David's prayer is full of agony wherein he cries, "Gather not my soul with sinners, nor my life with bloody men" (Ps. 26:9). But the perfect Jesus, what a grief the sight of sin must have caused him!

Our hands grow calloused with toiling, and our hearts with sinning; but our Lord was, as it were, like a man whose flesh was all one quivering wound. He was delicately sensitive of every touch of sin. We go through thorn brakes and briars of sin because we are clothed with indifference. But imagine a naked man compelled to traverse a forest of briars—and such was the Savior, as to his moral sensitiveness. He could see sin where we cannot see it and feel its heinousness as we cannot feel it. There was therefore more to grieve him, and he was more capable of being grieved.

Side by side with his painful sensitiveness of the evil of sin, was his gracious tenderness toward the sorrows of others. If we could know and enter into all the griefs of this congregation, it is probable that we should be of all men most miserable. There are heartbreaks in this house this morning, which, could they find a tongue, would fill our hearts with agony. We hear of poverty here; we see disease there; we observe bereavement; and we mark distress. We note the fact that men are passing into the grave and (ah, far more bitter grief) descending into hell. But somehow or other, either these become such common things that they do not stir us—or else we gradually harden to them. The Savior was always moved to sympathy with another's griefs, for his love was ever at flood-tide. All men's sorrows were his sorrows. His heart was so large, that it was inevitable that he should become "a man of sorrows."

We recollect that besides this our Savior had a peculiar relationship to sin. He was not merely afflicted with the sight of it and saddened by perceiving its effects on others, but sin was actually laid upon him. He was himself numbered with the transgressors. And therefore he was called to bear the terrible blows of divine justice. He suffered unknown, immeasurable agonies. Divine power strengthened him to suffer, else mere manhood would have failed. The wrath whose power no man knows spent itself on him. "It pleased the Father to bruise him, he hath put him to grief."

Behold the man, and mark how vain it would be to seek his equal sorrow.

The title "man of sorrows" was also given to our Lord to indicate the constancy of his afflictions. He changed his place of abode, but he always lodged with sorrow. Sorrow wove his swaddling bands, and sorrow spun his winding sheet. Born in a stable, sorrow received him. Only on the cross at his last breath did sorrow part with him. His disciples might forsake him, but his sorrows would not leave him. He was often alone without a man, but never alone without a grief. From the hour of his baptism in Jordan to the time of his baptism in the pains of death, he always wore the sable robe and was "a man of sorrows."

He was also "a man of sorrows," for the variety of his woes. He was a man not of one sorrow only, but of *sorrows*. All the sufferings of the body and of the soul were known to him—the sorrows of the man who actively struggles to obey; the sorrows of the man who sits still and passively endures. The sorrows of the lofty he knew, for he was the King of Israel. The sorrows of the poor he knew, for he "had not where to lay his head" (Matt. 8:20). Sorrows relative and sorrows personal; sorrows mental and sorrows spiritual; sorrows of all kinds and degrees assailed him. Affliction emptied its quiver upon him, making his heart the target for all conceivable woes.

Let us think a minute or two of some of those sufferings.

Our Lord was a man of sorrows as to his poverty. Oh, you who are in want, your want is not so abject as his. He had not where to lay his head, but you have at least some humble roof to shelter you. No one denies you a cup of water, but he sat upon the well at Samaria, and said, "I thirst" (cf. John 4:7). We read, more than once, that he hungered. His toil was so great that he was constantly weary, and we read of one occasion where they took him, "even as he was," into the ship—too faint was he to reach the boat himself, but they carried him as he was and laid him down near the helm to sleep. But he had not much time for slumber, for they woke him, saying, "Master, carest thou not that we perish?" (Mark 4:36–38). A hard life was his, with nothing of earthly comfort to make that life endurable.

Remember you who lament around the open grave, or weep in memory of graves but newly filled, our Savior knew the heart-rendings of bereavement. Jesus wept, as he stood at the tomb of Lazarus (John 11:35).

Perhaps the bitterest of his sorrows were those connected with his gracious work. He came as the Messiah sent of God, on an embassage of love, and men rejected his claims. When he went to his own city, where he had been brought up, and announced himself, they would have cast him headlong from the brow of the hill (Luke 4:28–29). It is a hard thing to come on an errand of disinterested love, and then to meet with such ingratitude as this. Nor did they stay at cold rejection; they then proceeded to derision and to ridicule. There was no name of contempt which they did not pour upon him. Nay, it was not merely contempt, but they proceeded to falsehood, slander, and blasphemy. He was a drunken man, they said (Luke 7:34). Hear this, ye angels, and be astonished! Yes, a wine-bibber did they call the blessed Prince of Life! They said he was in league with Beelzebub, and had a devil, and was mad (John 10:20)—even though he had come to destroy the works of the Devil! (1 John 3:8). They charged him with every crime their malice could suggest.

There was not a word he spoke but they would wrest it; not a doctrine but what they would misrepresent it. He could not speak but what they would find in his words some occasion against him. And all the while he was doing nothing but seeking their advantage in all ways. When he was earnest against their vices it was out of pity for their souls. If he condemned their sins it was because their sins would destroy them. But his zeal against sin was always tempered with love for the souls of men. Was there ever man so full of good-will to others who received such disgraceful treatment from those he longed to serve?

As he proceeded in his life, his sorrows multiplied. He preached, and when men's hearts were hard, and they would not believe what he said, "he was grieved for the hardness of their hearts" (Mark 3:5). He went about doing good (Acts 10:38), and for his good works they took up stones again to stone him. Alas, they stoned his heart when they could not injure his body.

He pleaded with them, and plaintively declared his love, and received instead from them a hatred remorseless and fiendish. Slighted love has griefs of peculiar poignancy. Many have died of hearts broken by ingratitude. Such love as the love of Jesus could not for the sake of those it loved bear to be slighted. It pined within itself because men did not know their own mercies and rejected their own salvation.

His sorrow was not that men injured him, but that they destroyed themselves. This it was that pulled up the sluices of his soul, and made his eyes o'erflow with tears: "O Jerusalem! Jerusalem! how often would I have gathered thy children together as a hen gathereth her chickens under her wings, and ye would not" (Matt. 23:37). The lament is not for his own humiliation, but for their suicidal rejection of his grace. These were among the sorrows that he bore.

But surely he found some solace with the few companions whom he had gathered around him. He did; but for all that he must have found as much sorrow as solace in their company. They were dull scholars. They learned slowly. What they did learn, they forgot. What they remembered, they did not practice. And what they practiced at one time, they belied at another. They were miserable comforters for the man of sorrows. His was a lonely life. I mean that even when he was with his followers, he was alone. He said to them once, "Could ye not watch with me one hour" (Matt. 26:40). But indeed he might have said the same to them all the hours of their lives, for even if they sympathized with him to the utmost of their capacity, they could not enter into such griefs as his.

A father in a house with many little children about him cannot tell his babies his griefs. If he did, they would not comprehend him. What do they know of his anxious business transactions, or his crushing losses? Poor little things, their father does not wish they should be able to sympathize with him; he looks down upon them and rejoices that their toys will comfort them and that their little prattle will not be broken in upon by his great griefs.

The Savior, from the very dignity of his nature, must suffer alone. The mountainside with Christ upon it seems to me to be a suggestive symbol of his earthly life. His great soul lived in vast solitudes, sublime and terrible, and there amid a midnight of trouble, his spirit communed with the Father, no one being able to accompany him into the dark glens and gloomy ravines of his unique experience. Of all his life's warfare he might have said in some senses "of the people there was none with me" (Isa. 63:3). In the end it became literally true, for they all forsook him (Mark 14:50)—one denied him and another betrayed him, so that he trod the winepress alone.

In the last, crowning sorrows of his life, there came upon him the penal inflictions from God, the chastisement of our peace which was upon him. He was arrested in the garden of Gethsemane by God's officers before the officers of the Jews had come near to him. There on the ground he knelt, and wrestled till the bloody sweat started from every pore, and his soul was "exceeding sorrowful, even unto death" (Matt. 26:38). You have read the story of your Master's woes and know how he was hurried from bar to bar, treated with mingled scorn and cruelty before each judgment seat. When they had taken him to Herod and to Pilate, and almost murdered him with scourging, they brought him forth, and said, Ecce homo—"Behold the man" (John 19:5). Their malice was not satisfied; they must go further yet, and nail him to his cross and mock him while fever parched his mouth and made him feel as if his body were dissolved to dust.

He cries out, "I thirst" (v. 28) and is mocked with vinegar. Ye know the rest, but I would have you best remember that the sharpest scourging and severest griefs were all within; while the hand of God bruised him, and the iron rod of justice broke him, as it were, upon the wheel.

He was fitly named a "man of sorrows!" I feel as if I had no utterance, as if my tongue were tied, while trying to speak on this subject. I cannot find goodly words worthy of my theme, yet I know that embellishments of language would degrade rather than adorn the agonies of my Lord.

There let the cross stand sublime in its simplicity! It needs no decoration. If I had wreaths of choicest flowers to hang about it, I would gladly place them there, and if instead of garlands of flowers, each flower could be a gem of priceless worth, I would consider that the cross deserved the whole. But as I have none of these, I rejoice that the cross alone, in its naked simplicity, needs NOTHING from mortal speech.

Turn to your bleeding Savior, O my hearers. Continue gazing upon him, and find in the "man of sorrows" your Lord and your God.

And now the last word is, he was—

Acquainted with Grief

With grief he had an intimate acquaintance. He did not know merely what it was in others, but it came home to himself. We have read of grief. We have sympathized with grief. We have sometimes felt grief. But the Lord felt it more intensely than other men in his innermost soul. He, beyond us all, was conversant with this black-letter lore. He knew the secret of the heart that refuses to be comforted. He had sat at grief's table, eaten of grief's black bread, and dipped his morsel in her vinegar. By the waters of Marah he dwelt (cf. Ex. 15:23), and knew right well the bitter well. He and grief were bosom friends.

It was a continuous acquaintance. He did not call at grief's house sometimes to take a tonic by the way. Neither did he sip now and then of the wormwood and the gall. But the quassia[2] cup was always in his hand, and ashes were always mingled with his bread. Not only forty days in the wilderness did Jesus fast; the world was ever a wilderness to him, and his life was one long Lent.

I do not say that he was not, after all, a happy man, for down, deep in his soul, benevolence always supplied a living spring of joy to him. There was a joy into which we are one day to enter—the "joy of our Lord" (Neh. 8:10)—the "joy set before him" for which "he endured the cross, despising the shame" (Heb. 12:2). But that does not at all take away from the fact that his acquaintance with grief was continuous and intimate beyond that of any man who ever lived.

It was indeed a *growing* acquaintance with grief, for each step took him deeper down into the grim shades of sorrow. As there is a progress in the teaching of Christ and in the life of Christ, so is there also in the griefs of Christ. The tempest lowered darker, and darker, and darker. His sun rose in a cloud, but it set in congregated horrors of heaped-up night, till, in a moment, the clouds were suddenly rent asunder, and, as

2. *Quassia* is a bitter medicine made from tree bark, used as both a tonic and an insecticide.

a loud voice proclaimed, "It is finished," a glorious morning dawned where all expected an eternal night.

Remember, once more, that this acquaintance of Christ with grief was a voluntary acquaintance for our sakes. He need never have known a grief at all, and at any moment he might have said to grief, *farewell.* He could have returned in an instant to the royalties of heaven and to the bliss of the upper world, or even tarrying here he might have lived sublimely indifferent to the woes of mankind. But he would not. He remained to the end, out of love to us, grief's acquaintance.

Now then, what shall I say in conclusion? Just this: let us admire the superlative love of Jesus. O love, love, what hast thou done! What hast thou not done! Thou art omnipotent in suffering. Few of us can bear pain. Perhaps fewer still of us can bear misrepresentation, slander, and ingratitude. These are horrible hornets which sting as with fire. Men have been driven to madness by cruel scandals which have distilled from venomous tongues.

Christ, throughout life, bore these and other sufferings. Let us love him, as we think of how much he must have loved us. Will you try, this afternoon, before you come to the Communion table, to get your souls saturated with the love of Christ? Lay them a-soak in his love all the afternoon, till like a sponge, you drink into your own selves the love of Jesus. And then come up tonight, as it were, to let that love flow out to him again while you sit at his table and partake of the emblems of his death and of his love. Admire the power of his love, and then pray that you may have a love somewhat akin to it in power.

General Index

Abraham, 53, 86, 113, 115, 132, 145, 152
"afflicted," 100, 117
Ahaz, 47, 168–70, 174, 179, 182; alliance of with Assyria, 169; campaign of religious syncretism, 169–70; hatred of God, 168–69; refusal of to ask for a sign from God, 168–69; sacrifice of his infant offspring by, 168
Amon, 184
anti-Semitism, 124
Aquinas, Thomas, 136
Archer, Gleason, 14
"arm of the Lord": the gospel as, 81, 83; as the symbol of God's power, 80–81
Assyrians, 15, 165, 169, 181; destruction of Assyria by a coalition of enemy armies (612 BC), 177–78; destruction of Israel by (722 BC), 165; taunting of the faithless people in Judah by the Rab-shakeh, 173
"astonished," 57. See also *shamem* (Hebrew: left desolate or laid waste; numbed, petrified, or paralyzed; appalled)
Augustine, 31, 136

Babylonians, 15; destruction of Judah by (597 BC), 178, 179n3, 187–88, 189; destruction of Babylon by the Medes, 15
Babylonian captivity, 178, 179n3, 188, 189–90; and Israel's neglect of the required Sabbath-year rest, 179n3
backsliding, 179–80
baptism, erroneous view of as the new birth (John 3), 148
"behold," 53; as an outcry ("Look!"), 53; as a simple command ("Observe this carefully"), 53; use of by Old Testament prophets, 53
Bethlehem, 69–70; and the Magi, 70
Bible, the: chapter and verse divisions in, 16, 22; division of into two sections (the Old Testament and the New Testament), 16
"borne," 96–97
Boston, Thomas, 137
bronze serpent, 171; as "Nehushtan," 171; as a symbol of Jesus's crucifixion, 28, 132

Caiaphas, 125
Calvin, John, 31, 129, 136
Campolo, Tony, 140n16
Chalke, Steve, 140n16
Chandler, Edward, 62
"chastisement," 101
Chrysostom, John, 135
confession of faith, 110–11, 156
confession of sin, 103, 104–5, 106. See also Israel/Israelites, future collective confession of

"stripes," 101

suffering servant, the, 139–42; astonishing exaltation of, 62–65; astonishing humiliation of, 56–62; astonishing revelation of, 53–56; as both divine and human, 133; contemptible beginning of ("a young plant"), 83–84; contemptible character of ("a root out of dry ground"), 84–86; contemptible end of ("despised" and "rejected"), 86–89; God's perspective on the servant's work, 147–56; as honored, 142–44; identity of, 25–27; silence of before his accusers, 116–19; silence of in the grave, 126–27; silence of in his death, 119–26; as a specific individual, 21, 22; suffering and exaltation of, 129–34; why Israel cannot be the servant, 125

"surely," 92–93

synagogues, Scripture readings in, 37; the *haftarah*, 37; omission of Isaiah 52:13–53:12 from, 37; the Torah, 37

Talmud, 25; account of Jesus's execution from the Jewish leaders'

perspective in, 122–24; denunciations of Jesus in, 87n17

temple, the, destruction of by the Romans (AD 70), 113

Tertullian, 135

thaumazō (Greek: to marvel, to adore), 62

trials, in first-century Israel, 120–22

unbelief, 78–80, 82–83. *See also* backsliding

Uriah, 162

Uzziah (also Azariah), 166–67; leprosy of, 167

Vos, Geerhardus, 138

Whitefield, George, 147

"Why Jews Don't Believe in Jesus" webpage, 98–99

works: good works as the fruit of faith, 148–49n2; as a "polluted garment," 76, 81; works-based religion, 48–49

Yiddish, derogatory expressions for Jesus in, 124

Zechariah, 162

Zedekiah, 69, 189; rebellion of against Nebuchadnezzar, 69, 189

Scripture Index